Building Collaborative Governance

Pracademic Lessons from the Basc

Building Collaborative Governance in Times of Uncertainty

Pracademic Lessons from the Basque Gipuzkoa Province

Edited by
Xabier Barandiarán, María José Canel & Geert Bouckaert

LEUVEN UNIVERSITY PRESS

Published with the support of the Diputación Foral de Gipuzkoa

Published in 2023 by Leuven University Press / Presses Universitaires de Louvain / Universitaire Pers Leuven. Minderbroedersstraat 4, B-3000 Leuven (Belgium).

ISBN 978 94 6270 367 4 (Paperback)
ISBN 978 94 6166 505 8 (ePDF)
ISBN 978 94 6166 506 5 1 (ePUB)
https://doi.org/10.11116/9789461665058
D/2023/1869/9
NUR: 759

Layout: Crius Group
Cover design: Frederik Danko
Cover illustration: Eduardo Chillida, *Besarkada XIV* [Abrazo XIV, Embrace XIV], 1997, corten steel. Courtesy of the Estate of Eduardo Chillida and Hauser & Wirth.
© Zabalaga Leku. San Sebastián, VEGAP, 2022. Photo: Archive Eduardo Chillida.

We wish to thank all those who have taken part in *Etorkizuna Eraikiz*, and likewise all those who believe in and practise collaborative governance.

Contents

Part I. Structural dimensions to institutionalise collaborative governance

Part II. Relational dimensions to learn and communicate about a culture of collaborative governance

***

Part III. Looking at results and conclusions

***

Preface
The Gipuzkoa model, a solid trajectory

Markel Olano, Diputado General de Gipuzkoa

Etorkizuna Eraikiz started out in the spring of 2016. Regional universities, representatives of organised society, businesses, associations and so on – we all pitched in towards a goal we found particularly attractive: addressing the construction of a new Gipuzkoa that would leave the problems of the past behind. Many of the queries we tabled at the time, such as new forms of mobility, the ageing of society and climate change, are now front-page news in the modern world.

Since then, Gipuzkoa has been hard at work to anticipate the future, and to guarantee the social and economic development of our society through cooperation. I wish to emphasise the notion of cooperation: one of the greatest contributions by *Etorkizuna Eraikiz* to the territory is probably the expansion of open, collaborative governance, conveying something which is so much a part of us – collaboration – to public policies, in order to provide answers for the territory's main challenges.

In a bid to explain the importance of collaboration, I home in on Rousseau's hunters' dilemma. In ancient times, a group of hunters are hunting a large stag, which will provide food for them and also for the rest of the village. To make the hunting expedition successful, however, there must be collaboration between all the members of the group. The threat lies in individualism: each hunter can abandon the stag hunt and instead go and hunt a hare, a task which is much easier. This means the group of hunters can eat, but the stag will run off, and the rest of the village will have no food.

Amid the gigantic challenges faced by Gipuzkoa and the modern world, what *Etorkizuna Eraikiz* is saying is that individual solutions do not work, and that we must work together to come up with a response to these problems. We are up against some magnitudes, processes of transformation which affect society as a whole, and any responses we may come up with for these processes must be shared and consensual.

In addition to the method of working, some significant results have been achieved. Our *Etorkizuna Eraikiz* programme has rolled out a new agenda which in the next ten years will enable us to become a more social, greener and more competitive territory, with a more powerful and innovative economy that will enable us to continue to transform the territory, and with a cohesive society establishing limits for social inequalities. In this regard, since 2016 more than 50,000 people have taken part in various initiatives and projects launched by *Etorkizuna Eraikiz*, and hundreds of social and economic agents have made some kind of contribution.

There can be no doubt that the current context poses some difficulties in achieving this objective. We have undergone a triple crisis in recent years – health, economic and social – and some major economic uncertainties and concerns are still in place. We do not know what tomorrow has in store for us, but what we do know is that we do not intend to simply sit on our hands and do nothing: we must reach an agreement on solutions to these problems, and strive to turn threats into opportunities.

Experimentation is the other distinctive characteristic of *Etorkizuna Eraikiz*. It basically consists of applying the scientific method to the construction of the future. The project has a number of laboratories acting as testing grounds for problems of the future: trial, error, more trials, and again until the proper result is achieved. In short, we face a gigantic social innovation exercise which, as already mentioned, seeks to involve society as a whole. It is no idle challenge, but we believe that our society has more than enough power and enthusiasm to face up to it.

However, in the current context, amid the various crises we face at the present time and will have to face in the future, our main priority is to protect those who are more vulnerable in order to prevent any regression in the welfare of families and the general public in Gipuzkoa. The Gipuzkoa Provincial Council is hard at work on this, on collaboration with other Basque institutions and Gipuzkoa society. At the same time, we are making an even greater effort, not only to maintain the current economic level, but to boost the future economy and generate quality employment.

However, a solid economy and a cohesive society are two sides of the same coin. Both constitute the core of the Gipuzkoa model. This is because we cannot maintain the level of welfare that characterises our society without a competitive economy based on state-of-the-art industry; and because the values linked to social welfare, such as education, gender equality and social cohesion, are basic values for the operation of a strong, competitive economy.

For the future of Gipuzkoa, it is essential to continue to develop this binomial if further progress is to be made. In view of the uncertainty and economic difficulties already affecting families and individuals in Gipuzkoa, this binomial, this Gipuzkoa model we hold so dear, marks out the path. It is a solid trajectory to address the current situation, giving priority to social protection and the welfare of one and all, and continuing to implement an advanced, innovative economy.

By taking action in relation to these two challenges, all of us will continue to build a social, competitive, green Gipuzkoa, a Gipuzkoa that will continue to be a territory with one of the lowest levels of social inequality in Europe. And, just like every time we talk about inequality, we address the issue from a broader perspective – social, economic, gender, linguistics, etc. – because the society of the future we all wish to build together must be cohesive in all its aspects.

List of abbreviations

ACBC Autonomous Community of the Basque Country
ARTD Action Research for Territorial Development
CG   Collaborative Governance
DFG   Diputación Foral de Gipuzkoa (Provincial Council of Gipuzkoa)
DPG   Dynamic Performance Governance
EE   *Etorkizuna Eraikiz*
EETT *Etorkizuna Eraikiz* Think Tank
EHU   Euskal Herriko Unibersitatea (University of the Basque Country)
OPSI Observatory of Public Sector Innovation
PCG   Provincial Council of Gipuzkoa
PGG   Provincial Government of Gipuzkoa
SDGs Sustainable Development Goals
UPV   Universidad del País Vasco (University of the Basque Country)

Glossary of *Etorkizuna Eraikiz* terms

2DEO: EE reference centre for audiovisual production in Basque language.

Adinberri: EE reference centre for healthy aging.

Agirre Lehendakaria Center: UPV social innovation centre specialising in systemic transitions towards sustainable human development.

Arantzazulab: Social Innovation Laboratory, EE reference centre for collaborative governance.

AROPE: a rate indicating risk of poverty and social exclusion.

Badalab: Linguistic and Social Laboratory, EE reference centre to preserve minority languages.

Bidelagunak: 'travelling companions' to support action learning groups at the PCG.

Boost: dynamic encounters with diverse citizen groups.

Comarcas: sub-provincial and supra-municipal administrative divisions; there are eight in Gipuzkoa.

Cupo: quota paid annually by the Autonomous Community of the Basque Country to the Spanish central state.

Diputación Foral de Gipuzkoa: Gipuzkoa Provincial Council.

EHU/UPV: University of the Basque Country.

Ekinez Ikasi: learning by doing. Active listening and learning processes developed with politicians and civil servants at the PCG following action learning methodology.

Elkar-Ekin Lanean: EE strategy to foster inclusive employability.

Etorkizuna Eraikiz Foroa: EE Forum, an open to citizens space for dialogue and reflection promoted by the Gipuzkoa Provincial Council and the EHU/UPV.

Etorkizuna Eraikiz: building the future.

Gipuzkoa Aurrera: antecedent of EE, developed between 2007 and 2011 to experiment with new ways of governance.

Gipuzkoa Deep Demonstration: EE strategy within the Gipuzkoa Lab to experiment in order to move towards social, economic and environmental sustainability.

Gipuzkoa Gantt: EE strategy to foster gene therapy.

Gipuzkoa Quantum: EE strategy to foster quantum computing.

Gipuzkoa Sarean: antecedent of EE, developed between 2007 and 2011 to improve competitiveness and wellbeing.

Gipuzkoa Taldean: Gipuzkoa in group, EE listening space.

Gipuzkoa Lab: EE experimentation space.

Gunea: area. Gunea room is a meeting point for the EE community located at the PCG.

Juntas Generales: General Assembly of the Province.

LABe: EE reference centre for digital gastronomy,

Mubil: EE reference centre for the development of intelligent and sustainable mobility.

Naturklima: climate observatory, EE reference centre to fight climate change.

Orkestra: Basque Institute for Competitiveness.

Parientes mayores or *banderizos*: families of rural landowners who during the Middle Ages waged a bloody clan war against each other, to the detriment of the entire territory.

Proiektuen Bulegoa: Projects Office of the Gipuzkoa Provincial Council.

Tabakalera: a cultural centre placed in the renovated former tobacco factory, where today *LABe* (one of the reference centres) is located.

Udal Etorkizuna Eraikiz: EE strategy seeking to promote collaborative governance at the municipal level and create a learning community together with the municipalities.

Udal Etorkizuna Eraikiz: strategy for socialising collaborative governance in the municipalities of Gipuzkoa.

Villa: chartered town.

Ziur: EE reference centre to foster cybersecurity.

Chapter 1
Introduction: *Etorkizuna Eraikiz*, a major case of collaborative governance

Xabier Barandiarán, *Diputación Foral de Gipuzkoa*
María José Canel, *University Complutense Madrid, Spain*
Geert Bouckaert, *KU Leuven, Belgium*

1.   Introduction: What is going to be looked at?

Etorkizuna Eraikiz (referred to as EE sometimes in this book) is an initiative led by the Provincial Council of Gipuzkoa (PCG), in the Basque Country, northern Spain, capital San Sebastián (or Donostia in Basque). It is aimed at fostering the community capacity to collaboratively understand and address current challenges. Through listening and experimentation, the programme comprises different projects in which public authorities and citizens (represented in entities such as business, societal, educational and civic organisations) co-participate to define and implement the province's agenda, and contribute to making sustainable policies. Throughout the book references to the characteristics of this programme will be made, and further information about the projects and activities is provided in the appendices (more specifically, see Appendix 1 for the link to the website).

Etorkizuna Eraikiz is an initiative which gives form and structure to the Provincial Government of Gipuzkoa's commitment to collaborative governance as a way of responding to the main strategic challenges of the province's future. The project was presented publicly in May 2016. There were ten initial pilot experiences. Since its launch, *Etorkizuna Eraikiz* has built a model encompassing various spaces for deliberation and experimentation between the PCG, organised society and citizens, with the aim of deliberating, reflecting, experimenting and collaborating to build their own responses to major challenges and build strategies for the territory in a collaborative manner.

From the very beginning, this government project developed activities and interaction with international leading scholars in the field to produce knowledge for the theory and the practice of collaborative governance, and its development has gone along with ongoing reflection and the support of academic knowledge. This volume builds upon the assumption that this government initiative is a challenging and productive attempt to involve society in policy-making, and that its analysis may provide knowledge both for the study and the practice of collaborative governance.

This chapter presents the approach of the edited volume, and frames it as a bench-learning case for pracademics. It presents the context both in terms of theory (locating the case within a literature review) and of the specific characteristics of the place and public administration which runs the government programme. On the whole, the chapter accounts for why this government programme from the Basque Country deserves attention and visibility in international fora, elaborating on the specific characteristics of the hybrid knowledge that is produced.

2.   The approach

There is already research that explores this government programme from different angles: intangible resources (Canel, Luoma-aho & Barandiarán, 2020), communication (Canel, Barandiarán & Murphy, 2019), learning (Murphy et al., 2020), listening (Canel, Barandiarán & Murphy, 2022), social capital (Barandiarán, Murphy & Canel, 2022), and trust (Barandiarán, Canel & Bouckaert, 2022).

There is not yet research which provides a comprehensive analysis of this government programme producing the hybrid knowledge that the case is suitable for. This volume is a hybrid practice/academic product in which an analysis is conducted by leading local and international scholars in the field of collaborative governance, in conjunction with those public leaders and managers who are fully embedded in its practical implementation.

Therefore, the data collected were produced from the actual implementation of a government programme on collaborative governance which: a) is fully articulated both theoretically – it is a model-based case – and in practice; b) has been fully implemented with the support of authority and resources; c) includes relevant public policies for social growth; d) covers the full range of the policy cycle; and e) includes sufficient information about actual achievements and results.

Work has been articulated around workshops in which 30 local and international scholars have interacted with actors participating in *Etorkizuna Eraikiz* (politicians, technical staff and societal organisations) looking at what worked and what did not work, exploring causes and elaborating on lessons learned. Scholars from universities from different parts of the world have been involved in the publication to frame and to connect the theoretical concept to the empirical practice of the Basque Country, with the purpose of creating a bench-learning case.

Based on the documentation provided by the policy-makers involved in *Etorkizuna Eraikiz*, on a review of the basic literature, and on the interaction between academics and professionals, the analysis:

- is carried out in groups of participants, in democratic collaborative partnership (Coghlan & Brannick, 2005, pp. 3–4), given that professionals and academics come together to address issues on an equal footing, and all have the same authority to provide solutions;
- aims to discover and provide results to improve practice and to tackle critical issues in the field of collaborative governance. In this sense, the discussion brings to the table the experience of *Etorkizuna Eraikiz* in contrast to similar experiences from other cultural contexts;
- provides knowledge about the five dimensions that the literature identifies in collaborative governance (Batory & Svensson, 2017): a) the case brings together governmental and non-governmental actors; b) the collaborative process is initiated and controlled by a public actor (a provincial council) with a non-governmental actor playing important roles; c) it is restricted to organised interests (stakeholders take an organisational form); d) collaboration runs through the entire policy cycle: design, decision-making and service delivery; and e) finally, the case includes normative assumptions to the extent that collaboration is undertaken with a public purpose, in order to increase society's involvement in public management, and participants are driven by a constructive and problem-solving idea.

The dynamics for the production of this book were the following. First, drafts of the chapters were prepared by both practitioners and local scholars who have been involved in the design and implementation of the collaborative governance of *Etorkizuna Eraikiz*. Second, together with informative materials about the different components of the initiative, the draft chapters were sent to scholars well in advance to prepare their contributions to the workshop. Three question-driven workshops were held in September and October 2022 in which around 50 practitioners from the PCG and scholars from different disciplines and cultural contexts met to discuss key issues on collaborative governance. A slot was allocated for each question. After the response given by practitioners, different attendees presented comments and further questions and discussion developed. The discussion served as input both for chapter authors (who produced the final version of their chapters after attending the workshops) and for external scholars (who delivered comments on what this initiative tells us regarding a specific angle of collaborative governance in contrast to literature or other initiatives across the world).

What is presented in the pages that come next is a pracademic publication, blended with evidence from practice, and the analysis from both practitioners and scholars. The ultimate goal is to produce hybrid knowledge which may: 1) be transferred to other initiatives in public administrations; and 2) nurture the scientific corpus in the corresponding academic field.

3.   *Etorkizuna Eraikiz* within the literature review of collaborative governance

Collaborative governance in its different terms and forms (co-production, collaboration, governance networks, citizen engagement efforts, citizen participation, multi-level governance, open government, transversalisation, united governance, private–public partnerships) is a topic that is currently high on the agenda of both academia and policy-making (Batory & Svensson, 2017).

Based on recent reviews and states of the art on collaborative governance (Batory & Svensson, 2017, 2019; Bianchi *et al.*, 2021; Voets, 2021), and on the sources that are referred to below, the present analysis could be profiled within the existing literature as follows.

The type of collaborative governance which is analysed in this volume is characterised by key features included in scholarly definitions of the concept (Agranoff, 2006; Ansell & Gash, 2008; Bingham *et al.*, 2005; McGuire, 2006; Emerson *et al.*, 2012; Emerson & Nabatchi, 2015a, among others): a public agency, directly engaging non-state stakeholders, in a collective decision-making process that is formal, consensus-oriented and deliberative; which entails new structures of governance as opposed to hierarchical organisational decision-making; and that engages across the boundaries of levels of government, and the public, private and civic spheres, in order to achieve common goals and to carry out a public purpose that could not otherwise be accomplished.

There is extant literature on the theoretical fundamentals of collaborative governance, such as the concept, models and frameworks (Ansell & Gash, 2008; Sirianni, 2010; Donahue *et al.*, 2012; Emerson *et al.*, 2012; Bryson *et al.*, 2015; Emerson & Nabatchi, 2015a and 2015b; Kapucu *et al.*, 2016; Lee & Ospina, 2022, among others). There is also literature looking at the practice (cases and implementation of models) (see, for instance, Ansell & Torfing, 2015; Ansell & Gash, 2008; Gugu & Dal Molin, 2016; Torfing & Ansell, 2017) which mostly draws on meta-analysis of literature about specific projects. The aspiration of the present analysis is to grasp the hybrid knowledge which may be produced from a comprehensive analysis of a whole case jointly analysed by practitioners and scholars.

Most recent research sources relate collaborative governance to concepts and issues such as accountability (Lee & Ospina, 2022; Sørensen & Torfing, 2021), governance networks, (Wang & Ran, 2021), meta-governance (Sørensen & Torfing, 2017), leadership (Imperial *et al.*, 2016; Sørensen & Torfing, 2018), sustainability and SDGs (Florini & Pauli, 2018; Hofstad & Torfing, 2015), innovation (Crosby *et al.*, 2017), legitimacy (Dupuy & Defacqz, 2022), and trust (Ran & Qi, 2019). There are certainly many concepts and aspects that come into play when looking at collaborative governance. The analysis of the three major conceptualisations provided by Voets *et al.* (2021) helps with identifying some key components of collaborative governance: the systemic conceptualisation (Ansell & Gash, 2008) pays attention to institutional design and facilitative leadership; the integrative framework (Emerson *et al.*, 2012) to feedback relationships and to broader system context and exogenous factors; and the propositions for the study of cross-sectoral collaborations (Bryson *et al.*, 2015) to the realities of power and authority, and to the role that accountability plays. This analysis has inspired the selection of issues to be presented in this volume.

The benefits of collaborative governance have been largely argued from a normative perspective but little explored in practice (Emerson *et al.*, 2012; Batory & Svensson, 2019; Waardenburg *et al.*, 2020; Bianchi *et al.*, 2021). In this sense, collaborative governance tends to generally be viewed positively in the literature, as something that enhances governmental ability to reach diverse policy goals. The analysis in this volume of what actually has and has not worked within the context of real needs may nurture the theory and normative assumptions on collaborative governance research.

Even though, as literature shows, the term 'collaborative governance' is interpreted normatively and culturally differently in different countries, the understanding undertaken in this volume includes key characteristics which are common to these different contexts: multi-actor collaboration, led by a public-sector organisation, aimed at building consensus among stakeholders, on a formal set of policies, designed and implemented to address key current challenges in social policies (Batory & Svensson, 2017). We understand that lessons learned could be transferrable to initiatives similar to this one in other countries.

Ultimately, the analysis of the proposed case can produce knowledge about several of the issues that scholars regard as key and still open on the topic (Bianchi *et al.*, 2021): what makes stakeholders collaborate; outputs and impact of collaborative governance; institutional factors; the role of leadership;

interaction management among different and diverse stakeholders to build trust and legitimacy; the organisation of policy implementation and service delivery; and the role played by culture, history and traditions in the design and implementation of collaborative governance initiatives.

4.   The context

The *Etorkizuna Eraikiz* project, promoted by the Provincial Government of Gipuzkoa, is a model that seeks to extend new ways of doing politics and managing the public sector through open and collaborative governance.

4.1. The territory

To understand *Etorkizuna Eraikiz*, it is first necessary to provide some background information on Gipuzkoa, the historical territory (or province) in which it was created and on whose society the project is based (see Appendix 2 for full information on the region).

Gipuzkoa has a land area of 1,980 square kilometres. It is the smallest province in Spain, but the fourth in terms of population density (360.51 inhabitants per square kilometre, standing only behind Madrid, Barcelona and Bizkaia). It is one of the three provinces forming the Autonomous Community of the Basque Country (ACBC), together with Araba and Bizkaia.

Gipuzkoa is a blue and green province. Blue, because it is situated on the shores of the Bay of Biscay, acting as a bridge between the Iberian Peninsula and the European mainland, a place of passage for a major European transport axis; and green because, despite its small size, it has a diverse and incalculable natural heritage, with 61% of the territory covered by woodland.

At the beginning of 2021, the territory had a population of 718,000. Of these, 51.1% were women, and 8.5% were foreign nationals. The population distribution is also unusual, since scarcely one in five of the inhabitants live in the capital. The province has 88 municipalities, among which there is a kind of municipal middle tier, with medium-sized towns (of around 10,000 inhabitants) spread throughout the territory, each with a strong local identity. Maintaining territorial balance from all points of view (transportation, services and infrastructure) is one of the key aspects of Gipuzkoa. Together with its small size, this means that it might better be described as an interconnected city rather than a province.

Like most western societies, Gipuzkoa, has an aging population. There are more people aged over 65 (165,000) than under 19 (136,000), and current trends suggests that the generation gap will continue to widen. Moreover, the province has one of the highest life expectancies in the world (86.4 years among women, the fifth in the world; and 81.1 years among men, eighth in the world). Its demographics continue to be weighed down by a low birth rate, with 1.26 births per woman (worldwide, only eight countries out of 197 have such a low rate).

4.2. Institutions and identity

The Provincial Council (*Diputación Foral de Gipuzkoa* as it is called in Spanish) of Gipuzkoa is the highest executive body in the province. The institution is elected by the General Assembly (*Juntas Generales*), which acts as a territorial legislative chamber. The origins of both institutions go back to the 14th century.

Initially, the General Assembly was an association of towns or *comarcas* (sub-provincial and supra-municipal administrative divisions; there are eight in Gipuzkoa) which were obliged to join forces for a variety of purposes (commercial, judicial, public order), as well as for defence. For example, in the case of Gipuzkoa, the towns allied with each other in an attempt to deal with violence between the *parientes mayores* or *banderizos*, families of rural landowners who during the Middle Ages waged a bloody clan war against each other, to the detriment of the entire territory.

The success of these *ad hoc* associations led to the consolidation of the General Assembly as a supra-local and permanent body for the entirety of the province, at which all chartered towns (*villas*) were represented. As the supreme assembly of the province, it had control over the public life of Gipuzkoa, and its powers were established in successive compilations of charters and laws. In the mid-15th century, the *Juntas* began to appoint certain individuals as commissioners to deal with a variety of public issues. Over time this commission assumed more and more powers, until it became what it is today, the Provincial Council of Gipuzkoa, the government of the historical territory.

The institutions of Gipuzkoa are therefore backed by more than six centuries of history (albeit with some interruptions). During this long period, they have faced numerous difficulties: wars, dissolutions and reduction of powers. To this day, part of Gipuzkoa's powers are in the form of historical rights, enshrined in the Spanish Constitution itself, which recognises the unique legal position of the Basque provinces and defines them as historical territories.

This 'historical' character means that besides the ordinary competences exercised by the provincial governments of the other provinces in Spain, the

Provincial Government of Gipuzkoa also exercises specific competences arising from its nature as a historical territory of the Basque Country, by virtue of its Statute of Autonomy. These include the possibility of collecting taxes through its own treasury department, as well as powers over all road infrastructure and social welfare, among other areas.

This special tax situation is governed by the 1979 Basque Economic Agreement, which regulates the unique fiscal and financial relations between the state and the three *foral* territories making up the ACBC. By virtue of this agreement, an overall quota is established that must be paid annually to the state by the ACBC. This quota is known as the *Cupo*. This arrangement has long been the subject of debate throughout the state. It should also be noted that although the state does not take a share of the revenue obtained by the *Foral* Provincial Governments, neither does it pay for the public expenses of the autonomous community, which the latter must meet itself. The Basque territories assume a unilateral risk in the sense that the results arising from management of the Agreement, good or bad, correspond only to the government of the Basque Country. Furthermore, the amount of the *Cupo* is not calculated on the basis of the revenues collected in the Basque Country. Rather, it is subject to variables that are exogenous to its management, such as the expenses incurred by the Spanish state in powers not assumed by the Basque Government, such as the army or international relations.

In addition to the historical aspect, Gipuzkoa has its own very marked idiosyncrasy due to its cultural and linguistic background. Indeed, it has the highest proportion of Basque speakers of any of the three provinces of the Basque Country (61% of the inhabitants of the ACBC who consider Basque to be their mother tongue live in Gipuzkoa), and is the one in which the language is best preserved.

4.3.   The so-called 'Gipuzkoa model'

A 'Gipuzkoa model' has become a term of common use, due to the historical importance of the idea and practice of 'collaboration' in institutionalising economic, social and political life in the territory, as the result of a marked cultural orientation towards associationism, community bonding and a high level of social capital. This strong and differentiated identity of the territory is also reflected in the existence of its own socioeconomic model, characteristic to the territory, which has come to be known as the 'Gipuzkoa model'. This is an arrangement that successfully combines the generation of wealth with social protection, and favours a balanced territory and a cohesive community, with a Basque culture and its own language, Euskara.

In the social area, thanks to this socioeconomic model, Gipuzkoa is a 'best-in-class' in terms of social inequality; in other words, it has a community with high levels of economic and social cohesion. Gipuzkoa has a Gini (the most widely used indicator for measuring social inequality) of 25.3, which is 5.4 points below the average for the European Union (EU28). Similarly, the AROPE rate, which indicates risk of poverty and social exclusion, is 19.2% in Gipuzkoa, 3.2 percentage points lower than the European average.

Gipuzkoan society understands the value of responsibility and solidarity in the distribution of wealth and is as a whole an active and involved society, with significant social capital, and a rich and diverse organised civil society. As an example of this, there are 4,500 associations in the territory performing voluntary work in a variety of fields, around a quarter of them in the third sector. In addition, 40,000 Gipuzkoan men and women (6% of the population) are involved in some type of volunteer work. Gipuzkoa is also an educated society: 43% of the population are in or have completed upper secondary or tertiary education.

In economic terms, the Gipuzkoa model is based on a strong industrial base, with the industrial sector representing 31% of GDP (industry + construction). The business fabric of Gipuzkoa is essentially based on SMEs, which account for 99% of the companies in the territory, with a marked innovative character and the capacity to compete even in global markets. Indeed, the region has world-leading companies in fields as diverse as new mobility and biosciences.

In terms of innovation, R&D expenditure in the territory amounts to 2.63% of GDP, significantly higher than the European average (+0.04%). In addition, the territory has a business, industrial, innovative and technological ecosystem of reference: a network of companies, clusters, agents, knowledge, education and innovation centres.

Another of the territory's characteristics is that it is home to a cooperative model that is exceptional in the world and it has the largest industrial cooperative group in the world (Mondragon Corporation). In 2021, the territory had 782 cooperatives, employing 27,755 people – around 10% of the total workforce.

5.   Basic information on *Etorkizuna Eraikiz*

Etorkizuna Eraikiz was born, therefore, in this fertile soil, a scenario that *a priori* presents many strengths, but which in the short and medium term was considered to be under threat from a series of challenges that could jeopardise the continuity of the province's socioeconomic model. The future challenges are in many cases the same as those facing the world as a whole, and the Western world in particular. This is the case, for example, with the issue of population aging, whose effects are even greater in Gipuzkoa.

Etorkizuna Eraikiz was also set up against an international backdrop of growing political disaffection, in the prelude to the rebirth of populism and extremist ideologies. *Etorkizuna Eraikiz's* proposal is based on a commitment to a new political culture, founded on collaboration between all types of agents. It invites participation and involvement in politics as a means of avoiding extremism and building bridges with an organised society and a citizenry which, in general, seems to view the political class and public administrations with suspicion.

When first launched in 2016, *Etorkizuna Eraikiz* was presented as a tool designed to maximise and get the most from the province's innovative potential in order to meet the future challenges facing Gipuzkoa. The project was initially allied with the universities and threw down the gauntlet to both citizens and organised society, in the form of a call to experiment, reflect and debate, and propose shared solutions to problems which, it was believed, affected everyone, not only in general terms, but also in the most specific aspects of everyone's lives.

From 2016 to the time of writing (late 2022), the world has changed a lot: we have suffered a global pandemic that paralyzed everything, war has broken out almost in the heart of Europe, and uncertainty is the most oft-heard word. The scientific and technological revolution of our times continues to accelerate, and the ways in which we relate to each other continue to change, undermining the certainties we used to rely on. Twentieth-century life, based on a stable job, affective relationship and family nucleus (with the corresponding more or less established order of going through the different stages of life) might be said to have collapsed. New generations are facing an altogether unclear path, with questions such as: What will I be working in? How long will I keep this job? Will I be able to afford an apartment? Will I have enough for my pension?

The *Etorkizuna Eraikiz* project has sought to help respond to these complex issues, generating a collective exercise for reflection and for sharing ideas and proposed solutions. More than 900 companies, associations, knowledge agents and organisations of all kinds have been involved in this effort; a total of 50,000 people who, in one way or another, have participated and continue to participate in the project (see Diputación Foral de Gipuzkoa 2021b; see also Appendix 6 for full information on the status of achievements; see also Appendix 8 for the *Etorkizuna Eraikiz* journal).

This volume seeks to describe what has been done and analyse what has been achieved. These introductory paragraphs will also serve to give an idea of the scope of this initiative, with information such as the following. Each year, the experimentation space *Etorkizuna Eraikiz* invites general society to submit proposals for addressing strategic issues of the future. Of these, to date a total of 150 experiments have been funded. Twenty-six of these experimental projects, involving all types of agents, are still in operation. Their purpose is to test in real environments different solutions to complex issues, such as new models of care for the elderly, work–life balance and relationships between the generations. Based on aspects that experimentation has shown to be of key importance, *Etorkizuna Eraikiz* has launched 11 strategies and reference centres. With their own structures and dynamics, they involve actors from different sectors of society, focusing on a stable basis in areas that are critical for the development of the territory (such as new mobility, climate change and aging), seeking to turn threats into opportunities for specialisation and local and international leadership.

In addition, *Etorkizuna Eraikiz* constantly maintains direct communication and participation channels with citizens (open budgets, cross-border budgets); has established a think tank, in which representatives of the public policy ecosystems participate, which is a space for reflection and debate on the threats, challenges and solutions facing Gipuzkoa and the direction the province should take, and whose work has an impact on public policies; is working to extend its model to all *comarcas* of the province through a territorial development laboratory; and shares its experience and knowledge with the municipal authorities of the province at a forum of municipalities. Finally, it is worth mentioning that *Etorkizuna Eraikiz* has opened its doors to the world, by employing promotion and socialisation strategies so that the initiative can be projected on the international stage, arousing the interest of other regions and counties as well as globally important academic institutions.

In short, *Etorkizuna Eraikiz* has established itself as a call to collaborative action in an increasingly changing and diverse world. This volume seeks to explore what can be learned from this experience.

Before presenting the structure of the book, Table 1-1 collects basic information about the chronology of this initiative. The information has been arranged in columns to present the chronology of the governance of EE, of the different spaces, of consequences on public policies, and finally of the activities undertaken to promote the initiative, both nationally and internationally.

Table 1-1. *Etorkizuna Eraikiz* chronology (2016–2022)

	Governance of *Etorkizuna Eraikiz*	Listening–Deliberation–Experimentation	Consequences on public policies	Socialisation and internationalisation
2016 → Vision, design and start-up	· Definition of the vision and basic design · The four universities from the region join the project · Creation of a Think Tank	· Start-up of the first four experimental projects · Start-up of the area of *Citizenship Projects* · Creation of four prospection groups		· Public presentations at *Tabakalera* and a number of districts in Gipuzkoa · University of the Basque Country EHU/UPV Summer Course; Congress · Contacts with international networks · Presence on social networks and media
2017 → Elaborating on specialisation	· Approval by the PGC of the so-called "new political agenda" (mid-legislature) · Signature of the Collaboration Agreement with district development agencies	· Experimental projects continue, and start-up of three new ones · New call for *Citizenship Projects*	· Design of the first reference centres: *Mubil, Ziur, Adinberri* and *Naturklima*	· University of the Basque Country EHU/UPV Summer Course; Congress · Contacts with international networks · Congresses and conferences · Presence on social networks and media

	Governance of *Etorkizuna Eraikiz*	Listening–Deliberation–Experimentation	Consequences on public policies	Socialisation and internationalisation
2018 → **Deployment**	· Creation of Gunea as a meeting point for the EE community · Streamlining, redesigning and formalisation of the EE *Think Tank*	· Start-up of two new experimental projects · Teaching and learning activities: "Action Learning" (internal), "Training in Open and Collaborative Governance" (Open University "UNED") · New call for *Citizenship Projects*	· Incorporation of the *Mubil, Adinberri, Ziur* and *Naturklima* foundation, allocation for start-up of 2DEO and the funding of *LABe (reference centre)*	· Thematic congresses · Contacts with international networks · University of the Basque Country EHU/UPV Summer Courses · Presence on social networks and media
2019 → **Consolidation of experimentation** (Election year: municipal and provincial elections)		· Start-up of six experimental projects · New call for *Citizenship Projects* · Consolidation of the *Territorial Development Laboratory*	· Start-up of *Elkar-Ekin Lanean*, to boost employability and combat social exclusion · Redesign of the pre-existing reference centre *Badalab* · Structuration of work teams for the reference centres and strategies, and operational deployment of activity	· Conferences · University of the Basque Country EHU/UPV Summer Courses; Congress · Reflection talks at *Loiola* (gathering all different actors of *Etorkizuna Eraikiz*) · Presence on social networks and media

	Governance of *Etorkizuna Eraikiz*	Listening–Deliberation–Experimentation	Consequences on public policies	Socialisation and internationalisation
2020 → **Institutionalisation**	· Approval of the Model and Management Plan for *Etorkizuna Eraikiz* · Creation of the *Proiektuen Bulegoa* Projects Office (with representation of the Gipuzkoa Provincial Council and of social and economic agents) · Systemic vision of the entire *Etorkizuna Eraikiz* portfolio	· Start-up of *Gipuzkoa Deep Demonstration* in collaboration with EIT Climate-KIC · Collaboration with the OECD Observatory of Public Sector Innovation (OPSI) · Start-up of nine experimental projects · Renovation of the approach of the *Think Tank*, adding the research-action methodology to the reflection process · Creation of the board of political parties · New call for *Citizenship Projects*	· Creation of the Social Innovation Laboratory *Arantzazulab*, Reference Centre for Collaborative Governance	· Conferences · University of the Basque Country EHU/UPV Summer Courses · Presence on social networks and media · Collaboration with the OECD Observatory of Public Sector Innovation (OPSI)
2021 → **New learning processes: the systemic vision**	· Enhancement of the portfolio vision and of the systemic vision · Creation of *Udal Etorkizuna Eraikiz*, socialisation of collaborative governance at municipalities in the territory	· Start-up of six experimental projects · New call for *Citizenship Projects* · Incorporation of cross-cutting sustainability to the *Etorkizuna Eraikiz* portfolio. Start-up of two missions: "the new mobility" and "sustainable food" · Consolidation of "action learning" methodology as a learning strategy for employees	· Design and start-up of the Linguistic and Social Laboratory *Badalab* (reference centre)	· University of the Basque Country EHU/UPV Summer Courses · Creation of *Etorkizuna Eraikiz Foroa* · *Loiola* plenary meeting (gathering all different actors of *Etorkizuna Eraikiz*) · International *Etorkizuna Eraikiz* Congress · Presence on social networks and media

	Governance of Etorkizuna Eraikiz	Listening–Deliberation–Experimentation	Consequences on public policies	Socialisation and internationalisation
2022 → Assessment and sustainability	· Systematisation and assessment of the proposals tabled (learning processes) in various listening processes · Creation of the Governance Laboratory · Process for the participative assessment of Etorkizuna Eraikiz from the perspective of impact	· Start-up of four experimental projects · New call for *Citizenship Projects* · Definition and deployment of two missions: "the new mobility" and "sustainable food" · Analysis of participation by young people	· New reference strategies: *Gipuzkoa Quantum* (to foster quantum computing) and *Gipuzkoa Gantt* (to foster gene therapy)	· University of the Basque Country EHU/UPV Summer Courses · *Etorkizuna Eraikiz Foroa* conference · *Loiola* plenary meeting (gathering all different actors of *Etorkizuna Eraikiz*) · International *Etorkizuna Eraikiz* Congress · Launching of Boost (dynamic encounters with diverse citizens groups) · Elaboration of the *Etorkizuna Eraikiz* case study · Presence on social networks and media

Source: authors' own elaboration.

6.   Structure of the book and key addressed issues

Three types of text compose this book. First, there are chapters in which several authors describe and analyse what has been done in *Etorkizuna Eraikiz*; second, workshop notes synthesise discussions about the addressed questions, identifying key thematic debates, critical issues and challenges; and finally, comments by external scholars refer to a specific angle or topic that emerges when looking at *Etorkizuna Eraikiz* against literature or other cases and experiences.

Building upon Voets *et al.*'s analysis (2021) of the state of the art of the conceptualisation of collaborative governance, three broad areas were identified for the distribution of contents: one refers to structures and processes, dealing with the institutional design and its development; a second one includes issues of culture and relational aspects; and a final third one looks at results and outcomes. Therefore, the book is divided into three parts. Part I covers the model and its institutionalisation. After presenting the conceptual basis (Chapter 2, Egoitz Pomares, Asier Lakidain and Alfonso Unceta), the chapters explore the journey from conceptualisation to practice (Chapter 3, Xabier Barandiarán, Sebastián Zurutuza, Unai Andueza and Ainhoa Arrona), with special attention to the role of a systemic vision in articulating the development of the model (Chapter 4, Naiara Goia, Gorka Espiau and Ander Caballero). After the chapters, summary notes from Workshop 1 are presented, around the following three questions:

1.   To what extent do structures of governance of *Etorkizuna Eraikiz* differ from hierarchical organisational decision-making?
2.   Which formulae did (and did not) work for decision-making with multi-level, cross-departmental, and public- and private-sector actors?
3.   Analysis of meta-governance: what for, who, what, how and with what impact.

Following the Workshop 1 summary, four comments from different scholars (Tina Nabatchi, Luis Aguilar, Peter Loge and Adil Najim) cover issues regarding the conceptualisation and institutionalisation of collaborative governance.

Part II focuses on relational dimensions, looking specifically at the role of experimentation (Chapter 5, Andoni Eizagirre, Miren Larrea and Fernando Tapia), of communication (Chapter 6, Ion Muñoa), and of listening and learning (Chapter 7, Anne Murphy, María José Canel, Ander Arzelus and

Olatz Errazkin). The summary notes from Workshop 2 revolve around the following questions:

1. Analysis of stakeholders. Who is in, who is still out? Issues of democracy.
2. The role of culture in interaction management. What worked and what did not work in aligning different stakeholders around common goals? Why do people engage in collaborative governance (efficiency, equality, social and economic growth)?
3. The role of leadership. How to organise leadership? What skills are needed for leading collaborative governance?
4. How has EE approached communication? What can be learned from it about the role communication plays in collaborative governance?

Following the Workshop 2 summary, comments from different scholars (Sonia Ospina, Eva Sørensen, Jacob Torfing and Vilma Luoma-aho) cover issues of leadership, accountability, relationships and democracy.

Finally, Part III is an initial attempt (other attempts will come in the future, once the data on final assessments are systematically and fully collected and analysed) to look at results, and it does so through a 'trust lens'. The questions presented in Workshop 3 are as follows:

1. Accounting for results. What indicators are there about *Etorkizuna Eraikiz*?
2. How do we shift from results to trust? How is the collaborative governance of *Etorkizuna Eraikiz* building and keeping trust? How do inclusion/ exclusion lead to trust?
3. How to further analyse results, outputs and impact of collaborative governance?

Comments from several scholars (Gregg Van Ryzin, Carmine Bianchi and Stephan Ansolabehere) provide inputs for evaluating collaborative governance, with a special emphasis on intangible outcomes.

In terms of practical details, the appendices collect full information about the region of Gipuzkoa, the different projects, status of achievements, some publications by *Etorkizuna Eraikiz* spaces, and the relationship with the 2030 SDGs Agenda; all of them include links to up-to-date information with which the reader will be able to follow up the development of this initiative. Finally, a combined list of references including all of those used in the different chapters is provided at the end.

PART I

STRUCTURAL DIMENSIONS TO INSTITUTIONALISE COLLABORATIVE GOVERNANCE

Chapter 2
Etorkizuna Eraikiz: The conceptual basis of the model

EGOITZ POMARES, *Sinnergiak Social Innovation, University of the Basque Country, UPV/EHU*
ASIER LAKIDAIN, *Sinnergiak Social Innovation, University of the Basque Country, UPV/EHU*
ALFONSO UNCETA, *Sinnergiak Social Innovation, University of the Basque Country, UPV/EHU*

1.   Introduction: models and methods in research

The word 'model' refers, in a literal sense, to an abstraction of reality. But it also evokes the representation of a phenomenon. Models can be viewed as maps that capture and activate knowledge. They can also be viewed as frameworks that filter and organise knowledge. Finally, they can be viewed as micro-worlds for experimentation, cooperation and learning (Morecraft & Sterman, 1994). Therefore, model construction always means simplification, aggregation, omission and some abstraction (Bossel, 1994).

According to Sheptulin (1983), certain characteristics can be identified that are common to all models:
- a model is a process of abstraction;
- the function of a model is to discover and study new qualities, relationships, principles or laws of the object of study; and
- a model is usually expressed as the design of strategies, forms, technologies, instruments or projects.

Models are widely used among the scientific community, although their use and meaning differs between Natural Sciences and Social Sciences.

In Natural Sciences, modelling is a research method that scientists use to replicate real-world systems, whether it is a conceptual model of an atom, a physical model of a river delta, a computer model of global climate, or any other type of model (Brogan, 1985).

One of the first steps in this area is to develop a mathematical model of the phenomenon under study. This model should not be oversimplified, otherwise the conclusions drawn from it will not be valid in the real world. Hypotheses are also defined to explain the phenomenon and used to try to predict other related phenomena. Modelling usually includes computational processes and advanced measurement systems (Morrison, 1991).

Despite efforts to resemble Natural Sciences, research on society does not operate to the same conditions of theorisation. As Latour (2000) argues, the Social Sciences have for decades operated as if the research methods of disciplines such as physics were methodological aspirations, capable of neatly explaining causal relationships. As Simon previously noted:

> The social sciences have been accustomed to look for models in the most spectacular successes of the natural sciences. There is no harm in that, provided that it is not done in a spirit of slavish imitation. In economics, it has been common enough to admire Newtonian mechanics [...] and to search for the economic equivalent of the laws of motion. But this is not the only model for a science, and it seems, indeed, not to be the right one for our purposes [...] We can (now) see the role in science of laws of qualitative structure, and the power of qualitative as well as quantitative explanation (1979, p. 493).

Much of social science research comes from the construction of simplified representations of social phenomena. As a result, the use of models is widely recognised and has become a predominant feature of modern political science (Clarke & Primo, 2012). Consequently, in the social domain, models are used as tools for construction of theories. They are employed to explain and predict the behaviour of real objects and systems, as simplified images of part of the real world, or as the representation of a phenomenon (Lave & March, 1993).

Unlike models, a method can be defined as a particular procedure for addressing a process of knowledge generation or configuration (Gough, Oliver & Thomas, 2013). Scientific knowledge requires methods capable of making valid observations and interpretations.

Generally, these methods are characterised by dividing observed phenomena into simplified units of analysis, and also by establishing connections between such units in order to find greater or smaller influences (Maxwell, 2017). Scientific methods, moreover, allow an unbiased comparison of existing theories, which can then be debated and modified. For this purpose, scientific methods must satisfy four key characteristics (Bhattacherjee, 2012):

– they must be based on logical principles of reasoning;
– inferences derived must match with observed evidence;

- other scientists should be able to independently replicate the research processes and obtain similar results; and
- the procedures used and the inferences derived must withstand critical scrutiny by other scientists.

2.   Models and methods applied to governance research

From the perspective of governance structures, the construction of models and/or methods is linked to processes of institutionalisation. Thus, collaborative governance provides moral and cognitive models for political interpretation and action through symbols, scripts and routines (Hall & Taylor, 1996).

Indeed, anthropology and sociology have made outstanding contributions to the analysis of organised collective behaviour in political institutions. So, from a classical perspective, to institutionalise is: 'to infuse with value beyond the technical requirements of the task at hand' (Selznick, 1957, p. 17).

As Ansell & Gash (2008) state, collaborative governance:

> is a governing arrangement where one or more public agencies directly engage non-state stakeholders in a collective decision-making process that is formal, consensus-oriented, and deliberative and that aims to make or implement public policy or manage public programs or assets (p. 544).

The institutional order is both the result of social interaction and the mechanism that structures that interaction. Thus, institutions are seen as grammar books for action (Burns & Flam, 1989); as instances that allow social actors to work together to achieve beneficial social goals (Elster, 1989); or as areas that seek to reconcile rationality on the part of individuals with rationality on the part of society (Bates, 1988).

The practical application of collaborative governance processes seeking institutionalisation, involving a plethora of agents that shape interactions between public administration and organised society, can be performed by way of three types of process (DiMaggio & Powell, 1983):
- coercive processes, where formal and informal pressures result in clearly delimited practices;
- mimetic processes, where uncertainty about the social environment leads organisations to imitate recognisable methods in other agents; or
- normative processes, where a group's standards of action are recognised, internalised and adopted as binding.

Processes of collaborative governance, whose conditions for success lie in the adoption and implementation of the actions prescribed by the model itself, should be seen as processes of institutionalisation in which the agents involved follow forms of interaction based on cooperation in order to cope with the uncertain conditions of their environment. Activities of this type are intended to blur the distinctions between the institution and its setting, in order to establish new spaces for interaction.

In this context, the models have a twofold utility: they function as prototypes, i.e. as something to aspire to achieve, while at the same time they provide a schematic plan of how the goal is to be achieved (Forcese & Richer, 1973).

Three key factors can be highlighted in the process of applying these models in practice:

- The first refers to the willingness of agents *vis-à-vis* methods of collaborative governance (Sørensen & Torfing, 2005).
- The second, according to Ansell (2008), is that collaborative political contexts can be viewed as the result of processes of institutionalisation that result in networks. These networks host agents that adopt complex relationships, where complexity is considered to comprise multiple, non-linear relationships with weak hierarchies (Taborsky, 2014).
- The third is that all of the above underlines the idea that networks have a dual character, in that they function as channels for the communication and mobilisation of resources in order to achieve common objectives, while at the same time forming social structures of influence that delimit the possibilities for action. In this regard, collaborative governance models have a social and instrumental dimension (Granovetter, 1985).

In any case, adherence to the principles of governance models and methods, whether from a perspective that views collective action as a set of strategies (Lieberman, 2002) or as an enterprise demarcated by habits and conformities (Scott, 2014), leads actions to be developed in consensual directions of public interest. Thus, the practices of collaborative governance establish the conditions for configuring a shared public agenda (Zuluaga & Romo, 2017).

In short, a governance model is a prescriptive abstraction which, beginning from a given architecture, requires an instituting process that links the agents involved with practices recognised by all. The degree to which the method of action is consolidated depends on the adoption and appropriation of the principles governing collaboration.

This being the case, collaborative governance differs from other forms of joint action in that it is a mimetic method for coping with uncertainty in its different forms (economic, political, social or environmental).

3. *Etorkizuna Eraikiz* ('Building the Future'): model and method

Reflecting on the current political disorder, Sánchez Cuenca (2022) writes that:

> We are going through a political crisis. It is not a crisis of the democratic ideal as such, which as yet has no competitors, but of its representative dimension. The crisis lies in representation and political parties, not in the democratic regime (p. 155).
>
> The political disorder must be seen as part of a global process of questioning the classic instances of social intermediation. Intermediation is in crisis or transformation in many areas of social life. In some cases, intermediation disappears and in others it loses its hierarchical character (p. 157).

These problems of intermediation have different implications. For our purposes, the problem of 'penetration' of the political institutions is particularly noteworthy. It takes the form of disaffection, resistance and opposition which may (though does not necessarily) crystallise into problems and conflicts. In any case, they directly affect whether society views its political institutions favourably or unfavourably.

When the problem of 'penetration' becomes acute and entrenched, when the political field normalises a way of functioning based on radical autonomy (Joignant, 2019), what emerges is a political crisis that is expressed in a deep gap between official politics and the citizens, the germ of institutional weakening.

In this context, governance is a means of reconciling official politics and society, an intermediate political space capable of connecting the two fields to try to channel more and more diverse social interests. As Dorf & Sabel (1998) rightly point out, governance falls within what they call 'models of democratic experimentalism'.

Based on these and other reflections, from 2015 work began on developing the *Etorkizuna Eraikiz* ('Building the Future') Programme in Gipuzkoa. It was initially formulated in the Strategic Plan of the Provincial Government of Gipuzkoa 2015–2019:

> Development of an exercise of shared prospection with agents from the province with regard to the fundamental challenges, in order to guarantee the economic, social and political future of the territory, which will serve to build public policies and address the strategic medium-term challenges of Gipuzkoa.

This statement of intent logically required a design, i.e. a model and a means of deployment. Generally speaking, governance initiatives are usually channelled through agencies. Ansell (2000) called this type of agency 'networked polity', i.e. a more or less stable extension of the world of democratic institutions into social networks, composed of interested organisations and interested citizens.

According to Ansell (2000), such agencies combine three constituent principles that usually govern the consortia constructed within the framework of European policy programmes:
- bottom-up functioning;
- public–private partnership; and
- strategic programming of the action.

A vast corpus of literature has been created around these three principles, which has developed different names and approaches: 'networked governance' (Mulgan, 2009); 'collaborative governance' (O'Leary, 2014; Sranko, 2013); 'public-private governance' (Kivleniece, 2013; Vogelpohl, 2012); 'new public governance' (Sørensen & Torfing, 2015); 'platforms for collaborative innovation' (Carstensen & Bason, 2012); 'i-labs' (Reynolds, 2015; Puttick *et al.*, 2014).

Etorkizuna Eraikiz drew on all these contributions to design its own model. The particular feature of *Etorkizuna Eraikiz* is that it is a model promoted and led by the Provincial Government of Gipuzkoa, adapted to the territorial and social reality of Gipuzkoa, which will create several relational spaces in which public issues and/or those affecting the development of Gipuzkoa will be addressed. *Etorkizuna Eraikiz* is a model designed to guide action, target-driven actions (purpose-driven actions) and subject to a decision-making process (based on non-hierarchical principles).

It is therefore an action that is located in the province of Gipuzkoa and guided by three priorities: to anticipate future challenges; to collaborate with the society of Gipuzkoa to address these challenges; and to promote 'experimentation' as a means of solving problems and designing public policies. This principle of experimentation promotes a specific form of relationship between cooperating citizens and organisations (whatever objective it may pursue), amongst players capable of organising, learning, prototyping, proposing and deciding collectively on a given issue (a specific purpose).

The *Etorkizuna Eraikiz* model is expressed through an architecture (conceptualisation and structuring of the various components), processes that support deployment (action) and transversal lines aimed at systematising and stabilising the action itself (guides).

Etorkizuna Eraikiz is therefore seen as a project structured towards change, which makes organisational and operational modifications and seeks to be jointly apprehended and practised by institutional and social stakeholders. A project with a vocation for transformation, resolution, knowledge generation and permanence (institutionalisation).

4. *Etorkizuna Eraikiz*: architecture, processes, institutionalisation

This section sets out the basis for understanding the functioning of the *Etorkizuna Eraikiz* collaborative governance model by describing its architecture, operating processes and the institutionalisation of the model.

4.1. Architecture

The architecture of *Etorkizuna Eraikiz* is the expression of the internal rationality of the model and its function is to build the operating logic within which the institutional and social agents act and interact. The architecture thus provides a framework for this relationship, structuring the way in which agents cooperate (Vommaro & Gené, 2016).

The operating logic of *Etorkizuna Eraikiz* is based on two 'spaces', which are arranged in networks with the aim of deliberating to configure a shared public agenda.

– *Gipuzkoa Taldean* (Gipuzkoa as a Team), the Listening Space
This is fundamentally designed to be a deliberative space that hosts different places and activities (Think Tank; Open Budgets; Citizenship Projects; Territorial Development Laboratory) in which challenges and priorities are identified and projects oriented to experimentation and resolution are proposed (Figure 2-1).

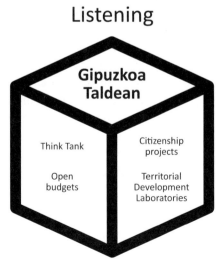

Figure 2-1. Listening Space

– *Gipuzkoa Lab*, the Space for Experimentation

This is the laboratory for developing projects through interdisciplinary partnerships, which always seeks to include a range of actors: public administration, organisations of different types depending on the theme, universities, international bodies and networks. The laboratory stimulates cooperation, learning and knowledge generation. Its primary function is to resolve challenges and to design and propose public policies (Figure 2-2).

The listening and experimentation spaces constitute the core of the governance model. They are the true

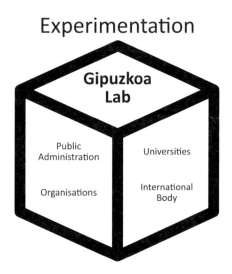

Figure 2-2. Space for Experimentation

expression of collaborative governance, since institutional and social actors cooperate through the identification of challenges, deliberation, prototyping, the search for solutions and the design of public policies. These deliberation and experimentation activities take place in contexts that operate on non-hierarchical principles. These are activities that occur in contexts that either have little or no hierarchy or are close to the existing hierarchy but not directly answerable to it.

As part of the model and complementing the practical expression of collaborative governance embodied in *Gipuzkoa Taldean* and *Gipuzkoa Lab*, the reference centres are entities that specialise in different areas of activity of particular importance for Gipuzkoa's future, including: cybersecurity, sustainable mobility, active aging, integration, sustainable transition, social innovation, linguistic innovation, digital gastronomy and audiovisual creation (see Appendix 5 for further and up-to-date information on these reference centres).

These centres are independent structures, although they are financed and supervised by the Provincial Government of Gipuzkoa. They produce specialised knowledge that is made available to the citizens and organisations of Gipuzkoa. Their goal and function is therefore 'strategic specialisation' (Figure 2-3).

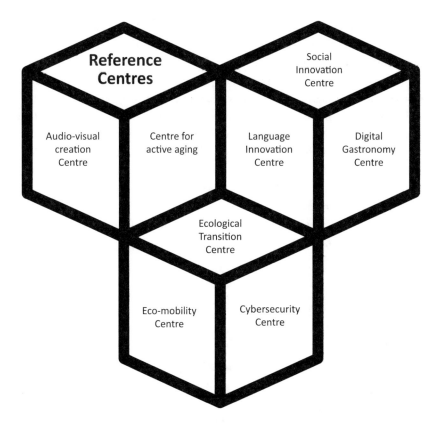

Figure 2-3. Specialisation section

4.2. Processes

The architecture of *Etorkizuna Eraikiz* builds an operating logic that substantially modifies some of the routines in which political action was developed – routines that are typical of an increasingly autonomised and hierarchical political space, whose inertia greatly hinders the ordinary participation of society in the deliberation, design and implementation of public policies.

It need hardly be stressed that a transformation such as that proposed by *Etorkizuna Eraikiz* rapidly vanishes if it does not have a support structure that guides, orders and channels the activity generated by the model's deployment.

This support structure is made up of 'processes', which are constituent elements of the model and also play an organising role. Once deployed, *Etorkizuna Eraikiz* produces knowledge, learning, experiences and results. And the mission of the processes is to provide a framework and order for the action.

The Management Process is in charge of facilitation, monitoring and evaluation of the development of the model. In this task, the portfolio and the monitor are essential tools.

The Dissemination Process promotes systematic socialisation and communication activities through a range of tools (websites, blogs, workshops, events, etc.).

The vocation of the Research Process is to formalise and structure into a knowledge repository the contents and findings of *Etorkizuna Eraikiz*'s activity.

The Internationalisation Process should ensure that *Etorkizuna Eraikiz* is linked to other similar international experiences, and promote comparison and lesson-learning. Internationalisation should thus be viewed not as an event, but as an ordinary activity.

These processes are interrelated through a stable General Process-Led Plan (Figure 2-4).

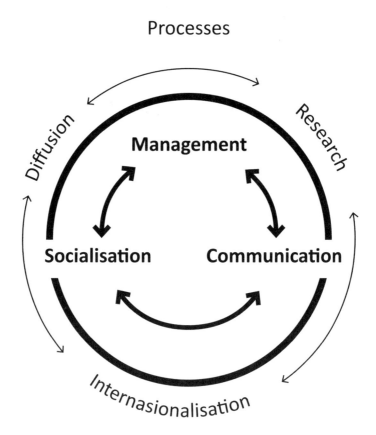

Figure 2-4. Support process

4.3.   Institutionalisation

The problem of institutionalisation converges with the problem of social action. Any analysis of the former necessarily leads to an interpretation of the latter. Moreover, to institutionalise is to produce a logic that acquires a life of its own, while partially or totally breaking down existing logics (Lourau, 1970). Moreover, institutionalisation has a material expression (rules, norms, places) and a symbolic expression (rituals, uses) (Castoriadis, 1983).

In order to evaluate the degree to which the *Etorkizuna Eraikiz* model is institutionalised, one must consider the degree to which it has achieved penetration in normative (including spatial) terms, and also in behavioural terms.

In regulatory terms, the Provincial Government of Gipuzkoa's approval of the Model and Management Plan of *Etorkizuna Eraikiz* on 28 January 2020 was vitally important. It gives *Etorkizuna Eraikiz* a normative anchor, and means that the model *exists* institutionally.

In behavioural terms, what is relevant is the way in which institutional and social actors perceive and experience the model (Lapassade, 1985) and the degree to which institutional and social actors are favourably disposed to acting in the manner prescribed by the model. The publication '*Etorkizuna Eraikiz* 2016–2020' (Diputación Foral de Gipuzkoa, 2021b) is the evidence that *Etorkizuna Eraikiz* is now a reality manifested through a wide range of actions.

The more objectified the model is (in terms of its architecture and routines), the less it needs to be explained – i.e. the more institutionalised both its architecture and its operating logic are. Institutional and social actors are coming to see *Etorkizuna Eraikiz* as a place where cooperative practices are routinely carried out.

At this point, it may be necessary to clarify that while *Etorkizuna Eraikiz* shows an appreciable level of institutionalisation, this does not necessarily mean that there is a high degree of social appropriation (Lau & Sears, 1986). In other words, for institutional and social agents to make a conscious and reflexive transition towards the governance model represented by *Etorkizuna Eraikiz*, it is not enough just to practise and experience its operating logic. In this respect, too little time has elapsed for the model to have comprehensively penetrated. This issue therefore remains outstanding and will depend on the degree to which the institutional trajectory of the governance model and the interests and attitudes of institutional and social actors converge.

5.   Conclusions

Western democracies have accustomed us to a way of structuring politics that is founded on the idea, practised to an ever more extreme extent, that any direct and continuous expression of the citizens' voice is impossible. In the absence of such a possibility, there is no choice but to delegate power to a few to act as a loudspeaker for the voices of the citizenry. The paradigm of this idea is embodied by political institutions. The truth is that, in practice, these institutions, formalised in governments, parliaments, parties, etc., have gradually become the property of professional politicians who practise politics in a way that is quite far removed from the people they represent (Bauman, 2001).

In such circumstances, governance models are proposals for transforming the current relationship between institutional actors and social actors. They seek to break with the situation created in many representative democracies, characterised by the existence of an official political space that is becoming increasingly autonomous of and distanced from society. The overarching sensation is of a citizenry being subjected to rather than represented by political power, and a civil society that lacks ordinary channels of expression and participation.

Governance models provide a new orientation for ways in which the items on the public agenda can be raised and debated and for the decision-making mechanisms with regard to such items. With the implementation of such models, one may expect greater participation and control by civil society over public affairs, together with a better reflection of citizens' priorities in public policies and other additional benefits.

We believe that governance models should seek to describe areas and procedures designed to transform the political praxis instituted. This simplification need not necessarily explain the theoretical foundations, but the strength of the model and its practical viability depend to a large extent on the underlying theory.

Etorkizuna Eraikiz is a model with a solid theoretical foundation that began with a diagnosis and which proposes an action-oriented design. It is also a localised model that takes into account the specific characteristics of Gipuzkoa, the place where it is intended to be deployed. *Etorkizuna Eraikiz* is determined not only to modify the political rhetoric but also to create the conditions for an action that will transform the established political space.

In this last regard, the success of the model should be judged not only in terms of its theoretical and propositional soundness but also – and most particularly – by its capacity for deployment and practical application. This involves acceptance of a new order and a new operating logic in the relationship between institutional and social agents, and in the deliberation and proposal oriented towards the design of public policies. As we have already explained, the response to these challenges has both a cognitive and an empirical dimension.

In the case of *Etorkizuna Eraikiz*, the empirical dimension appears to show a great deal of activity governed by the spatial, functional and relational logics established by the model. The cognitive dimension (assimilation, appropriation and validation of the new order) requires a degree of reflexivity in institutional and social agents that is still far from being achieved.

Going forward, the continuance of the *Etorkizuna Eraikiz* model will depend on three areas: problems concerning the behaviour of social actors; problems concerning the behaviour of the institutional actors themselves; and problems arising from the relationship between institutional and social actors (Freund, 2018).

In any case, non-reflective practice is a necessary condition for the deployment of a governance model, but it is not in itself a sufficient condition for its appropriation and stabilisation.

Chapter 3
The institutionalisation of *Etorkizuna Eraikiz*: From conceptualisation to practice

Xabier Barandiarán, *Provincial Council of Gipuzkoa*
Sebastián Zurutuza, *Provincial Council de Gipuzkoa*
Unai Andueza, *Provincial Council of Gipuzkoa*
Ainhoa Arrona, *Basque Institute of Competitiveness*

1.   Introduction

The preceding chapter, which describes the conceptual model of *Etorkizuna Eraikiz* (referred to hereinafter as EE), states that institutionalising collaborative governance means creating a new logic that will transform the existing one and take on a life of its own. It achieves this goal to the extent to which the model is collectively grasped and put into practice. The purpose of this chapter is to describe the form taken by that joint practice during the first six years of EE (2016–2022), in order to explain the logic it has gradually acquired on its path to transformation, knowledge generation and permanence.

More specifically, this chapter:
– provides background on EE, identifying key aspects without which the momentum and subsequent development of the initiative cannot be understood;
– describes its practical development, i.e. the way in which the spaces, cross-cutting processes and management mechanisms around which it is structured are arranged;
– explains the responses that have been provided to any needs that have emerged when the model was applied, with reflections from the actors involved; and
– discusses the lessons learned from the experience.

Three of the authors of the chapter are members of the EE promotion team, and the fourth has worked as a researcher. The first author is currently advisor to the Deputy General, was Chief of Staff to the Deputy General in two government terms (2007–2011 and 2015–2019), and is at present the main person responsible of the initiative; the second author is Strategy Director of the Cabinet of the PGC; the third author is Managing Director of Strategic Projects; and the fourth author is a researcher at Orkestra and part of the research team collaborating in the EE's Governance Laboratory and the Think Tank.

The text includes the individual reflections of each of the authors, together with lessons shared by all of them. However, in order to facilitate reading of the text, it has been written in a common voice.

2.   Preliminary considerations: background and approach to collaborative governance in *Etorkizuna Eraikiz*

Although EE was launched in 2016, its momentum and subsequent development cannot be understood without some reference to the background that made it possible to sow the first seeds that would later blossom into today's initiative. In addition to the theoretical bases described in the previous chapter, we think it is important to explain the concept of collaborative governance adopted at EE. With this objective in mind, we set out below some key elements to contextualise this initiative for the institutionalisation of collaborative governance by the Provincial Government of Gipuzkoa in a broader time frame and in its specific theoretical conception.

2.1.   Early experiments with shared leadership, public–private partnerships and citizen participation

The origins of EE can be traced back to 2007, the first year of the government in which some of the current policy-makers in the programme promoted three principles through political discourse and action that would later form the basis of the idea of collaborative governance in EE: shared leadership, public–private partnership and citizen participation.

During the 2007–2011 term of government, the first initiatives were developed that were to take shape in the first attempt to experiment with new forms of governance – the *Gipuzkoa Aurrera* and *Gipuzkoa Sarean* projects and a provincial decree on citizen participation. Gipuzkoa Aurrera was a public–private platform that sought to promote major strategic challenges in Gipuzkoa. It was a first approach to experimenting with shared leadership and public–private collaboration by the government team that would later develop EE.

This initiative included Gipuzkoa Sarean, a project that sought to strengthen the social capital of the territory in order to improve competitiveness and wellbeing (Barandiarán & Korta, 2011). A working group was created between different institutions and universities. This group identified a number of actions for developing social capital in different areas of society, thus highlighting the importance of values in the economic, social and political development of Gipuzkoa.

Following the 2011 elections, the project continued under a new government and its action was redirected towards the construction of a new governance for territorial development. The project – currently known as the Territorial Development Laboratory (see section 4.2) – has contributed to the construction of a collective capacity for collaboration by generating spaces and dynamics between a certain group of agents, mainly local development agencies, the Provincial Government and researchers (Diputación Foral de Gipuzkoa, 2015; 2020), through the methodological development of action research for territorial development (Karlsen & Larrea, 2014). This methodology enabled conceptual ideas on collaboration to be given shape in a real construction of governance, and was later of key importance in the practical structuring of EE (see more details on the project and methodology in Chapter 5).

2.2.   Collaborative governance as a response to new challenges

In 2015, part of the political team that in 2007 had promoted the early initiatives experimenting with new forms of governance returned to office at the Provincial Government. This team proposed a collaborative governance strategy. It understood that globalisation and its conditions of development had brought a new political agenda to the table, including challenges such as climate change, diversity management, the fight against inequality and the new individual and collective living conditions resulting from digitalisation. Society and its institutions were faced with a new political agenda that was developing against a backdrop of uncertainty, disruption and lack of stability.

Moreover, the political leadership of the Provincial Government considered that the liberal democracy that has characterised Western societies was undergoing a transformative crisis, as a result of new geopolitical, economic and social realities, with major consequences, such as the generation of more individualistic and consumer-oriented societies, the weakening of social capital, a growth in social inequality, difficulties for political structures to influence multiple spheres, and political disaffection. It was thus felt that the current configuration of state governance presents enormous difficulties in developing effective public policies in a context of enormous deregulation and profound disengagement of society from the political community.

In this situation, the Provincial Government decided to adopt the principle of collaborative governance as a strategy that would lead the institutions towards a new form of political direction and means of managing public policies, based on collaboration and shared leadership. This entailed a new form of communication between policy-makers, organised society and civil society. The concept more coherently included the initial ideas of shared leadership, public–private collaboration and citizen participation advanced in the first term of government. Moreover, it matched the collaborative logic that has characterised the development of Gipuzkoa in many areas.

2.3.   Collaborative governance in *Etorkizuna Eraikiz*

Although there are many good reasons for choosing collaborative governance as a principle for governance and problem-solving strategy (Ansell, 2019), at EE it is seen as a way of establishing the structural and cultural conditions that will guarantee democratic quality for deliberation and for the shared action of public, private and social actors interacting in a specific public policy context.

While there are many ways of approaching collaborative governance (Ansell & Gash, 2008; Batory & Svensson, 2019; Bingham, 2011; Emerson, Nabatchi & Balogh, 2012), the team responsible for EE sees it as *the process of deliberation and shared action that links public institutions, organised society and civil society, with the aim of strengthening the public policy ecosystem in the context of a shared public space, through the generation of social capital and a new political culture.*

We can particularly draw attention to three fundamental implications of this definition, which have been key to the development of EE:
–   *Redefining the deliberative space and the distribution of power.* Incorporating diverse actors in public deliberation has made it necessary to analyse how this new space is configured in democratic terms. Who do the participants in the deliberation process represent? It was felt that in this new space, the government's leadership role does not disappear, since it is the government that holds the democratic representation of public institutions and guarantees the preservation of the public nature of the process while respecting fundamental democratic values and principles. However the incorporation of organised society and civil society into a new space for deliberation and shared action means building a new public space, which adds new spaces to that represented by the public

institutional system. These spaces are also public in nature but do not derive directly from the institutional system.

– *Generation of social capital* to activate a new political culture that provides a response to an institutional structuring in terms of collaborative governance. It was seen that social capital is a resource that is developed in human relationships (institutionalised and formalised to a greater or lesser extent) and which translates into norms that generate reciprocity and trust-based social behaviours. Consequently, it enables collaboration between public, private and social actors.

– *Governance and social innovation*, since collaborative governance incorporates wider society into the development of new spaces for creation, deliberation and active experimentation, to respond to the multiple needs that arise in the field of public policies in a context of complexity and uncertainty.

The EE model was built on this vision of collaborative governance, viewed as a strategy to extend democracy – which redefines the public space and power and seeks to strengthen social capital in order to create the necessary conditions for active experimentation and social innovation – and the vision of the role of social capital and the bases described in Chapter 2.

2.4. Key elements that enabled the promotion of *Etorkizuna Eraikiz*

Academic works that have systematised experiences in collaborative governance (see, for example, Ansell & Gash, 2018; Emerson *et al.*, 2012) identify a series of factors that help explain the onset of this type of experience, such as political dynamics, levels of trust, incentives and leadership. It is not the purpose of this chapter to analyse the role of these factors in the origins of EE. However, we do consider it important to share some characteristics of the initial leadership that we believe to have been of key importance in the implementation of the first actions in 2007 and the subsequent launch of EE in 2016:

– *A dream/vision among top policy-makers*. During the 2007 term of office (and subsequently in the 2015 and 2019 terms), the Deputy General and his chief of staff were individuals who had been formed politically in academia and in the political party to which they belonged. However, they had little experience of public management. Paradoxically, this circumstance provided an opportunity to propose strategies such as collaborative governance and shared leadership which sounded far removed from everyday politics and administration and were seen as pertaining more to theoretical paradigms.

– *New political agenda and a new way of doing politics.* From the beginning of the 2015 government, it was considered necessary to work as a team to achieve the targets that had been set for the legislature. A sociological study carried out in the Provincial Government at the beginning of the term of office revealed the need to develop a new political agenda and a new way of doing politics in the territory. A new political agenda entails addressing major transformations to respond to territorial challenges (such as climate change, digitalisation, population aging, social inequality, etc.); and a new way of doing politics has to do with the development of a collaborative culture that overcomes political divisions, partisan interests and the political disaffection of the citizenry with the political community. Thus, in the early days of EE, the political team began to discuss shared leadership, public–private partnership and citizen participation, and to develop actions based on these principles; subsequently, these would be articulated in the concept of collaborative governance.

– *Incorporation of reflexivity and long-term vision.* The need to transform the political agenda and the way of doing politics (and ultimately, the political culture) meant that from the beginning of the term of office it was necessary to incorporate greater reflexivity into public policy processes and also a long-term vision to achieve objectives in a context that was considered to be complex and uncertain. As we shall see in the rest of this chapter, the team managed to implement this reflexivity.

– *Understanding power as a means for action, with the consequent detachment from it.* The Deputy General saw power as an instrument for achieving results. These authors believe that it would not otherwise have been possible to promote the creation of spaces to share this power with other agents and wider society.

– *The importance of people.* All of the elements mentioned above show that, beyond strategies, functions and plans, the characteristics and values of the people in charge can be decisive when it comes to guiding an initiative such as EE.

– *Power and capacity for action.* In addition to all of the above, those who wanted to put into action a concrete vision of politics and democracy were at the top of the hierarchical pyramid in the Provincial Government and had the capacity to implement the actions that would build that vision. The results of the 2015 election (the electoral support for the new political leadership was overwhelming) created better conditions for launching an initiative such as EE.

The launch of EE, whose principal features are described below, cannot be understood without the previous factors and background described above.

3.   Principles and objectives of *Etorkizuna Eraikiz*

EE's objectives are: 1) to identify the challenges of the future, in dialogue with society; 2) to collectively build the public agenda of the province, in spaces of stable collaboration; 3) to cooperate in the design of and experimentation with public policies, in order to define joint solutions to the territorial challenges, learning to work collaboratively; and 4) to drive the transformation of the Provincial Government, accompanying the transition to a culture of collaborative governance.

In order to achieve its objectives, EE is based on four principles:

– *Institutional leadership.* The programme is promoted and led by the Provincial Government, the agent that proposes and finances it, as well as actively participating in its development.
– *Based on the specific characteristics of the territory in which it operates.* It is founded on characteristics such as the dynamism of its *comarcas* (a *comarca* is a sub-provincial, supra-municipal administrative division), a dense fabric of associations, and a tradition of collaboration and involvement in the public sector.
– *Creation of open spaces for learning, exchange and experimentation*, where people and organisations interact, collaborate and work together to generate proposals and address challenges.
– *Generation of democracy, trust and public value*, through new spaces for deliberation and experimentation that strengthen participatory democracy, seek to increase the generation of trust and a collective capacity to improve policies and services, and better respond to the challenges faced.

4.   Collaborative spaces for deliberation and experimentation

EE has built a model in which several spaces are developed that provide a framework for different forms of collaboration, with different purposes and the participation of different types of actors. EE can be viewed as a collaboration system, structured into three collaboration platforms that generate and develop a range of collaborative arenas and projects. In this conceptualisation we acknowledge the contribution of Tina Nabatchi, who suggested at the workshops that EE should be conceived as a collaboration system with collaborative platforms that are articulated in projects. We have further added the concept of 'arena' to capture the diversity of initiatives included in the platforms

We see collaboration platforms as "programmes with dedicated competences and resources for facilitating the creation, adaptation and success of multiple or ongoing collaborative projects or networks" (Ansell & Gash, 2018) and collaboration arenas as "temporary, purpose-built institutionalizations of interaction that comprise a mixture of resources, rules, norms, and procedures that both shape and are shaped by actual processes of collaboration" (Ansell & Torfing, 2021). Although the categories could be applied differently (for example, EE or even one of its arenas, the Think Tank, could be conceived as a collaboration platform), and despite the fact that there are some slight differences in practice (the three platforms of EE are not organisational bodies but conceptual spaces for articulation), we believe this to be a suitable conceptual approach, which we use to describe the model in order to facilitate the reader's comprehension.

Specifically, the EE model has three major platforms (see Appendices 3, 4 and 5 for further information):

– *Space for listening*: *Gipuzkoa Taldean* is the main space for deliberation and proposal. It includes several listening, dialogue and deliberation initiatives.
– *Experimental space*: *Gipuzkoa Lab* is the main space for experimentation and learning. It is the laboratory for advanced experiments for the future.
– *Specialisation area*: reference centres and strategies are specialised public, private or social centres (foundations, consortiums, etc.) whose purpose is to strengthen sectors that are strategic for the province of Gipuzkoa (in the field of mobility, aging, cybersecurity, the Basque language, etc.).

The platforms are described below.

4.1. Space for listening: *Gipuzkoa Taldean*

This is the space for active listening to society, to enable its participation in the deliberation and co-creation of public policies. It consists of several collaborative arenas and projects:

– *Think Tank*. The mission of this arena is to co-generate transferable and applicable knowledge that will have an impact on a new agenda and a new political culture in the Provincial Government. It takes the form of four reflection/action groups, in which stakeholders from organised civil society participate alongside staff from the Provincial Government: The Work of the Future, Green Recovery, The Futures of the Welfare State and New Political Culture. The methodology used is action research (see Chapter 5 for more details).

– *Citizenship Projects.* An initiative for citizens to propose and lead their own experimentation processes. This is achieved through an annual call for funding for social innovation projects, usually proposed and developed by local entities (associations, universities, companies, NGOs), generally grouped into consortiums.

– *Territorial Development Laboratory.* A space that promotes multi-level collaborative governance for territorial development, which is developed within the framework of a collaboration agreement with municipalities and their regional development agencies.

– *Participatory budgeting.* A tool through which citizens are offered the possibility of making proposals. Based on the ideas received, a series of projects are shaped and submitted to public scrutiny to determine which initiatives will be financed.

– *Ekinez Ikasi* ('Learning by Doing'). With the support of the methodology of action learning, active listening and learning processes are developed for internal groups of the Provincial Government of Gipuzkoa (see Chapter 7).

– *Udal Etorkizuna Eraikiz.* A programme that seeks to promote collaborative governance at the municipal level and create a learning community together with the municipalities, centring on new ways of governing.

– *Panel of Political Parties.* A space in which all parties represented in the provincial parliament participate to deliberate on the political agenda of the future and adopt decisions on a shared basis.

4.2. Experimentation space: *Gipuzkoa Lab*

A platform where active experimentation projects are developed, bringing together key actors from civil society, universities, public administration and those with the capacity to generate knowledge at an international level. The aim is to incorporate a new political agenda into the Provincial Government's public policies. The reference frameworks for the establishment of this new agenda and the projects proposed are the 2030 Agenda, the missions of the European Union and the RIS3 strategy of the Basque Government.

An experimental project is an initiative that is aligned with one or more strategic areas of EE; that seeks to respond to one or more challenges; that is developed by an interdisciplinary partnership made up of different agents from the territory and agents from outside the territory (university, international agent or network, one or more organisations from the network of agents in the territory, and the Provincial Government); and is oriented towards practical experimentation as a mechanism for transformation. The practical experimentation takes a triangular approach, relying on research, internationalisation and dissemination, and aims to generate applicable policy proposals.

5.   Reference centres and strategies

The reference centres and strategies are collaborative work spaces that cooperatively address social and economic projects of a strategic nature for Gipuzkoa, and are characterised by: 1) strategic specialisation, since they promote the development of strategic areas for the future of the territory; 2) being aimed at positioning Gipuzkoa in their respective fields; and for this purpose 3) leading and facilitating the implementation of the strategies; 4) seeking to increase the capacity to respond to complex challenges, based on transversality and plurality; and 5) generating their own ecosystems, creating networks and dynamising agents from the sector.

Table 3-1 shows the different reference centres and the way they are organised.

Table 3-1. Reference centres and strategies of *Etorkizuna Eraikiz*

Name and theme	Aim	Organisation and participating agents
MUBIL Intelligent and sustainable mobility	Centre for the development of activity, science and knowledge in intelligent and sustainable mobility.	Public foundation (Provincial Government, Donostia-San Sebastián City Council, *Ente Vasco de Energía*) Collaboration with private agents and research and training centres in the development of activities
ADINBERRI Active aging	Strategy to enhance the innovative potential of the territory at the service of active and healthy aging, from a social and economic perspective.	Public foundation (Provincial Government) Collaboration with institutions, agents from the social and healthcare system, academia, industry and society in the definition of strategies and performance of activities.

Name and theme	Aim	Organisation and participating agents
ZIUR Industrial cybersecurity	Centre for reinforcing and developing the cybersecurity capabilities of industrial companies in Gipuzkoa and strengthening their competitiveness.	Public foundation (Provincial Government, Donostia-San Sebastián City Council) Collaboration with institutions, industrial companies and research centres for organising actions.
NATURKLIMA Climate change	Multidisciplinary centre that seeks to generate institutional, technical and social capacities to address the impact of climate change and generate innovation for socio-ecological transition.	Provincial Government foundation Collaboration with public institutions, social entities and private organisations working in the fight against climate change.
2DEO Audiovisual production in Basque	Strategy that seeks to increase the production and consumption of audiovisual products in the Basque Country, promoting new creative contexts, experimenting with new production models and formats, and increasing the number of channels for dissemination.	Laboratory integrated in a cultural centre (*Tabakalera*), managed by the centre's team Collaboration with industry players in organising actions.
LABe Digital gastronomy	A space for experimentation and testing based on research, catering and the components industry to apply new knowledge in the gastronomy sector.	Strategy coordinated from the structures of the Provincial Government Developed in conjunction with a reference agent (Basque Culinary Centre), a cluster of kitchen appliance components and an association of hoteliers.
ARANTZAZULAB Social innovation and governance	A space for reflection and experimentation on the challenges of Basque society, which promotes research, experimentation and socialisation aimed at social transformation.	Foundation made up of the Provincial Government, a local town council (Oñati), a religious order (Franciscan Province of Arantzazu), a business corporation (Mondragon Corporation) and a local bank (Fundación Kutxa) Collaboration in organising actions with public institutions, universities, knowledge agents, international agents and organised society.

Name and theme	Aim	Organisation and participating agents
BADALAB Minority languages	Experimental space for the revitalisation of minority languages and equal opportunities among speakers.	Consortium formed by the Provincial Government, Renteria Town Council, Soziolinguisti-kako klusterra, Euskalgintzaren kontseilua, EITB, EHU/UPV, Euskaltzaindia, *Arantzazulab* and Langune. Collaboration with public, private and social agents for organising activities.
ELKAR-EKIN LANEAN Inclusive employability and activation	Integrated multi-departmental strategy for employability and inclusive activation through economic reactivation and competitiveness, quality employ-ment and social policies.	Strategy developed from the structures of the Provincial Government Strategy management and governance bodies that include representatives of public institutions and economic and social agents. Collaboration in organising actions with public institutions and third-sector and economic agents, universities and training centres.
GIPUZKOA QUANTUM Technologies	Strategy to form a hub around quantum technologies in Gipuzkoa, aligning existing agents in this field.	Strategy led by the Provincial Government, in collaboration with BERC Donostia In-ternational Physics Centre (research centre) and Multiverse Computing (private company) Collaboration with other institu-tions in defining the strategy.
GIPUZKOA GANTT Gipuzkoa Advanced New Therapies Territory	Collaborative project to turn Gipuzkoa into an international benchmark in advanced therapies (cell, gene and RNA), with an industrial vocation, generating a specialised ecosystem in this sector.	Strategy developed from structures of the Provincial Gov-ernment, in collaboration with a research centre, two companies and a public entrepreneurship agent (Viralgen, VIVEbiotech, BioDonostia and BIC Gipuzkoa)

Source: authors' own elaboration.

The reference centres and strategies constitute a key area of EE, and more information is provided on them in different chapters of this volume – as part of the conceptualisation of the *Etorkizuna Eraikiz* model (Chapter 2), and as a contribution to the 2030 Agenda (Chapter 8). This chapter analyses how these centres develop collaborative governance, an issue that is dealt with in greater detail in the paragraphs below.

Each centre and reference strategy has its own form of organisation and decision-making, adapted to its objectives and sectors. Thus, some have generated *ad hoc* teams and centres under different legal forms (foundations, consortiums), and others have teams from the structures of the Provincial Government or another collaborating agent. For example, *Badalab*, the centre specialising in minority languages, takes the legal form of a consortium, with exclusively public funding, but decisions are made collegially among the public institutions and social organisations making up the centre. The centre for social innovation, *Arantzazulab*, is part of a foundation in which the Provincial Government, a town council, a local bank, a business corporation and the religious order to which the venue in which it is located belong all participate, and its financing and decision-making processes are shared. The cybersecurity centre, *Ziur*, is a public foundation, owned by the Provincial Government and the City Council of Donostia-San Sebastián.

In addition to their contribution to addressing specific challenges, the centres contribute to the construction of collaborative governance in Gipuzkoa through the inclusion of a collaborative logic in the main strategies of the territory. Specifically:

– They extend the practice of territorial governance, through the incorporation of a collaborative logic. This occurs on two levels. On the one hand, there is a collaborative rationale in the organisation and the decision-making and management bodies, as in the case of *Badalab*, where, as already mentioned, decisions are shared. On the other hand, although to varying degrees, there is a collaborative logic in the development of the actions carried out within the framework of the centres. One example is the initiative to address loneliness (*Hariak*), promoted by the centre for active aging, *Adinberri*, which has been developed in collaboration with public and social institutions and experts, with a steering group of 51 people, in a process in which more than 400 people have participated. The centres also encourage a collaborative logic among the agents of the sectors they stimulate. For example, *Badalab*, the centre for minority languages, seeks experimental structuring and relationships between different agents and speakers through its programmes and experimental spaces.

– They succeed in uniting, aligning and coordinating visions and capabilities. They bring together the key players in their fields, in some cases
   mobilising resources, knowledge and capabilities to build solutions.
   For example, gastronomy agents have diverse priorities in the area of
   digitalisation and so the centre for digital gastronomy, *LABe*, has worked
   on defining common fields of interest for all stakeholders. The strategy of
   employability and inclusive activation, *Elkar-Ekin Lanean*, was defined
   in a process of dialogue between a diverse group of agents. It promotes
   alignment and agreement on visions, knowledge and resources among
   the agents, through, for example, regional networks of inclusion in which
   third-sector entities, economic agents and local public entities collaborate.
   The *Ziur* cybersecurity strategy also collaborates with proximity agents –
   development agencies, business associations, clusters, etc. – to work with
   small businesses. Another example is the design and implementation of
   an integrated care model developed by the centre *Adinberri*, connecting
   health, social, community and private services.
– These promote relationships between different departments and different
   tiers of government. For example, the *Elkar-Ekin Lanean* strategy has
   been built on the idea that inclusion is a multidimensional challenge
   that requires a comprehensive, multi-sectoral and multi-level approach.
   It must include the economic-business and social vision and needs to
   activate different levers, such as issues of taxation and procurement,
   which depend, in institutional terms, on different departments of the
   Provincial Government, the municipalities and the Basque Government.
   The strategy has therefore been defined and developed in collaboration
   with these institutions and their representatives participate in its management structures.
– They lead knowledge and experimentation in strategic areas. For example,
   the *Naturklima* strategy has a climate observatory and produces annual
   reports on the circular economy. The *Ziur* centre has observatories to
   identify cybersecurity threats and best practices in its field –which are
   also shared with companies, in collaboration with local agents – and tests
   out cybersecurity technologies and products. *Mubil* does the same in the
   field of intelligent and sustainable mobility. The social innovation centre,
   Aranzatzulab (see more details in Chapter 4), has created a meeting place
   for Basque universities to carry out research on collaborative governance,
   has a residency programme for international researchers, and carries out
   various tasks for generating knowledge in practice, as an initiative to
   connect spaces of co-creation in the region and generate new knowledge.

In short, the strategies and reference centres achieve objectives and results that would not be possible without joint action and contribute to the design and implementation of public policies. Although led by the Provincial Government, these are co-developed together with the main agents of the system and with society.

6.   *Etorkizuna Eraikiz* governance and cross-cutting processes

To promote and facilitate their development, management and facilitation bodies have been created for the main EE initiatives, as well as bodies and strategies to manage the model with a comprehensive overall vision.

Specifically, EE has governance structures that include: a) bodies from the Provincial Government for strategic orientation, design, monitoring and implementation; and b) the 'Project Office', comprising representatives from the EE ecosystem (six people from the Provincial Government, two representatives from universities, four representatives from other public institutions, companies, associations and the social sphere), who play an advisory role, especially for experimental projects. In addition, the Governance Laboratory, created in 2022, seeks to deepen the relational logic, collaborative governance and a systemic vision of EE (see Chapter 4).

Together, these bodies seek to foster institutional designs and leadership that facilitate collaboration and experimentation, connectivity between processes, and management, socialisation and communication activities.

In addition, as noted in Chapter 2, EE has three cross-cutting processes (dissemination, internationalisation and research) that must be integrated in all areas of the initiative to enrich the production of information, knowledge and learning in the construction of shared solutions. To support these processes, the Provincial Government has signed collaboration agreements with international institutions (such as the OECD), has created an international network on collaborative governance, has designed an International Plan to position EE at a global level, and has consolidated stable relations with the French Basque Country. It has also signed annually renewed collaboration agreements with all the universities in the territory, and the universities participate in almost all of EE's projects.

Before getting into the description of the practice, Figure 3-1 is a graphic representation of the model.

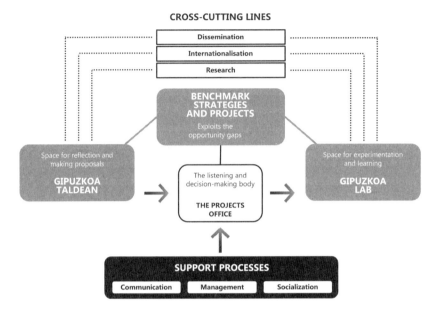

Figure 3-1. Graphic representation of *Etorkizuna Eraikiz* model. Source: authors' own elaboration.

7.   From theory to practice: evolution and learning

Since the initial conception of the model, EE has evolved, taking a form which, based on the same principles, with the same objectives, and within the same general framework, has sought to respond to the needs and problems that have arisen, making additions and adjustments to the concept initially proposed. The most significant changes are outlined below, with the lessons learned from its practical construction.

7.1.   Collaborative governance involves generating stable collaborative ecosystems for developing territorial strategies

The reference strategies and centres, described in a previous section, were not included in the model initially designed on the theoretical basis described in Chapter 2. However, the team in charge considered that the areas in which the Provincial Government was planning to develop strategic commitments should be addressed with a logic of collaborative governance, i.e. the main strategies of the territory should be co-led by organised society and the Provincial Government.

For its development, the members of the team identified the key players in each (previously defined) strategic area of Gipuzkoa, to approach them with the proposal for developing this endeavour jointly. In this way, the different reference centres and strategies took shape, each with its own specific form, according to the specific features of the different sectors.

As mentioned in section 5, the reference centres and strategies help to develop collaborative governance in two ways: firstly, the organisation, structure and operation of each centre entails the collaboration of agents from different sectors, giving rise to a new institutionalisation; and secondly, each of the projects carried out is essentially a collaboration.

7.2. Development of the process involves reformulating the initial spaces: from a classic Think Tank model to a space for action research

Initially, the Think Tank was conceived as an instrument to provide the Provincial Government with a greater capacity for reflection. Having been conceptually defined, the challenge was to build the space in practice and the team in charge began in the way it knew best, in a classical way: it proposed a strategic reflection with four groups of agents on four major themes, on which a series of reflections were made and, subsequently, some projects were launched.

After that first experience, the team decided to rethink the suitability of the model. The reflection had had an instrumental function oriented towards selecting the projects for experimentation and we concluded that we had to look for another way of institutionalising reflection. Based on the idea that it was necessary to establish a new arrangement for the relationship between knowledge and public policies (see next section), and on the experience acquired in the Territorial Development Laboratory (see Chapter 4), in 2020 it was decided to use action research as a working methodology.

Two years on, the Think Tank is now not only a space for reflection, but also a space for transformation, since reflection is oriented towards action and policy transformation (see Chapter 5). For example, a new model of care has been jointly defined (as set out in a White Paper), which the department of social policies is incorporating into its public policies. In addition, the Think Tank has taken on a central role that was not initially envisaged, becoming a key element for experimenting with collaborative governance and generating reflections and lessons that can be useful for other EE spaces.

7.3. A new relationship with the university is both a condition and a result of a new collaborative governance

The arrangement that is usually proposed in public organisations (and which was also initially proposed in the Provincial Government) with regard to the relationship between knowledge generation and public policies is a classic linear scheme: ideas are put forward and it is up to the policy-maker to take ownership of them and work with them. This is what has traditionally been called the *knowledge-driven model* (Weiss, 1979).

Within the framework of EE, we performed a reflection exercise that led us to reconsider the role of academia and the relationship between the Provincial Government and the universities. It was felt that the logic had to be changed, in such a way that the Provincial Government would set out the needs arising from the policies, to which the university could respond. However, it is difficult for a public institution to overcome existing inertia, and it was therefore decided to leave the previous dynamics in place, in the belief that they would be gradually diminished, and to generate a new working arrangement within the framework of EE. In addition to the arrangement described above (in which the Provincial Government sets out the needs to the University), other spaces have also been established in which research needs are co-defined in the process itself, in a continuous dialogue between policy and research (see Chapter 5).

This new arrangement has been extremely important, not only because it has allowed the development of several collaborative projects between the Provincial Government and the university, but also because it conceptually establishes a change in the relationship between the two, as well as in the logic of incorporating knowledge into policies.

7.4. The importance of change in the Provincial Government

One dimension that has gained strength in the institutionalisation of EE is the importance of working to transform the Provincial Government to ensure that it takes on board the approaches and values of collaborative governance.

Change in the Provincial Government had been a goal from the outset, but it did not constitute a field of action, since EE's focus had been on the spaces of articulation with society. During the implementation process, it became increasingly clear that it was vitally important to transform the culture of the organisation. EE's spaces for deliberation and experimentation contribute to this transformation, since the development of projects requires working collaboratively. However, it was considered necessary to make an additional effort in order to avoid what some people called a 'twin Provincial Government', which relates with external agents in one way – collaboratively – within the framework of EE, and in another way based more on a traditional hierarchy.

The first step was to incorporate programmes from the Governance Department into the EE initiative, so that they could be developed on the basis of a collaborative logic. An Interdepartmental Committee was also created, which is enabling steps to be taken towards mainstreaming. In addition, studies have been intensified to enable the Provincial Government to strengthen its capacity for reflection. The *Ekinez Ikasi* (action learning) programme, mentioned above and described in Chapter 7, has made it possible to increase reflexivity about practice and enrich interactions with a dynamic of mutual listening and assistance, and has had an impact on the way problems and collaborative work are approached. Finally, a pilot project is being carried out to foster a culture of collaboration and speed up transformation of the Provincial Government towards collaborative governance.

7.5. The evolution towards a 'polycentric architecture': of management as a support to meta-governance

The initial model designed for EE included two spaces (listening and experimentation), and a body – the Project Office – connecting the two. The relational logic was conceived as follows: the listening spaces would generate ideas, from which the Project Office would select several to be experimented with in the experimentation space, in order to generate lessons that could be incorporated into policies. The Project Office was made up of representatives from the stakeholders' ecosystem (universities, public institutions, companies, associations, Provincial Government), and was to be the body in charge of monitoring the EE, as well as analysing and selecting proposals. The Provincial Government's Strategy Directorate was to have a supporting role.

However, reality showed that the Project Office as initially conceived was not feasible. The participating organisations felt they did not have sufficient knowledge, capacity or time to perform the assigned decision-making function; they felt that their role should be consultative and advisory, and this is the function currently performed by the office. What had appeared to be a good formula for structuring the model in an ideal theory-based design proved not to be so in practice.

Moreover, the institutionalisation of collaborative governance in EE was more complex than the initial model envisaged. It has generated what Sonia Ospina, Professor of Public Management and Policy at New York University, called a 'polycentric architecture', in her address to a conference organised by *Etorkizuna Eraikiz* in December 2021. The model includes a diversity of collaborative spaces, which generate their own collaborative ecosystems, and which interact in a logic of diverse relationships, influencing policies through diverse mechanisms.

In this complex situation, the team conducted a reflection in 2021 and stressed the importance of managing the entire initiative systematically and going further in the governance of governance, i.e. *meta-governance* (Sørensen & Torfing, 2009). The collective processes of reflection and evaluation performed in the annual plenary of EE in 2021 reinforced this idea, and issues emerged such as the need to work with a systemic vision and the importance of articulating the relationships between the different areas. Following a process of reflection between a team of policy-makers and researchers (including the authors), in 2022 it was decided to create the group called the Governance Lab, whose mission is to strengthen the systemic and holistic vision of EE and to further extend the ways of working on collaborative governance across the initiative (described in more detail in Chapter 4).

7.6.   Structures inside or outside the Provincial Government? A hybrid model that could increase the potential for innovation and policy change

One of the debates when designing the model was whether EE should be managed and integrated into the structures of the Provincial Government or whether a specific agency should be created for its governance. After considering the advantages and disadvantages, the former option was chosen. Thus, even though resources are allocated and special bodies and dynamics are generated for its development, it was decided to place EE within the structures of the Provincial Government, under the direction of the Strategy Directorate.

In practice, however, a hybrid model has been constructed that can draw on the benefits of both options. EE is managed from the structures of the Provincial Government. This involves a series of difficulties, such as the reduced capacity to facilitate collaboration and innovation processes, confusion in the type of tasks for public managers, and other types of resistance typical of hierarchical and compartmentalised structures. However, this approach facilitates the link between the work of the deliberative spaces and the work of the departments and decision-making bodies, thus increasing the possibility of transformation.

At the same time, the EE reference centres have structures that develop their strategies in a semi-autonomous manner. Some centres, such as *Adinberri*, *Arantzazulab* and *Badalab*, are particularly well advanced in the development of experimentation dynamics, which allows innovation spaces to be generated that are one step removed from the institutional inertia of public bureaucracies.

If it is necessary to find institutional designs in each place that seek their own balance between different criteria (Ansell & Torfing, 2021), in the case of EE a formula has been constructed that allows innovation capacity to be balanced with capacity for influence in policy-making with a model that hybridises internal and external structures.

7.7. The ambition to establish collaborative governance as a principle of governance beyond the Provincial Government: *Udal Etorkizuna Eraikiz*

The multi-level perspective is integrated especially into certain EE deliberation and experimentation spaces, such as the *Territorial Development Laboratory* and the *Elkar-Ekin Lanean* strategy, in which collaboration dynamics are established between public bodies of different territorial scales, adopting a multi-level governance perspective. Indeed, some territories, like Gipuzkoa, are characterised by a strong framework of local institutionality, whereby several public bodies play an important role in building collective responses to territorial challenges.

From this perspective, and with EE's aim being to foster a new political culture in Gipuzkoa, it was considered relevant to develop a line of work that would promote collaborative governance beyond the Provincial Government, i.e. at a local level between different municipalities. The *Udal Etorkizuna Eraikiz* programme was launched for this purpose. It aims to extend the culture and forms of collaborative governance to a local level, and to generate a community of change and learning with local councils.

Although the programme is still in its infancy, it may have great potential for establishing collaborative governance as a principle of public governance in Gipuzkoa, as well as for strengthening inter-institutional collaboration between the Provincial Government and the municipalities, further extending the multi-level perspective of EE.

8. Final reflections

Since EE was launched in 2016, institutionalising it has entailed a confluence between the initial design and the decisions that have been made in practice, as part of the learning process that has characterised the implementation and development of a model to foster collaborative governance in Gipuzkoa.

Beyond the specific challenges that emerge from practice, such as the strengthening of shared leadership, EE must continue to face the challenge of experimenting in order to further extend the democratisation of politics.

Power sharing has become a strong area in the institutionalisation of society in advanced democracies, but it has not yet permeated the system of public institutions. Democracies are usually considered to be consecrated through the election of representatives from the citizenry and their integration in public institutions, which then develop dynamics that do not further impinge on the democratic system.

Collaborative governance means questioning the current public system, and the development of an initiative such as EE therefore runs into some resistance. It constitutes a process of deconstructing traditional power, which entails moving away from the bureaucratic system and designing new spaces, and thus represents a new way of doing politics.

It is therefore reasonable to presume that the further the implementation of the model goes, the more problematic and entangled the path will become. Collaborative governance is a challenge to classic power, and it will bring with it conflict, anger, reflection and complexity. However, if a society aspires to re-empower the democratic system in order to address the crisis of liberal democracy, it is essential to create new deliberative spaces and further embed democracy through them. In this future construction, a model such as EE must encourage reflexivity, and question and challenge itself with questions such as: who is participating and who should participate? In this way, this process of questioning becomes a driver for a constant furthering of collaborative governance.

9.   Lessons for practitioners

-   Flexibility is of key importance in co-constructing a model of collaborative governance practice. It needs to be redesigned on the hoof to respond to emerging challenges and incorporate lessons learned during imple-mentation. At EE, this flexibility has enabled, among other changes, a collaboration platform to be incorporated for developing territorial strategies (reference centres); a key deliberation arena (the Think Tank) to be transformed from a space for listening and generating ideas into a forum for action research, and a decision body (the projects office) to be reformulated as an advisory body.

- The logic of collaboration needs to be introduced in the public sector and addressed throughout the organisation. Particular effort is required to change the organisational culture and to involve political and technical staff from all areas so that they work together collaboratively.
- Fostering a collaborative system in which different platforms, arenas and projects are promoted requires the creation of a good system of 'governance of governance' (*meta-governance*), to endow the system with the capacity to reflect and work on institutional designs and leadership, not only of each of the platforms and spaces, but of the system as a whole.
- Although collaborative governance arrangements need to be context-based, a hybrid formula such as that constructed in EE, in which platforms are articulated from the structure of public organisations, while at the same time promoting autonomous platforms and arenas that eschew the traditional logic of administration, can be a helpful formula for generating innovation and having a real impact on policies.
- It is essential to change the form of relationship between the public administration and academia, and to involve universities in collaborative governance, so that specialised knowledge can be included in identifying territorial challenges and in the construction of responses to address them.
- If the ambition is to change the political culture of a territory, moving it towards collaborative governance, it is essential to adopt a multi-level territorial perspective. This means involving other governments and public institutions from the territory in collaborative platforms and projects. However, it also entails considering the promotion of collaborative governance at different territorial scales – in the case of EE, at a local level and in the municipalities.

Chapter 4
What a systemic vision can do to help develop collaborative governance: The example of *Etorkizuna Eraikiz*

Naiara Goia, *Managing Director Arantzazulab*
Gorka Espiau, *Managing Director Agirre Lehendakaria Center*
Ander Caballero, *Department of Government, Harvard University, and Agirre Lehendakaria Center*

1.   Introduction: a systemic vision through collaborative governance

This chapter explores the potential of systems analysis for addressing global policy challenges in the 21st century, and more tangibly, its application to *Etorkizuna Eraikiz*. We introduce the concept of collaborative governance as a mechanism to help public institutions view, manage and construct a new public agenda with a systemic vision.

1.1.   Presentation and context: a new political agenda in the face of 21st-century challenges

Complexity lies at the very heart of the challenges of our 21st-century society. Our world is undergoing profound political, economic and social changes, and globalisation has brought new interdependencies into the policy arena. Governments are no longer the only parties who control the success or failure of policies, or the way in which citizens perceive their actions. Against this backdrop, we are faced with 'wicked' problems, so called because they have no single cause or solution (OECD *et al.*, 2020).

Traditional approaches are no longer appropriate for addressing the scale and interrelatedness of emerging complex challenges. With dynamic and evolving characteristics, on a multi-level, multi-actor and multi-sectoral scale, today's challenges can no longer be addressed effectively within the boundaries of single organisations.

To effectively operate in this fast-changing context, governments need strategic vision, transformative leadership and firm commitment at the highest political level. This requires a new democratic governance model which can take on global challenges such as climate change, the COVID-19 pandemic and social inequalities and deliver on the 2030 Agenda for Sustainable Development (OECD, 2021a).

If we are to successfully respond to the challenges of this new world and have some hope of shaping desirable outcomes, we need to embrace new ways of looking at the world and new ways of organising. Our challenge is thus to evolve new organisational structures and capacities. Here, collaborative governance is presented as a governance model which can better tackle the systemic and complex magnitude of the challenges that institutions deal with, understood as "a process in which government, private organisations, and civil society interact to decide, coordinate, and carry out the direction and governance of their community" (Arellano, Sánchez & Retana, 2014, p. 121).

First, this section introduces the concept of the systemic perspective, and the benefit of incorporating it into the management of the *Etorkizuna Eraikiz* strategy. Second, some of the objectives that led to the incorporation of this vision into the strategy framework are described. Finally, we present a number of ongoing activities and mechanisms that integrate a new systemic approach through collaborative governance to enhance the outcomes of the *Etorkizuna Eraikiz* programme. The chapter also showcases the internal governance structures ('meta-governance') which embrace the systemic vision and are designed to achieve a sustained overall impact over time.

1.2.   Introduction to systemic vision and systems thinking

This is a century of global and complex issues. The world is undergoing profound structural changes, and the challenges we face are systemic and of an unprecedented scale. They cannot be addressed through *ad hoc*, short-term, sectoral interventions. Rather, we must assume that the systems are dynamic, and evolve and behave in ways that are largely determined by their own properties and characteristics (Hynes, Lees & Müller, 2020)

Nevertheless, the organisational structures and management systems of the public sector, for the most part, have not focused on cross-organisation outcomes. The effects of interventions are usually analysed within their specific domains or policy silos, rather than addressing broader interdependencies and outcomes, and inter-departmental relations. This runs contrary to the new mission-oriented policies approach (Kattel & Mazzucato, 2018), which argues that public policies are horizontal by nature and require different capabilities and methodologies than currently exist in the public sector. Thus, public administration needs to be modernised to ensure a transformation of working methodologies and forms of organisation. Here, the starting hypothesis is that systems thinking can help achieve mission-oriented policies and a better adaptation to evolving societal, technological and economic changes.

Although there is no single definition of systems thinking in the system dynamics community, there is some consensus in the literature about seven key characteristics: Recognising Interconnections (understanding how parts relate and seeing the whole system); Identifying Feedback (recognising existing interconnections and feedback); Understanding Dynamic Behaviour (understanding the relationship between feedback and behaviour); Differentiating Types of Flows and Variables (understanding the difference between levels and rates); Using Conceptual Models (explaining and observation using general systems principles); Creating Simulation Models (describing connections using mathematical models); and Testing Policies (testing hypotheses to develop policies) (Stave & Hopper, 2007).

Authors ranging from academia to social innovation practitioners have described the fundamental concepts of systems thinking, all of which are based on similar elements, such as: Interconnectedness (mutually connected elements); Synthesis (understanding the whole and the parts at the same time, together with the relationships and the connections that make up the dynamics of the whole); Emergence (the outcome of the synergies of the parts; this encompasses non-linearity and self-organisation and the term 'emergence' is often used to describe the outcome of things interacting together); Feedback Loops (flows between elements of a system); Causality (deciphering the way things influence each other in a system); and Systems Mapping (identifying and mapping the elements of 'things' within a system to understand how they interconnect, relate and act in a complex system) (State & Hopper, 2007, p. 10). Once we have identified these elements, unique insights and discoveries can be used to develop interventions, shifts or policy decisions that will dramatically change the system in the most effective way (Acaroglu, 2017).

In short, systems thinking involves studying all components and their influence on one another as a whole. It is the opposite of our traditional analytical approach of reasoning and functioning in silos, where we break things down into separate parts and try to manage them individually.

Applying a systemic approach to complex problems can help us understand the interrelationships between system components and identify the interventions which can lead to better results. If we understand that public problems and purposes are part of a system that is continuously shifting, we need methods to help institutions adapt. System thinking tools could well be the solution for our 21st-century challenges.

As Daniel Innerarity, who has played an advising role in *Etorkizuna Eraikiz*, put it in his address to the *Etorkizuna Eraikiz* Think Tank's New Political Culture Deliberation Group (Provincial Government of Gipuzkoa, 2020):

> The basic idea is that today's society faces problems which go beyond the classic instruments of governments. This is reflected in two things: (i) The concepts we use to talk about politics were designed at a time very different from our own (300 years ago). Rousseau in his *Social Contract* was thinking about the Geneva of his time. We must therefore rethink these concepts, and decide whether they are valid for us. (ii) The self-interested use of simplicity. There are political actors who seek a very self-interested simplification of reality. There are right-wing and left-wing simplifications, populists and technocrats: the basic positions on each side are that you either have to listen to the people or that you have to bring in an expert. Thinking in complexity when understanding politics involves thinking systemically. That means that we live in societies in which all factors are necessary for a general picture. You have to think about everything to be able to think about one thing. And there is a dynamic contrary to today's prevailing inter-specialisation. The one who knows best is the one who is able to have an overall vision, which is very difficult at the moment, because the number of actors and factors is innumerable. Complex democracy is a democracy that allows the interaction of many values and many factors.

Using a collaborative governance model, a public-sector institution involves other community stakeholders to carry out a strategic learning process aimed at framing public value, its drivers and the strategic resources needed to affect community outcomes (Ansell & Gash, 2008). Collaborative governance, therefore, is in itself a public governance mechanism for addressing political disaffection and respond from a systemic vision to the needs of the various ecosystems that make up the design and implementation of public policies.

1.3.   Anticipatory innovation governance

In order to explore in greater depth the systemic vision of the *Etorkizuna Eraikiz* programme, in 2020 and 2021, the OECD Observatory of Public Sector Innovation (OPSI) joined forces with the Provincial Government of Gipuzkoa and regional innovation stakeholders. Through sense-making workshops, action research and advice, the OECD-OPSI helped the Provincial Government to orient better its innovation portfolio and governance structures, particularly toward more anticipatory innovation.

The *Etorkizuna Eraikiz* programme was evaluated using the OECD-OPSI model for public-sector innovation, which is based on the level of uncertainty and directionality of (desired) change. The model defines four facets: enhancement-oriented innovation, mission-oriented innovation, adaptive innovation, and anticipatory innovation. Each facet requires different strategies and working methods to be successful. According to the OECD-OPSI model, systems thinking works best in the context of purpose-driven change, when the goals and problems are known or can be collectively defined (OECD, 2017).

Following an exploratory stage involving desk research, generative workshops, interviews and validation activities, the OPSI identified a series of initial actions needed to launch the intentions and ambitions of *Etorkizuna Eraikiz* (Diputación Foral de Gipuzkoa, internal report by the OECD/OPSI, 2021a) These included: (i) networks and partnerships (develop increased connections between the various nodes in the innovation ecosystem); (ii) public interest and participation (develop new listening and deliberative processes, particularly with community and civic groups); (iii) legitimacy for anticipation (set ambitious missions with firm timelines and give structure to bold commitments for Gipuzkoa); (iv) tools, methods and organisational capacity; (v) institutional structures and sense-making; and (vi) exploration and experimentation.

2.   Goals for systemic governance at *Etorkizuna Eraikiz*

The *Etorkizuna Eraikiz* strategy seeks collaborative governance with a systemic vision to increase the impact of the collective construction of the Gipuzkoa public agenda by: (i) promoting synergies between different spaces (*Gipuzkoa Taldean, Gipuzkoa Lab and Reference centres and strategies*) and ongoing projects, and (ii) improving the scalability of successful activities. To do this, governance spaces and strategies must be developed to ensure their impact on policies (what is known as 'meta-governance').

Etorkizuna Eraikiz articulates this meta-governance through the management boards of the Council, an Advisory Board and a Governance Laboratory. These spaces promote institutional designs and leadership that facilitate collaboration and experimentation; connectivity between projects, initiatives and spaces; management activities; and socialisation and dissemination of the learning acquired.

The mission of *Etorkizuna Eraikiz* is to promote collaborative governance throughout Gipuzkoa. It works to strengthen the dynamics of collaboration at a municipal level as well as inter-institutional collaboration between the Provincial Government and municipal authorities, thus becoming a model for the whole territory. In this way, *Etorkizuna Eraikiz* seeks to generate public value and strengthen the capacity of the territory to respond to challenges collectively.

The practical activities developed in recent years have helped shape the *Etorkizuna Eraikiz* model. The initiative is currently promoting diverse inter-related spaces and ecosystems of cooperation and experimentation. The result is a complex 'polycentric architecture' in which the interaction and interrelation between spaces and initiatives and their impact on the public agenda and public policies can occur through diverse channels. As the spaces, initiatives and processes have gained momentum, the challenges associated with each initiative have increased, and the challenges related to the overall approach of the strategy have intensified.

Over the last two years, a number of reflections have been made and diverse listening processes with agents of the Provincial Government's public policy ecosystem have been conducted (by agents, we are referring to stakeholders involved in the *Etorkizuna Eraikiz* spaces and projects). These sessions have addressed the needs and challenges of *Etorkizuna Eraikiz*, among other things. Here we highlight three listening and reflection processes:

– November 2021: *Etorkizuna Eraikiz* Loiola Plenary (the main stakeholders of the Provincial Government ecosystem). This Plenary has become a systematised space dedicated to the evaluation of the *Etorkizuna Eraikiz* model, and a gathering place for co-creation and collective learning among participants.
– December 2021: *Etorkizuna Eraikiz* Conference (bringing together international experts).
– January–December 2021: Qualitative evaluation by Agirre Lehendakaria Center (the main stakeholders of the Provincial Government's public policy ecosystem).

A number of recommendations and proposals for improvement were identified in these sessions/assessments:

1. Work on a global and systemic approach.
2. Build capacity to strengthen collective leadership and systemic management, learning management and belonging, in the Provincial Government's public policy ecosystem.
3. Promote inclusiveness: integrate individuals, attract young people and companies, increase the number of actors.

4. Socialise and communicate.
5. Involve the Provincial Government departments in *Etorkizuna Eraikiz* and connect them to the *Etorkizuna Eraikiz* system.
6. Define the logic of the initiative and the roadmap and formulate the theory of change.
7. Promote internationalisation and learn from international best practice.
8. Develop methodologies and ways of working.
9. Consolidate projects to guarantee the sustainability of the *Etorkizuna Eraikiz* programme over time.
10. Evaluate and measure results.
11. Increase the impact of experimentation activities on public policy-making.

Several of these recommendations (1, 2, 5, 6, 8 and 11) refer to incorporating a systemic vision in the design, management and governance model of the *Etorkizuna Eraikiz* strategy itself. This can be broken down into the following challenges:

– Interrelations between *Etorkizuna Eraikiz* spaces/initiatives (mutual knowledge, coordination, synergies, joint action, etc.).
– Relationship between *Etorkizuna Eraikiz* and the traditional role of the Provincial Government.
– Relationship between sub-elements of *Etorkizuna Eraikiz*: reference centres, experimental projects, community projects.
– Multi-level governance, coordination and definition of the role of municipalities (local councils).

These recommendations, which highlight the need to incorporate a systemic vision and foster relationships based on collaborative governance throughout the territory, were gathered from the testimonies of some of the *Etorkizuna Eraikiz* ecosystem actors, exemplified in the following excerpts:

> Interconnections. There are many projects and agents acting independently, a crossover is needed. (ALC, qualitative evaluation, January 2022)
> Management and systematisation of the learning process to have systemic management [...] *Etorkizuna Eraikiz* has a polycentric, complex architecture, with an ambition to work from a systemic perspective. But what does it mean to have a systemic perspective? In what space or line of activity line is this implemented? How and where are existing lessons in this field systematised? Where is the learning exchange for network management taking place? (Sonia Ospina, *Etorkizuna Eraikiz* Conference, December 2021)

We need to reinforce and work on a systemic approach to establish links between projects, academia, and internationalisation processes, defining mutual action. Relationships between projects must be strengthened. (Loiola Plenary, November 2021)

The procedures proposed by *Etorkizuna Eraikiz* to transform politics and the public agenda need to be understood, accepted, practised, and legitimised in a collective way. (*Etorkizuna Eraikiz* Conference, December 2021)

In addition to the listening and evaluation processes described above, the management board of the *Etorkizuna Eraikiz* initiative also engaged in some internal reflections. As a result, several decisions were taken intended to institutionalise *Etorkizuna Eraikiz* with a systemic vision. More specifically, based on a variety of frameworks, a reflection was made on the importance of thinking in terms of 'meta-governance', and the new way of conceptualising the *Etorkizuna Eraikiz* model. The new model incorporated this idea, but with a subtle shift in the way of conceiving *Etorkizuna Eraikiz*. This included the existing logic (listening–experimenting–decision-making) but viewed in more complex terms. The result was an updated version of the *Etorkizuna Eraikiz* model which incorporated new spaces such as the Governance Lab (described in more detail in the following sections).

The conclusion that can be drawn from these reflection processes is that in order to guarantee effective and efficient functioning of the entire system, organisational structures and strategies that promote 'meta-governance' beyond 'management' must be developed. This highlights the importance of system-wide leadership, design and development strategies, in effect comprising system-wide 'governance'.

Such an approach entails a deeper systemic way of thinking and working for the activities sponsored and supported by *Etorkizuna Eraikiz* programme. It creates space for accepting uncertainty and complexity, understanding interdependencies, assessing consequences, and learning by doing, so that we can provide more systemic and deliberative responses to social transformation.

3.   Collaborative and systemic governance at *Etorkizuna Eraikiz*: achievements

This section describes the activities carried out in order to respond to the challenge of understanding and implementing *Etorkizuna Eraikiz* as a system, and details the achievements to date. It showcases the internal governance structures (so-called 'meta-governance') which embrace the systemic vision.

Etorkizuna Eraikiz is a collaborative system itself, a network of networks. A characteristic that is particularly relevant when it comes to dealing with systems is the horizontal accountability. It is not the subject of this chapter, and we will not go into detail in this section, but it is worth mentioning that an important aspect of *Etorkizuna Eraikiz* is the promotion of collective leadership. The understanding of leadership at *Etorkizuna Eraikiz* is distributed and it promotes self-organisation. This is a key asset for the development of the *Etorkizuna Eraikiz* framework as a system. *Etorkizuna Eraikiz* has several centres of authority that are connected, and this aspect creates the conditions for greater levels of collective leadership and self-organisation. The different structures and platforms (such as the reference centres) have shared responsibility and decision-making. There is a recognition of a cession and sovereignty in decision-making – the leaders recognise authority at the lowest levels and accept decentralisation for decision-making. This is a key achievement to deploy collaborative governance with a systemic vision.

Besides, to address the challenge of implementing more systemic governance, several decisions were made intended to institutionalise *Etorkizuna Eraikiz* with a systemic vision. The goal was to amplify the transformation throughout the territory and achieve a global and sustained impact over time. Many structures were incorporated to contribute to the systemic approach in *Etorkizuna Eraikiz*, as well as other processes that provide frameworks for interacting and sharing with individuals and groups (socialisation) participating in the whole project, and wider reach and dissemination (communication).

Here we focus on four spaces included in the project that have made a clear contribution to this challenge:
- The meta-governance space: Governance Laboratory.
- *Etorkizuna Eraikiz* Think Tank's New Political Culture Deliberation Group.
- The social innovation laboratory *Arantzazulab*, a reference centre in governance.
- A selection of innovation processes that support the systemic view of the *Etorkizuna Eraikiz* model.

3.1. Governance Laboratory

The Governance Laboratory was launched within the framework of *Etorkizuna Eraikiz* at the beginning of 2022. Under the umbrella of the Strategy Directorate of the Provincial Government of Gipuzkoa, this space is designed to make connections, working synergies and mutual learning through (combining) reflection and action. It is a 'body' that ensures that the processes and projects of *Etorkizuna Eraikiz* are developed through collaborative governance.

Figure 4-1 depicts the structure of the *Etorkizuna Eraikiz* model and the location of the Governance Laboratory in the new meta-governance space.

The Governance Laboratory is made up of the following members: Director General for Strategy; Advisor for External Action; Head of Service of the General Directorate of Strategy; Technician of the General Directorate of Strategy; Representative from Orkestra responsible for the 'action research' methodology; Methodology Coordinator of the Think Tank; Managing Director of *Arantzazulab*; and General Director of Citizen Participation.

To guarantee the philosophy of collaborative governance in the processes and projects of *Etorkizuna Eraikiz* and promote connectivity and relationships between different initiatives, the laboratory undertakes the following functions:

– Ensure the initiatives of the *Etorkizuna Eraikiz* spaces are developed following the logic of collaborative governance and design instruments and initiatives to measure compliance with this goal.

For instance, there is ongoing collaboration between the Governance Laboratory team and the Think Tank's New Political Culture Deliberation Group to define a set of key criteria that characterise the collaborative governance model promoted by the Provincial Government. The goal is to evaluate the degree to which these criteria are being applied to the different spaces and projects included in the *Etorkizuna Eraikiz* strategy.

– Promote dynamics to manage *Etorkizuna Eraikiz* with a systemic vision. The idea here is to identify parallel processes that are being developed within *Etorkizuna Eraikiz*, so as to define co-creation and co-learning spaces among them.

– Work on the challenges of the *Etorkizuna Eraikiz* governance model.

The Governance Laboratory follows the methodological approach implemented by the Territorial Development Laboratory, which is a co-generative framework of action research for territorial development

The establishment of this Governance Laboratory is evidence of the positive evolution of the model and demonstrates the achievement of the strategy itself. The laboratory provides an effective space to implement collaborative governance in the public policy ecosystem of Gipuzkoa and guarantees the systemic vision and objectives of the *Etorkizuna Eraikiz* activities.

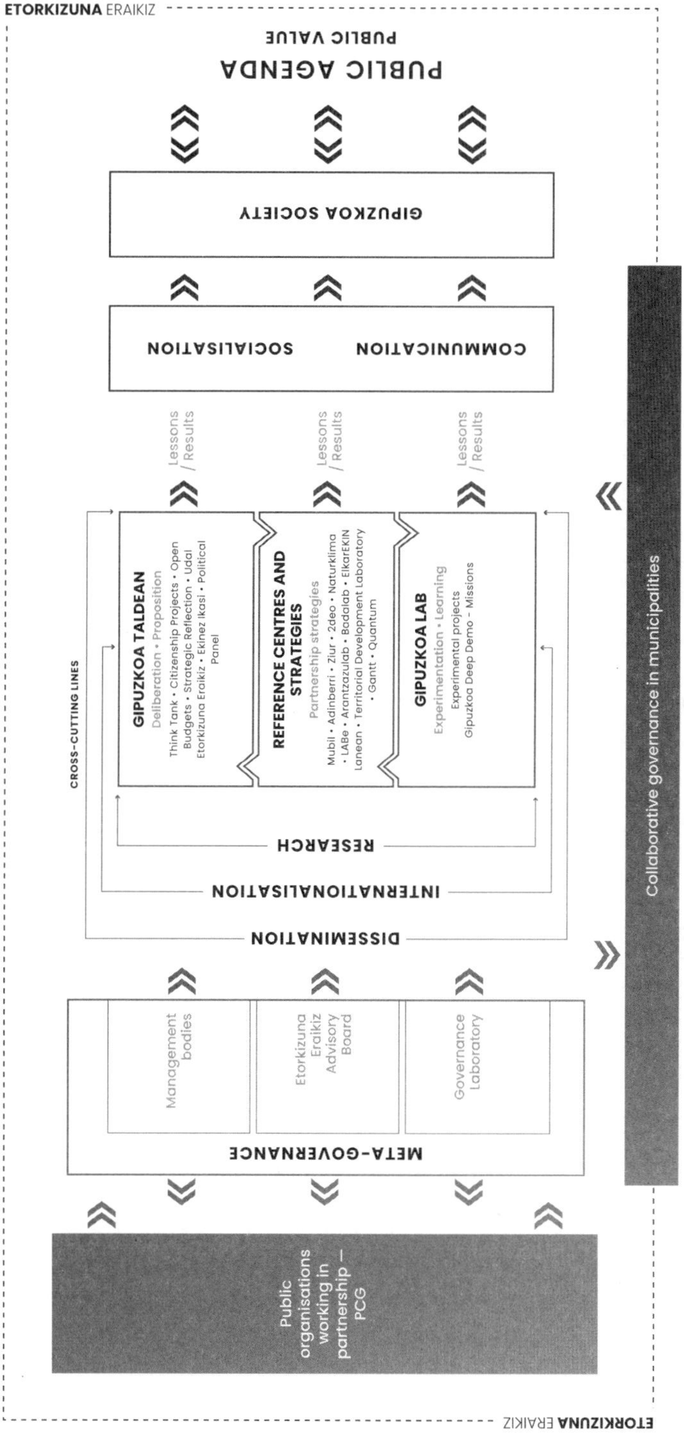

Figure 4-1. The Governance Laboratory within the *Etorkizuna Eraikiz* model. Source: authors' own elaboration.

3.2. *Etorkizuna Eraikiz* Think Tank: New Political Culture Deliberation Group

The mission of the *Etorkizuna Eraikiz* Think Tank is to co-generate knowledge to influence the transformation of the policy ecosystem of the Provincial Government of Gipuzkoa. This ecosystem is made up of several organisations outside the Provincial Government but linked to its policies. Consequently, co-generation has been developed through dialogue between people working in these institutions and various policy-makers from the Provincial Government (see Chapter 5 for a more detailed description of the *Etorkizuna Eraikiz* Think Tank).

The *Etorkizuna Eraikiz* Think Tank also integrates and promotes research, knowledge dissemination and methodological development activities, which are coordinated by the Think Tank's management team. This facilitates lesson-learning between the four groups addressing interconnected challenges. From these and the initiatives of *Etorkizuna Eraikiz* and the Provincial Government of Gipuzkoa, learning and activities are generated which involve society and the academic community in formulating answers to the big questions the Think Tank seeks to address.

The New Political Culture Deliberation Group addresses the conceptualisation of collaborative governance as a mechanism to institutionalise the construction of political reality by incorporating organised society and civil society into the system of public deliberation. It is a mechanism of public governance intended to address political disaffection and respond, from a systemic vision, to the needs of the various ecosystems that make up the design and implementation of public policies.

The Think Tank therefore contributes to the construction of a systemic vision in *Etorkizuna Eraikiz* (through the connection of the challenges of the four deliberation groups). At the same time, it co-generates knowledge on collaborative governance among multiple stakeholders, thus facilitating its development and outreach.

3.3. Social innovation: *Arantzazulab* – a reference centre for governance innovation

Arantzazulab is a laboratory for social innovation and a reference centre for collaborative governance operating within the framework of *Etorkizuna Eraikiz*. It is a space designed for reflection and innovative experimentation on the future and the challenges Basque society is facing (see Appendix 4 for further information).

Social innovation is a key concept linked to collaborative governance systems. Underpinning this concept is the assumption that there is a need for collaborative governance to respond to the crisis of liberal democracy, and that this lab can incorporate society into the deliberation process by developing new spaces for reflection and action. In other words, new governance is needed to formulate new questions and satisfy new demands in the search for new answers. And this must be done through experimentation. Collaborative governance for social innovation can overcome a hierarchical and functionalist vision of public administration, enabling collaboration, creativity and social innovation to be incorporated into the network.

Arantzazulab promotes and facilitates initiatives to develop new knowledge, new values and new ways of doing things. The social innovation it promotes centres on innovation and on exploring new forms of collaborative governance. Through this approach, the lab facilitates the participation and empowerment of people in the public agenda. Social challenges are tackled through community involvement and collaboration between stakeholders by means of four strategic pillars: 1) collaborative governance; 2)) activation of the ecosystem; 3) openness and internationalisation; and 4) research, training and delivering new knowledge to society. The three main activities of the lab are: Research, Experimentation and Dissemination.

Since opening its doors in October 2019, *Arantzazulab* has pursued its mission "to lead the development of Collaborative Governance knowledge in the Basque Country, and support the Basque institutional system, community, and social stakeholders". This body of knowledge is developed from both a theoretical perspective (promoting research and the participation of experts in the field) and a practical perspective (facilitating experimentation initiatives).

The singular nature of the lab has attracted attention both locally and internationally, since there are few labs focusing specifically on governance innovation. Creating and backing *Arantzazulab* demonstrates the Provincial Government's firm commitment to promoting collaborative governance and seeking a collective construction of the province's agenda through collaboration between multiple stakeholders and citizens.

The laboratory operates on the basis of a collaborative governance approach. Firstly, it is supported by other key territorial institutions, which provide an important endorsement of its objectives. Secondly, it establishes regular collaborative relationships with other units and spaces from *Etorkizuna Eraikiz*, such as the Think Tank, the Governance Laboratory, *Gipuzkoa Taldean* and the unit for experimentation and the Research Dissemination Programme.

The activities of the lab are designed to provide added value to the Provincial Government of Gipuzkoa so that the knowledge and results generated can be integrated into its processes, strategies and public policies. Thus, the lab acts as a reference centre in governance, by connecting, co-creating and disseminating the knowledge acquired through collaborative governance among stakeholders. The end goal is to ensure that the procedures proposed by *Etorkizuna Eraikiz* to transform politics and the public agenda are understood, accepted, practised and legitimised collectively. Some of the most significant projects contributing to *Etorkizuna Eraikiz*'s objectives and fostering a collective understanding and construction of the public agenda through collaborative governance include:

–   The development of a solid framework of collaborative governance, which in addition to conceptualisation, will facilitate understanding of the key characteristics, factors and criteria. This framework will assist other actors and institutions in the region to understand, assimilate and apply this collaborative governance approach to their own contexts.

–   A research project on reimagining the future of collaborative governance (partnering with international researchers and experts in the field). This project develops understanding of the different types of actors, roles and conditions necessary for transformation to occur, and identifies experiences that capture information about governance, management, financial and other organisational models and ways used to operationalise the transformation activities.

–   Experimenting with different modes of collaborative governance and of implementing collaborative governance in practice, to empower the community and to create shared deliberation spaces with people and civil society (deliberative democracy processes, the development of a co-creation ecosystem, etc.).

In short, *Arantzazulab* can be viewed as a key achievement for reinforcing the *Etorkizuna Eraikiz* strategy and ultimately for extending collaborative governance in the region.

3.4.   Other innovative processes which support the systemic vision of *Etorkizuna Eraikiz*

The following innovation processes also contribute to developing the systemic vision of *Etorkizuna Eraikiz*:

3.4.1. Gipuzkoa Deep Demo
One of several Deep Demonstration initiatives worldwide, Gipuzkoa Deep Demo is the result of a strategic partnership between the Provincial

Government of Gipuzkoa and EIT Climate-KIC's collaboration with the *Etorkizuna Eraikiz* programme (EIT Climate-KIC is a knowledge and innovation community, working to accelerate the transition to a zero-carbon, climate-resilient society, and is supported by the European Institute of Innovation and Technology). The partnership aims to bring a deeper systemic way of thinking and working to the activities sponsored and supported by *Etorkizuna Eraikiz*.

With this project, the Provincial Government has the opportunity to harness and showcase the experiences of collaborative governance, social inclusion and equality measures that make up the *Etorkizuna Eraikiz* programme, placing them at the heart of a comprehensive portfolio of actions to address the transformations needed to decarbonise the Basque Country and build climate resilience.

An heuristic device has been designed to produce portfolios developed in collaboration with the Climate-KIC team ('problem space'). It is a high-level abstraction or representation of *Etorkizuna Eraikiz* as a system, connecting and structuring the innovation actions of the territory into a portfolio logic. It represents the various ongoing activities, together with the constitutive elements upon which *Etorkizuna Eraikiz* seeks to act (Adaptation, Social Cohesion, Decarbonisation). This device also serves the dual purpose of reinforcing the systemic vision and taking action in the system. The structural elements of the system are represented, bringing visibility to the constituent elements and markers that require action in order to promote change.

3.4.2. Udal Etorkizuna Eraikiz
The *Udal Etorkizuna Eraikiz* project consists of socialising and implementing the *Etorkizuna Eraikiz* model in the municipalities of Gipuzkoa. The result is a collaborative network of anticipatory collaborative governance between the municipalities and the Provincial Government, which makes it possible to listen, learn and decide collectively.

Within this initiative, *Arantzazulab*, in collaboration with the Governance Department of the Provincial Government, is mapping the institutions and projects that promote collaborative governance in Gipuzkoa. This will ensure an in-depth understanding of their trajectory and activity and establish the basis of their networking process. The initiative will also help us understand the opportunities and challenges that collaborative governance creates for the institutions of Gipuzkoa. Furthermore, it highlights the challenges of multi-level governance, in terms of coordination among institutions and different administrative levels and identifies the role of municipalities.

4.   Challenges and opportunities

We have presented some of the achievements and mechanisms implemented to date that contribute to addressing the challenge of achieving more systemic governance. However, this is only the beginning, and challenges remain in terms of embedding and enhancing this systemic and collaborative governance vision across a broader range of *Etorkizuna Eraikiz* initiatives. Some of these challenges are set out below.

4.1.   Collaborative governance and systemic vision

Some of the questions arising in the Governance Laboratory are: How do we effectively ensure that the different initiatives and spaces of *Etorkizuna Eraikiz* work under collaborative governance? When can we say that an initiative works under collaborative governance? Who does the monitoring?

As regards systemic vision and holistic management: How can we promote a systemic approach? How can we promote the management of *Etorkizuna Eraikiz* from a holistic perspective? How should we facilitate connections, synergies and shared lesson-learning between spaces? Which ones should be encouraged?

In one way or another, these issues will be addressed in the *Etorkizuna Eraikiz* Governance Laboratory (the meta-governance space described earlier) with a regular review of the functioning of the collaborative governance structures.

4.2.   Systemic knowledge management and learning sharing

Where is the learning process managed? How do we effectively manage networks between actors (or even measure and assess the quality and impact of partnerships)?

Here the role of that research seems clear – as a cross-cutting line extending to all *Etorkizuna Eraikiz* initiatives. In addition, it is crucial that we optimally coordinate the knowledge on and research into key challenge areas conducted by the various actors in the ecosystem (academia, reference centres, etc.). We must work further to extensively disseminate and leverage the knowledge being developed in reference centres and labs engaging in experiments.

As regards the knowledge on collaborative governance itself, this tool – which underpins the *Etorkizuna Eraikiz* strategy – must be carefully managed. In this respect, the various stakeholders co-generating knowledge on collaborative governance have a key role to play (*Arantzazulab* as a reference centre on governance, the Think Tank and more specifically the New Political Culture Deliberation Group, and the cross-cutting research lines to *Etorkizuna Eraikiz*). A coordinated plan among all of them will guarantee not only the incorporation of knowledge, but also the extension of this governance logic across the many institutional levels and actors of the ecosystem.

4.3. New tool for systems thinking and anticipatory governance

How can we identify new tools, processes and human capabilities available locally or externally to help with anticipation, learning from experimentation and scaling up experiments? We should learn what is available, curate a tailored toolbox and develop capacity and skills in these methods that will contribute to the ambitions of collaborative governance.

4.5. Scalability and Impact

How can we evaluate the impact of systemic initiatives? How can *Etorkizuna Eraikiz* efficiently consolidate lessons learnt from experiments? Can developmental evaluation tools help reassess the initial goals and identify opportunities for scaling up experiments?

5. Conclusions: lessons learned and next steps

Collaborative governance is becoming a distinctive identifying feature of *Etorkizuna Eraikiz*, and by extension, the Provincial Government of Gipuzkoa. In this chapter we have highlighted the importance and need for the public sector – and more specifically the Provincial Government of Gipuzkoa through *Etorkizuna Eraikiz* – to incorporate a systemic vision through collaborative governance to rise to 21st-century challenges. To make this practice actionable, *Etorkizuna Eraikiz* must adapt budget cycles, overcome organisational silos, and create specific structures to foster and ensure the stability of collaborative governance processes and systematise the learning process and successful scaling up of projects. These structures are tasked with supporting management, securing funding, disseminating results and ensuring that governance processes are properly implemented. They can be located within government itself, outside government, or a combination of the two.

We have also introduced the necessary processes to embed and enhance this systemic vision across multiple *Etorkizuna Eraikiz* initiatives. A selection of some of the initiatives and existing governance structures that reinforce the systemic view of the *Etorkizuna Eraikiz* model have been presented.

The systemic approach discussed here is underpinned by collaborative governance and contributes to the objective of co-creating a new political agenda in the region and developing new sustainable public policies with multiple stakeholders. In short, this approach entails a deeper systemic way of thinking and working within the activities sponsored and supported by the *Etorkizuna Eraikiz* programme. Furthermore, it creates a space for accepting uncertainty and complexity, understanding interdependencies, assessing consequences, learning by doing and shaping, and making more systemic, deliberative responses to social transformation.

6.   Lessons for practitioners

Etorkizuna Eraikiz as a collaborative system:
–   *Etorkizuna Eraikiz* is a collaborative system, a network of networks. The model is mainly relational.
–   We can see it as a complex open living system, in which the dynamism of the system is a good quality.
–   *Etorkizuna Eraikiz* is therefore a framework and defining it as such is going to facilitate its replicability.

Systemic vision: horizontal accountability and collective leadership:
–   When you have a network, horizontal accountability becomes important (it is based on trust not on authority). *Etorkizuna Eraikiz* has in fact several centres of authority that are connected. In order to develop collaborative governance, collective leadership is a key factor.
–   Collective leadership is rooted in collaboration, trusting relationships and shared power. The source of leaderships is not individual. This gives people the motivation and the alignment (ignites the passion for people to move forward).
–   Collective leadership is about leading in collaboration with others and in service of the collective.
–   One of the elements that make *Etorkizuna Eraikiz* replicable is the systemic approach.

Evaluation of the system:

– When we think about the whole *Etorkizuna Eraikiz* system, the evaluation of the outcome or the process is very difficult.
– We could think about different levels of evaluation (at project/platform/systems level). The evaluation should have a certain degree of participation.
– Multiple methodologies could be used to carry out the evaluation (e.g. a combination between traditional, developmental and systemic participatory action research).
– Conducting a *stakeholder analysis* could help to ensure the inclusion of a broader range of people.

Workshop 1
Synthesis of interactions between scholars and practitioners

What follows is a synthesis of the discussions, including major ideas, comments, further questions and challenges that emerged from the interaction between the local/international scholars and the practitioners (politicians, civil servants, stakeholders) embedded in *Etorkizuna Eraikiz*.

1. To what extent do the structures of governance of *Etorkizuna Eraikiz* differ from hierarchical organisational decision-making?

Initial response and reactions

Responses to this question centre on attempts to categorise EE. What is *Etorkizuna Eraikiz*? From the interaction between academics and practitioners, the following characteristics emerge:

- Usually, collaborative governance initiatives are small or refer to concrete projects. In contrast, EE is broad in scope; it involves experimentation on a whole-regional scale.
- It is comprehensive: it includes governance, markets and networks.
- It is a dynamic network of networks, including different sources of authority, but all of them are related and share goals.
- It is a multi-level system; a constellation of projects, centres and strategies.
- It is an open, living system. Open, living systems survive because they can adjust to new challenges; there are constant cycles that emerge from turbulence, uncertainty and change. EE could be categorised in this context as an open and living system which survives through its attempt to respond to new challenges.
- It is a 'relational model' in which full commitment and strong relations among the different actors predominate.
- Decision-making is blurred, but always refers back to the Provincial Government. EE shows the need for collaborative governance to ensure an entity with authority, legitimacy and responsibility to supervise, as

well as to generate the conditions to combine blurred decision-making with coordination for a certain degree of centralisation.

Thematic debates

The following comments and suggestions emerge from the discussion:
- Understanding the why of something (more than the what or the how) helps to understand its development. Why was it decided to go from hierarchical decision-making to collaborative governance?
  - The acknowledgement that the government's own capacity to address challenges was limited. Governments lack legitimacy, resources, information, knowledge. EE was launched because of: a) the complexities of the social system; and b) an awareness of interdependence between the Provincial Government and the citizens of Gipuzkoa.
  - The crisis in democracy: EE's goal was to empower the political community and enhance the legitimacy of the institutional system.

Further questions, critical issues and challenges

- To deal with the tension between vertical and horizontal structures.
- To deal with the tension between efficacy, effectiveness and accountability.
- To deal with diversity: differences play a positive role.

2.   Which formulae did (and did not) work for decision-making with multi-level, cross-departmental, and public- and private-sector actors?

Initial response and reactions

Responding to this question requires to differentiate formal and informal rules. There are formulae of efficiency (i.e. agreements on costs) and formulae for dialogue (i.e. are all opinions equally valid?). Each formula expresses a process of collective decision-making. Decision-making in CG results from the dialogue between different public and private agents.

Further questions, critical issues and challenges

- How are decisions actually made?
  - Decision-making has not followed a clear linear path. The dynamics include contradictions; processes and formulae have been improved on the go.
  - The dynamics have been based on an awareness of the need for change and trust in the actors involved; there is uncertainty about the transformation that may actually be achieved.
  - The basic unit of EE is always the project. Projects are organised according to a structure: experimentation projects are functionally dependent on the Strategy Unit; reference centres are functionally dependent on the Directorate of Strategic Projects. All this means both a centralised and decentralised form of decision-making: those at the top allow for autonomy amongst leaders who are not at the top.
- To generate spaces for dialogue and facilitate interaction. The good thing about EE is that rules are not very formalised. Rules for participation have to be adjusted to specific contexts. Therefore, what is important is not to formalise the rules, but to specify them. Specified rules have to help develop capacitation facilities, conflict management, identification of different interests and opinions.
- To manage the tension between representation and efficacy. Collaborative governance is a collective product, but the decision about collectivity has to be taken by a legitimate elected authority. It is the representative authority that has to make decisions about the use of public resources.
- To deal with the tension between hierarchical structures and relational aspects. The strength of ties and bounds as compared to the strength of relations.
- Costs. Collaborative governance is costly. It is suggested that other initiatives of blended financing be reviewed, because they may foster ownership of the projects.
- To deal with the tension between the need for authority and the need for ample representation. Failures and problems of EE are attributed to the large number of participants, actions and collective decisions. Design and management of the implementation process are important to maintain commitment among the different actors, to prevent and avoid people quitting.

3. Analysis of meta-governance: what for, who, what, how and with what impact?

Thematic debates

From the presentation of the meta-governance of EE, the following comments and suggestions emerge from the discussion:
-   Evaluating the impact of meta-governance includes looking at the following properties: 1) quality of dialogue; 2) clarity of goals (absence of ambiguity); 3) clear definition of observable empirical aspects; 4) directionality of cause; 5) certain amount of measurable data with regard to social situations; 6) use of technological systems; 7) clear information on the profile of the citizens who are (to be) involved: resources, social status, social reputation, respectability, trustworthiness, knowledge; 8) the use of results for improvement; 9) transparency, openness; and 10) clear leadership, clear management.
-   Any evaluation of EE should also look at the way different actors view the situation/the problem.

Difficulties for evaluating EE's impact:
-   Most of EE's outcomes are intangibles: changes in relations between politicians and technicians, between the DFG and the university, between the DFG and the media, between the DFG and business and societal organisations; changes in the culture of collaboration, etc. This kind of impact should not be measured only with positivistic approaches.
-   Because EE is a multi-level system, evaluation needs to be made at different levels.
-   Time is needed between causal intervention and the resolution of the problem. Has there been enough time to evaluate the impact of EE?

What needs to be defined to evaluate impact:
-   The level: evaluation at the level of projects, centres or systems?
-   Will it be participatory evaluation?
-   Who are/can be the informants of evaluation? All parties should be included: the collaborators, the citizen perspective, politicians, the political party, civil servants.
-   Both the results (achievements) and the process (fairness, transparency, dialogue).
-   One single methodology or multiple methodologies and methods?

Further questions, critical issues and challenges

- Is election vote data to be included for evaluation? To implement government programmes you have to be in government. However, orienting government to win the elections is controversial; it might even be detrimental.

Comments from scholars

Comment 1
Etorkizuna Eraikiz: A collaborative governance framework for learning and acting

TINA NABATCHI, *Joseph A. Strasser Endowed Professor in Public Administration, Maxwell School of Citizenship and Public Affairs, Syracuse University, US*

1.   Introduction: looking at problems through the lens of 'clocks and clouds'

There can be little doubt that as we move through the 21st century, governments around the world are looking for new ways of doing business. The governance processes of old – many of which were developed in the 19th and 20th centuries – are no longer sufficient for accomplishing all the tasks of government or meeting the needs of its people. Research suggests that a new political culture – one that embraces collaboration as key for learning and acting – can play a meaningful role in improving both the form and function of government. *Etorkizuna Eraikiz* ('Building the Future') has emerged as an impactful approach to governance in Gipuzkoa Province that is reshaping not only how government works, but also the work of government itself. This essay draws on the metaphor of clocks and clouds (Popper, 1966) to explore how *Etorkizuna Eraikiz* serves as a collaborative governance framework for learning and acting throughout Gipuzkoa Province.

In 1966, the great philosopher of science, Karl Popper, divided the world – and ultimately the problems of social science – into two categories: clocks and clouds. As he explained, clocks are a mechanical phenomenon. They are regular, orderly and predictable. They are neat and structured. To understand a clock – or problems with a clock – you take it apart. You study its components, measure its pieces, count the teeth on its gears. Through disassembly, examination and reassembly, you can fix a clock. A clock problem may be challenging, but ultimately, it is solvable.

Clouds are very different. Clouds are a natural phenomenon – they are irregular, disorderly and generally unpredictable. They are messy and ever-changing. You cannot take apart a cloud. It does not have constituent pieces. Instead, to understand a cloud, you must study it as a whole, along with all of the factors – humidity, wind, temperature, air pressure and so on – that created the cloud in the first place. The same is true for a cloud problem – you cannot study it in isolation, but rather must study it in relation to the factors that directly and indirectly shape the problem. Moreover, you cannot fix or control a cloud, and therefore, cloud problems cannot be 'solved' in the traditional sense of the word – they only can be addressed in better or worse ways.

Many of our public problems are clock problems. Clock problems may be complex, challenging and sometimes controversial, but they are well defined and can be structured. They can be solved with standardised techniques and procedures. Authority for addressing them is typically in the hands of one (or a few) actors who have disciplinary or specialised expertise, and who agree on the problem, the relevant knowledge, values and norms, and the goals for the solution. For example, getting a piece of mail from San Sebastián in Gipuzkoa Province to Syracuse, NY in the United States is a complicated endeavour, but we can work through postal hubs, map transit routes and develop pricing mechanisms. Likewise, creating a programme for vaccine distribution and administration is difficult, but we can look to other health service providing activities and medical distribution programmes, examine other acquisition and logistics problems, and replicate or alter those processes.

As we continue to move through the 21st century, however, we increasingly are dealing with cloud problems: climate change, sustainable development, migration and refugee challenges, human trafficking, poverty and wealth inequality, the social governance of new and emerging technologies, and partisan divides, democratic rollbacks, and the rise of populism and authoritarianism, to name but a few. These problems – like other cloud problems – do not stand alone. They are deeply enmeshed and intertwined with other problems and affect and are affected by myriad other factors. These problems cannot be broken down into tidy pieces. They do not have gears with teeth that fit neatly together.

In part, this is because cloud problems do not have clear problem definitions – how the problem is defined depends on who is asked. There are no standardised techniques and procedures for problem-solving. Instead, the 'solution' continuously evolves in parallel with a set of interlocking issues and constraints that are themselves continuously evolving. These problems cannot be addressed by a single actor or government agency working alone. Authority and responsibility for addressing cloud problems is dispersed, diffused and diluted among multiple actors and organisations in the public, private and civic sectors. Moreover, these myriad actors usually have conflicting expertise and clashing views on the knowledge, values and norms that are relevant, not to mention the goals for the solution. Thus, traditional, expert-driven or managerialist approaches are generally ineffective for addressing cloud problems. Such approaches seldom work because cloud problems are not purely scientific and technical. They also involve social complexity, political complexity and decision complexity. They involve cognitive uncertainty, strategic uncertainty and institutional uncertainty. They involve competing, conflicting and socially embedded perspectives, values and norms, and often, addressing the problems requires attitudinal and behavioural changes among the public itself.

In short, cloud problems, which increasingly are the norm in modern governance, are not only complex, challenging and controversial like clock problems – they also are unstructured, intractable and filled with conflict and uncertainty. So, how do we address cloud problems? In previous work, I have suggested ten interconnected principles for addressing cloud problems through collaborative and participatory governance approaches (Nabatchi, 2022). *Etorkizuna Eraikiz* (EE) – a strategy for collectively building the future through collaborative problem-solving and governance in Gipuzkoa Province – beautifully illustrates these principles.

2.   Ten principles for addressing cloud problems: some illustrative examples from *Etorkizuna Eraikiz*

Principle 1: Adopt a learning strategy. A learning strategy accepts that the problem is messy, that technical methods for solving the problem are inadequate, and that the boundaries of the problem are diffuse because the problem is interrelated with other problems. EE has taken a learning approach from day one. When the Basque Nationalist Party came into power in Gipuzkoa Province in 2007, it realised it needed to find new ways to approach provincial challenges and set out to build partnerships and collaborations that spanned levels of government, bridged the public, private and civic sectors, and engaged everyday people. Throughout its work, the government sought to build experiments that not only would provide new information and insights on existing and emerging problems, but also would allow for continuous learning.

Principle 2: Embrace diverse knowledge and new patterns of knowledge production. A learning strategy accepts that multiple forms of knowledge are necessary to address problems and that new forms of knowledge need to be generated. In developing its learning strategy, EE leaders quickly recognised that knowledge is the currency of collaboration (Emerson & Nabatchi, 2015a).

Thus, their engagement efforts sought to integrate knowledge in multiple forms: scientific knowledge, technical knowledge, specialised knowledge, political knowledge, cultural knowledge, lay knowledge and common knowledge, among others. Moreover, their activities used not only convergent thinking in which problems are solved through established rules and logical reasoning, but also divergent, lateral and emergent thinking, wherein problems are addressed respectively through the application of strategies that deviate from commonly used or previously taught strategies, the re-examination of basic assumptions and perspectives, and the revelation of unforeseen possibilities through idea comparison and combination.

Principle 3: Welcome the participation and input of multiple actors. The success of learning strategies relies on the participation and input of multiple actors. From the start, EE developed processes for engagement and dialogue among a diverse set of stakeholders. Today, EE activities engage politicians, government administrators, policy-makers, civil society actors, academics, business representatives and entrepreneurs, scientific, technical and other experts, and members of the public – or perhaps better, the many publics.

Principle 4: Encourage multidimensional methods engagement. To welcome multiple actors, multidimensional methods of engagement must be created. EE has been particularly successful at this. Specifically, EE has three central components: (1) *Gipuzkoa Taldean*, a think tank that centres its work on four areas (the economy and future employment, climate change and the green economy, the future of the welfare state and care, and the new political culture and governance); (2) *Gipuzkoa Lab*, a space for deliberation and experimentation on proposals and projects that aim to address community issues, challenges and problems; and (3) *reference centres and strategies*, a series of public–private and social work spaces that aim to strengthen strategic sectors in the province. In turn, each of these components has numerous projects, programmes and activities that engage people and organisations throughout the province. Both individually and holistically, the three central components of EE and their associated projects form parallel and serial learning processes that support a range of activities from narrower inter-organisational collaborations to broader public participation processes. Moreover, some of these processes are organised by government officials, others by business or civic leaders, and still others by everyday people.

Principle 5: Treat people like adults. Often government and the participatory processes it runs takes a parochial stance on participation, designing processes that are paternalistic, patronising or placating (Nabatchi & Leighninger, 2015). EE does not. It gives people the respect, recognition and responsibility they deserve as citizens and provides them with information and choices, a chance to tell their stories, a sense of political legitimacy, opportunities to take action and participation experiences that are enjoyable, easy and convenient (Nabatchi & Leighninger, 2015). In doing so, it has engaged people in meaningful ways, and perhaps more importantly, in ways that increase the likelihood they will stay engaged over time.

Principle 6: Provide good process. Cloud problems are as much about social and political issues as they are about scientific and technical issues. Accordingly, processes must be designed to enhance human relations and social interactions. Good process is evident in each of the three EE components. For example, the various programmes and activities of the *Gipuzkoa Taldean, Gipuzkoa Lab* and *reference centres* tend to use facilitated dialogues that start with deliberation and principled engagement, cultivate shared motivation and build the capacity for joint action (Emerson & Nabatchi, 2015a).

Principle 7: Focus on interests, not positions. Positions are what a person or group wants – they are the demand being made or the solution being offered. Interests are the needs, values or concerns that underlie a position – they are why a person or group is making a particular demand or offering a specific solution (O'Leary & Bingham, 2007). For any given issue, people generally have only one position but many interests, with some interests being stronger than others. Perhaps more important is that people with conflicting positions often share basic interests, which can form the foundation for constructive discussions and productive action. Reports from EE leaders suggest that through processes of engagement, dialogue, deliberation and action planning, groups have addressed immediate conflicts and have moved beyond their self-interest to think about the broader public good.

Principle 8: Develop theories of change and action strategies. Through good process, people are likely to develop shared goals and agree on the mechanisms for achieving those goals. This is done through the development of a theory of change – one that articulates assumptions about what might work to address the problem, and the joint actions needed to realise their purpose and goals (Emerson & Nabatchi, 2015a). Theories of change and action strategies are central to the *Gipuzkoa Taldean, Gipuzkoa Lab* and *reference centres*. In each of these components, groups use a 'research-action' process in which they learn about a problem, build knowledge and understanding, generate solutions, implement actions and then assess the results so they can revise, amend or adapt as necessary.

Principle 9: Reframe 'failure' as a 'learning opportunity'. Since its start in 2007 (and despite a hiatus from 2011 to 2015), EE has attempted many governance changes through the implementation of new processes, programmes and policies. Not all of them have worked. However, through the process of trying,

EE actors have grown to understand that just because something did not work does not mean it was a waste of time. Indeed, a core (though perhaps unspoken) principle of EE is the idea of failing forward, that is, learning from what did and did not work to make improvements, adapt and try again. Keeping in mind the broader goal – creating tools that inform governance and improve public action – has given EE the opportunity to learn from failure.

Principle 10: Nurture creativity, innovation and experimentation. Each of these ten principles speak to the need to do things differently, and doing things differently means being open to creative expressions, innovative ideas and experimental activities. EE recognised, from the start, that these are the tools for generating breakthroughs on cloud problems, Thus, creativity, innovation and experimentation were baked into the EE vision and have generated surprising and powerful ideas that have moved the province toward substantive, meaningful and impactful governance.

Each of these ten principles and the accompanying EE illustrations deserve much more attention, not only because the actors involved in EE – from the top of government to its frontlines and from business and civic leaders to everyday citizens – have worked hard and long to make change a reality, but also because communities and governments around the world could learn a lot from their efforts. Indeed, as a collaborative governance framework for learning and acting, EE sheds light on practical approaches for addressing cloud problems and many other challenges of modern governance.

Comment 2
The challenge of combining legitimacy and effectiveness when building collaborative governance

Luis F. Aguilar, *National Researcher Emeritus, Mexico*

The focus of the text is the effectiveness of collaborative governance, which implies its legitimacy and enhances it as well, building up citizens' trust in the capacity of democratic governments to steer and lead. Knowledge is the essential condition of effectiveness, which involves data, correct concepts, tested causal assumptions, correct calculus of effects and costs, and evaluation. Since collaborative governance is the product of dialogue and consensus between public, private and social actors, cognitive rules and discourse ethics rules are required and are fundamental to making feasible and effective its objects, actions and timelines. In the final section of this comment an agenda regarding effectiveness is proposed.

1.   The assumption

The origin and significance of collaborative governance are explained by three intertwined facts of contemporary society – *complexity, insufficiency* and *interdependency* – from a theoretical standpoint. Today's most important social issues, projects and problems are indeed complex in terms of their composition, causality and set of connections, which makes it practically impossible for a single agent, public or private – whether a public institution, a market corporation or a social organisation – to have the cognitive, financial, technological and power resources to fully understand and manage the variety of components, dimensions, causal chains, developments and web of relationships. The independent agents of contemporary society determine their goals freely, but at the same time are interdependent, as they do not own sufficient resources to define properly the composition of their individual and communal goals and projects, and to carry out them successfully.

This performative insufficiency moves independent agents to establish relations with people who have the resources they need, to exchange and combine resources, to collaborate, to associate. *Complexity, insufficiency* and *interdependency* in the public field are the root causes of the origin and significance of intergovernmental and public–private–social (multi-actor and multi-level) collaborative governance to manage the current complex problems, issues, aims and undertakings.

Despite their significant powers and assets, democratic governments do not have sufficient financial, cognitive, technological or human resources to steer their societies, to solve critical problems and to achieve their intended valuable social goals. Nor, in some countries or in specific issues and circumstances, do they have the political and moral resources of social trust and credibility. Governments understand that they need the resources, assets, competences and endowments of other states, governments, economic corporations, social organisations and intelligence services, and therefore decide to interact with them to build agreements on social goals and public policies and to have access to the resources that make them feasible. Though this normal condition of governmental is very well recognised, the political culture of several societies hinders collaborative public governance.

In *Etorkizuna Eraikiz*, as in similar experiences, the main reason why governments and citizens decide to join together, to be partners, to collaborate, is the acknowledgment of their *insufficiency* to control or solve by themselves the problems of individual, organisational and community life, as well as the acknowledgement that mutual *interdependency* relationships with other agents are necessary to reach the goals that matter to them and, accordingly, they make the rational decision to exchange information, combine resources and work together.

The drive that motivates *Etorkizuna Eraikiz* to differ from traditional hierarchical governance is, in my opinion, the implicit or explicit honest recognition of the Gipuzkoa Provincial Government that it is, by itself, with its own ideas, preferences, resources and means, limited, insufficient, to lead the communities and sectors of Gipuzkoan society towards conditions for a safe and healthy existence' work in a changing international and national environment. And there is, at the same time, an appreciation that the resources that the government lacks are indeed available among Gipuzkoan and/or Basque corporations, civil society organisations, media, universities, neighbourhoods, churches, families, etc. The Gipuzkoa Provincial Government recognised that a dialogue with all these actors, though they differ in their beliefs and preferences, is crucial to building agreements on the relevant social future of Gipuzkoa and on the actions to attain it.

2.   The question

The collaborative governance of *Etorkizuna Eraikiz* has significantly contributed to restoring the legitimacy of democratic governments, the value of public life and the importance of politics itself, overcoming the years of public disinterest and political disaffection of numerous citizens, sceptical of the competence, credibility and trustworthiness of politicians and administrative and legislative bodies. Nonetheless, the social concern has changed, and not only in Gipuzkoa Province. A shift from concern about the legitimacy of the government to concern about the effectiveness of the legitimate government has happened among citizens. A democracy of results matters, and values, institutions and discourse are not enough. That is the question: is collaborative governance more effective, more cost-effective, than the public policies implemented by the past hierarchical approach of the Gipuzkoa Province Government? Which core properties and elements are the source of the effectiveness and social usefulness of collaborative governance performance?

Legitimacy and *effectiveness* are two essential properties of democratic governance, but they develop under different logics of action and 'rationalities'. While the political legitimacy of governance refers to the value and normative order of the state, the effectiveness of governance refers to the cognitive social system of science and technology and to 'best practices' which prove to be efficient and effective when coping with some social problems.

Legitimacy and *effectiveness* complement one another, but are not mutually inclusive, since governmental effectiveness implies legitimacy, but legitimacy does not imply effectiveness. Legitimacy is certainly a fundamental condition of effectiveness, since illegal rulers, by their position or by their actions, are condemned to be questioned and rejected by societies that coexist and progress under the rule of law. Consequently, illegality will not grant authorities the authority to rule, and citizens will not feel themselves obliged to obey their commands and policies. Nevertheless, a government does not have the capacity to govern a society merely on the legitimacy of its position and performance, even if the head of government is the subject of massive electoral support or a strong political coalition. Ruling a society, leading a society, has a different logic of action. Governance is *a performative action*, an action for effecting social results, for producing the intended social goals at lower costs and greater benefits. Therefore, governance shapes itself as a *rational* action, focused on clear and well-ordered goals, and feasible too. To be performative, the governance of legitimate governments must rely on data on social issues, on knowledge of the latter's composition, causes and relationships, on actionable technologies, financial skills, performance management and capacity to dialogue with their citizens and negotiate compromises with their opponents.

3.   The answer

Knowledge is the essential condition of the effectiveness of governance, supported by the assumption and/or evidence that some social facts regularly lead to some actions in the natural world, in the social system, and in the interactions between society and nature. Conjecturing, searching, discovering, testing cause-and-effect relationships is the human activity of knowledge. *Effectiveness–Causality–Knowledge* are intertwined necessary conditions. Collaborative governance is no more than a good intention and an extraordinary commitment, unless the joint decision on the content of the governance, made by public, private and social partners, is supported by proven data, a logically and empirically correct definition of the social problems, tested cause-and-effect relationships, and accurate estimations of the effects, costs and timescale of the causation process.

However, collaborative governance is distinctively a process and result of dialogue between a number of actors, political and technical leaders, and stakeholders from organised society, who differ in their beliefs, viewpoints and preferences, and which involves expositions and critical objections, questions and explanations, data and opinions, doubts and elucidations. This dialogue is the distinctive feature of the *Etorkizuna Eraikiz* collaborative governance model. The deliberation, proposition, implementation, experimentation and learning about the activities and contents of collaborative governance decisions (strategic projects, programmes, services, organisations) are outcomes of an innovative systemic dialogue, encouraged and supported by established and committed multi-actor organisations (i.e. the EE Think Tank, *Gipuzkoa Lab, EE reference centres*), which drive and coordinate different forms and subjects of dialogue through action research methods.

This dialogue between the stakeholders regularly paves the way for attaining a balanced understanding and agreement on the choice of governance priorities, objectives, actions, projects, actors, timelines and costs. But dialogue can also make the debate more tense and complicated when controversial issues are addressed in critical circumstances, breaking any interest in further participation (high 'transaction costs') and preventing a joint decision. Therefore, *ground rules of dialogue, cognitive rules* and *discourse ethics rules* are essential to manage the intellectual, moral and political differences and divergences during the debate and to create a trustworthy atmosphere allowing communication, understanding and agreement on governance goals and actions. Since the course of the interchange and debate cannot be fully planned in advance, the ethical and cognitive rules must be stated as principles, as guidelines for conversation, far from meticulous and fixed written regulations.

Discourse ethics rules, particularly in the domain of the public discourse, are fundamental in order to guarantee the fair access of citizens to public deliberation, to control falsehoods, and to prevent asymmetries, discriminatory inequalities, exclusions, and unfair power games and manoeuvres during the conversation, enabling respect and trust between the participants and favouring agreement on the content of governance. But in addition, it is necessary to produce and agree upon *norms of cognitive correctness*, as the effectiveness of governance rests on sound logical and empirical concepts, arguments, analysis, explanations and estimates; these are crucial in order to prevent incorrect concepts, mistaken causal assumptions, biased opinions, unverifiable criticisms and untenable dogmatic positions.

The choice of feasible goals and effective actions for governance must be based on objective data, tested causal assumptions, accurate surveys, precise cost and effect calculations, cost–benefit analysis and performance measurements, supported by the results of social and natural sciences and by technological systems, since the production, quality and testing of current knowledge is coupled with digital technology systems, their underlying algorithms and the developments in artificial intelligence. Hence, *knowledge management* is necessary to support and assist the 'tacit knowledge' of most citizens on their own issues and to draw on the 'explicit knowledge' of experts and researchers.

The institutional, political, cultural and socioeconomic elements are indubitably factors of effectiveness of governance, but the decisive factor is knowledge. Goals cannot be achieved, problems cannot be solved, opportunities cannot be taken, investments are unviable and challenging future scenarios is unfeasible if government and society have no, or partial or biased, data on the social facts, inaccurate definitions of their composition and relationships, mistaken causal assumptions, and a poor idea of the options capable of producing the intended goods and services and making the investments productive and the future scenarios of social wellbeing feasible.

The social system of knowledge has robust information and knowledge on many but not all public issues. Many public decisions are made in conditions of 'uncertainty', under 'bounded rationality'. This is a subject which deserves a careful elaboration. In conditions of limited information and knowledge on public issues, public decisions cannot be but relatively effective, or effective to some degree, so that governments are called to inform, explain and justify before citizens the decisions, as well as the subsequent limited quality and extent of products, outcomes and impacts.

4.   The agenda

The *Etorkizuna Eraikiz* collaborative governance model comprises the following dialogue and agreement activities, which must be maintained, refined, strengthened and regulated:
-    Clear order of the preferences, goals and priorities on the public issues to be governed (e.g. social problems to control or solve, opportunities to take advantage of, unfair life conditions to remove). *Ambiguities and*

confusion regarding the choice of goals are to be avoided as they condemn the government to fail.

- Clear definition of the specific components and properties of the social situations regarded as problems and of the specific components and properties of the social situations stated as goals to be achieved (e.g. control and solution of social problems and needs, creation of safe and satisfying life conditions), outlining at the same time their observable and measurable empirical features.
- Clear definition of the components and properties of the causal actions to bring about the intended social situations of governance, outlining their observable and measurable empirical features. In conditions of *uncertainty* the choice of incremental or experimental actions is a rational option.
- Ascertainable and measurable data on the attributes of the social situations (problems, goals, affairs, opportunities, sociodemographic characteristics and social trends) that are the subject of stakeholders' interest and of public governance.
- Tested causal assumptions on the causation process, supporting the choices to perform the intended governance goals.
- Use of technological systems of information, enabling the production, analysis and storage of open data, transparency and traceability of the decision-making process, as well as of the causation process.
- Clear information on the profile of the citizens taking part in the governance decision-making, and their competences, resources, degree of involvement, social reputation and expertise on social issues.
- Permanent evaluation of the governance process, focusing on the logical and empirical soundness of its presuppositions, data, concepts, causal processes, actions, outputs, outcomes and costs, and on the use of its results to innovate regarding the collaborative governance decision-making.
- Openness and transparency of the governance decision-making, involving the pre-decisional stage of joint deliberation and the post-decisional stage of communication, implementation and experimentation of the decisions.
- Clear leadership and management, throughout the collaborative governance decision-making process, underlining knowledge management.
- Clear and agreed rules of dialogue and ethical and cognitive rules.

Comment 3
Historical background in the Basque Country for diverse social capital as a precondition for *Etorkizuna Eraikiz* collaborative governance

PETER LOGE, *School of Media and Public Affairs, The George Washington University, US*

The new *Etorkizua Eraikiz* is successful in part because, at heart, it is very old. Weaving the new with the thread of the old is something from which leaders elsewhere can learn.

One way to view a nation or a people is as a story of itself. As Ben Rhodes (2022) puts it, "[e]very nation is a story. It's almost never a simple one, and the story's meaning is usually contested. National identity itself depends upon how we tell the story – about our past, our present, and our future." The stories we tell each other about where we came from and who we are define us as nations and people. As McGee (1975) writes, "[t]he people *are* the social and political myths they accept" (p. 247).

These stories or myths can be especially important when a society faces challenges. Economic, political and social threats can lead to proposed new solutions. Advocates and leaders may say that a new moment requires bold new approaches. But in uncertain times, voters may not want new ideas – in the face of chaos or confusion, people tend to seek the safe and familiar. The most successful new ideas are those that draw on cultural traditions and social memory (Weaver, 1953); the new as an extension of the familiar.

A forthcoming paper on Basque identity argues that the centrality of community is a defining feature of what many Basques say it means to be Basque; commitment to community is a running theme in the Basques' stories of themselves (Loge & Caballero, forthcoming 2023). This story is not without merit. In explaining the economic success of the Basque Country, Sebastián Royo (2009) writes, "[c]ivil society is strong, articulated and well organized in the Basque Country" (p. 17). A result of this strength is that "the Basque Country has been particularly successful at forging new sustainable institutions and interfirm networks where the need for cooperation and the development of capabilities to respond to collective-action problems were lacking" (Royo, 2009, p. 2). Royo and others who write about the Basques point to this focus on collective decision-making and cooperation as having roots in the ancient Basque *fueros*. As one political scientist wrote in 1893, "[i]t is the *fueros* of the Basques that have played the largest part in history as charters of liberty" (Strong, 1893, p. 318).

Basques and Basque scholars will tell you that the *fueros* themselves grew out of even older Basque traditions.

In this light, the new works because it draws on the old. A leading expert on, and force behind, *Etorkizuna Eraikiz*, Xabier Barandiarán, writes that one reason *Etorkizuna Eraikiz* works is that it is consistent with traditions and values in Gipuzkoa, and helps reinforce democracy, trust and public value (Barandiarán, 2022, p. 10). *Etorkizuna Eraikiz*, like the Mondragon (a cooperative business project launched in 1956, Whyte & Whyte, 2014), succeeds because it is an "old well from which new water flows." (Loge & Caballero, forthcoming 2023), and the phrase seems apt here as well. Some authors suggests that a cultural commitment to community is a reason for the success of the Basque gastronomy (Minder, 2016; Rodriguez, 2016). *Etorkizuna Eraikiz* fits a telling of the Basque story; it is the next logical chapter in the very long book of the Basques.

The roots of *Etorkizuna Eraikiz* run deep in Basque soil, but they did not grow on their own. Officials in Gipuzkoa developed the model and persuaded people that it was a good idea. If the idea is to continue, people in Gipuzkoa need to agree that the province should continue to invest in it. One way to make a case for *Etorkizuna Eraikiz* is to remind people that the new is an ancient tradition meeting a modern moment. If the new rhymes with the old, it is more likely to continue. In this case, the goal is to make *Etorikizuna Eraikiz* a logical extension of who the Basques were, a defining characteristic of who they are and, thus, who they will be.

On the surface, this analysis may present a road map for leaders in Gipuzkoa and Euskadi, but it may not appear to offer much to other regions or countries. If *Etorkizuna Eraikiz* is uniquely Basque, there is not much others can apply to their situations. The model may seem like a rare species of bird that only lives on one remote island and has failed to reproduce in zoos.

Such would be the case if the community-first story were the only one that could be told of the Basques, if no other people could tell a similar story, and if it were the only story that would work. Of course, none of those things may be true.

The lesson for other nations is not to move to Donostia, as tempting as that might be. Instead, those that want to learn from this application of collaborative governance should construct something like *Etorkizuna Eraikiz* that fits a local narrative, and explain the model in the context of the narrative. Nearly every society has a story of coming together to respond to hardship or to ensure that a rising tide lifts all boats. For example, in New Zealand, "[e]ffective collaboration is achieved by using the correct (*Tikanga*) decision-making processes, through a greater understanding and appreciation of Māori values that can be supported by a variety of kaupapa Māori-based assessment tools" (Harmsworth, Awatere, Robb & Landcare Research, 2015, p. 1). In the United States, policy-makers could draw on stories of entrepreneurship and communities uniting to rebuild after disasters.

Etorkizuna Eraikiz works in Gipuzkoa because it is a new take on an old Basque story. The lesson for those in Gipuzkoa is to keep the new grounded in the old. The lesson for those looking to learn from Gipuzkoa is to find a similar cultural or social well from which to draw new water.

Comment 4
Collaborative governance as jazz: Three propositions

ADIL NAJAM, *Frederick S. Pardee School of Global Studies, Boston University, US*

Etorkizuna Eraikiz should be understood as a grand experiment by the provincial government of the province of Gipuzkoa in the Basque Country in Spain, to "change the way of doing politics". Indeed, one of its five strategic goals is nothing less that to "reinvent the Government of Gipuzkoa by opening agile means of civic participation, multi-agent collaboration and transparency" (Gipuzkoa Provincial Council, 2022).

Even discounting for high-sounding political proclamation, there are at least two noteworthy dimensions of *Etorkizuna Eraikiz* ('Building the Future' in English) – both identified by my fellow authors in this volume – that make this experiment ripe for scholarly analysis. First, as Sørensen (this volume) points out, the Gipuzkoa experience is unusual in not only involving politicians at high levels but in being initiated and promoted by the political leadership, in particular Markel Olano, the Deputy General of the Gipuzkoa Provincial Council. Second, *Etorkizuna Eraikiz* is exceptional in that it is not a peripheral exception but a norm within the current Gipuzkoa government setup. Importantly, for the purpose of analysis, we are able to observe and study a wide and varied set of "organizational structures and institutionalized paths" operating as a "network of networks" within government authority (Ospina, this volume).

Preliminary as my own observations are – based on interviews and presentations from selected *Etorkizuna Eraikiz* leaders, document review and some site visits – they are rich enough to formulate the following three tentative propositions that would be worth testing by future scholars as *Etorkizuna Eraikiz*, and other such experiments, evolve over time.

1. Proposition 1: Collaborative governance is best viewed as jazz, not as a symphony

Governance, and certainly policy processes, are sometimes depicted as a machine (Hjern & Hull, 1982; Najam, 1995; Peters *et al.*, 2022): a set of defined processes, actors, structures, rules and norms that interact along fairly well-defined (often sequential) pathways to create organisational coherence. Even alternative models mostly tend to maintain the goal of 'order' and seek to replace one set of actors, structures, rules, etc., with another (Najam *et al.*, 2006). To use a different metaphor, such models tend to view governance as a symphony: a defined set of stakeholders working towards a common goal, off a common set of notes, or script.

The *Etorkizuna Eraikiz* experience presents us with a different conception of collaborative governance: as jazz – working towards a set of common goals, but not off a common set of notes, or script. This is akin to ideas of 'improvisational governance' which also sometimes uses the metaphor of jazz (Bastien & Hostager, 1988; Hartog, 2015). However, in our case, jazz is not just a choice but a prerequisite for effectiveness. It is also, not just a 'different style' of governance, but governance with different – and an expanded set of – actors. As we will note shortly, this is a necessary condition for the evolution of governance to new collaborative complexities.

This shift in metaphor can be consequential. Scholars, as they should, tend to study governance *post facto* and *de facto*. Hence, our natural tendency is to seek structure and organisation, and to be wary where either is weak or temperamental. Politicians and practitioners, as in this Gipuzkoa case, whose goal is implementation and impact face no such compulsions. Much like Eduardo Chillida (a famous Basque sculptor, 1924–2002) imagining his sculptures, they are not scared of contradiction, nor frightened by messiness. This fearlessness – this ability to embrace jazz, and with it institutional contradiction and even messiness – may well be a condition for meaningful collaborative governance.

2.   Proposition 2: Beyond representation, collaborative governance can be designed to enhance government effectiveness

Representation is often, and rightly, a principal driver of collective governance (Rich & Moberg, 2015; Steelman *et al.*, 2021; Peters *et al.*, 2022). Indeed, because form is deemed to follow function, this is why stakeholder analysis is so important in the study of collaborative governance and the breadth and depth of stakeholder inclusion is amongst the very first questions that any such analysis confronts. This is how it should be, and is, also in Gipuzkoa.

However, in the case of *Etorkizuna Eraikiz*, a search for effective implementation, identifiable impact and policy innovation are seen not just as 'collateral benefits' of collaboration, but as defining goals embedded within the ten commitments outlined at the very outset of the enterprise. This may be explained in part by the fact that this experiment not only involves political leadership but is designed by it. It is not surprising, then, that the 'problem' *Etorkizuna Eraikiz* sets out to 'solve' is not just one of "forc[ing] institutional representativeness", but even prior to that to be "better placed in [...] the race for social welfare" (Gipuzkoa Provincial Council, 2022). The focus on collectiveness comes not just from democratic inclusion (i.e. 'good' governance), but also from innovation and impact ('effective' government).

The elevation of this very practical political goal of enhancing government effectiveness should not be a surprise given the structure and antecedents of *Etorkizuna Eraikiz*. Importantly, it leads to the proposition that what is sometimes viewed as a welcome corollary benefit of collaborative governance can be a principal design objective of collaborative governance. This prioritised search for government impact and policy innovation is most evident in the structure of the *Etorkizuna Eraikiz* model, which is based on two major spaces (*Gipuzkoa Taldean* and *Gipuzkoa Lab*) and an organised liaison (*Proiektuen Bulegoa*). On this point, the designers of *Etorkizuna Eraikiz* are very clear: "[Our] purpose is to work collectively to detect the future challenges facing the province of Gipuzkoa, design the best means of addressing them, experiment with possible responses in real contexts with the aid of different agents and apply the results in the public policies of the regional government" (Gipuzkoa Provincial Council, 2022).

3.   Proposition 3: Changing the logic of collaborative governance could change democracy

Preposterous as this proposition may sound, it is meant to be a provocative celebration of collaborative governance as embodied in the ideas of *Etorkizuna Eraikiz*, and not some ominous foretelling. Clearly, the idea of collaborative governance and its place within democratic evolution has itself been evolving (Ansell & Gash, 2008; Bang & Dryberg, 2000; Morse, 2011). However, collaborative governance is still often viewed as a necessary, but not essential, additive to the processes of democracy and democratic governance: A 'fix' that can fill in the vacuum of unrepresented voice; a 'scheme' to incorporate ignored stakeholders; a 'solution' to eroding governance legitimacy. In these times of citizen disaffection, experiments like *Etorkizuna Eraikiz* may be suggesting that collaborative governance is not just an improvement but an actual evolution of democracy – an evolution that responds to the very unmet citizen needs that are otherwise leading to distrust in and disdain for government (Fukuyama, 2015).

Conceivably, if discontent with increasingly distant, tedious, mechanistic and procedural governance is what is driving citizens across the world towards populist authoritarianism, then maybe an evolutionary response should be to make governance less distant, less tedious, less mechanistic and less procedural, i.e. a lot more collective, a little more like jazz.

Taking at face value the proclamation of *Etorkizuna Eraikiz* designers that theirs is nothing less than an attempt to change the 'political culture' of the province, the obvious question to ask is: why? One possible response is embedded in our second proposition above: it is to enhance policy impact and effectiveness. A second possible response is even more grandiose, but also even more striking: to create a better democracy. If we allow ourselves the liberty to play with this idea just a little bit more, we can conceive of an evolutionary path for democracy in practice where the right of citizen vote, once met, triggered a demand for greater citizen voice, especially for 'policy affectees' (i.e. early experiments in collaborative governance) and is now – aided by the emergence of new technologies of involvement and galloping individual empowerment – evolving into a clamour for citizen involvement in policy, not just 'policy-making' (through vote and voice) but also in 'policy implementation'.

In such a conception, the expanded logic of collaborative governance would imagine a citizenry that is no longer content with periodically 'choosing' who makes policy, nor with having a 'voice' in what policy should be, but is demanding the opportunity to jump into the messiness of conceiving and actualising policy implementation. Such a citizen is no longer satisfied by being a spectator at a symphony; instead, she seeks to jump into the jazz orchestra, to be a part of the music itself. Clearly, such a citizenry is emerging – particularly amongst the young, and not just in Gipuzkoa.

4.   A final word

Inspired by the audacious ambition of *Etorkizuna Eraikiz* itself, this essay has deliberately gone out on a limb to be certainly ambitious and possibly audacious. It is not – because it cannot be – an evaluation of the experiment in Gipuzkoa. It is, instead, a reflection on what could possibly be derived from this experiment. It presents a perspective on how to look at collaborative governance, i.e. jazz, and also three bold propositions that are inspired by a review of this experience but demand much more research before they can become anything more than propositions.

One hopes that the future trajectory of *Etorkizuna Eraikiz* itself, but also myriad other experiments around the world, will provide the space and the evidence for such investigations. Meanwhile, one wishes *Etorkizuna Eraikiz* the very best. May its audacious ambitions continue to be realised.

PART II

RELATIONAL DIMENSIONS TO LEARN AND COMMUNICATE ABOUT A CULTURE OF COLLABORATIVE GOVERNANCE

Chapter 5
Active experimentation through action research: The experience of the *Etorkizuna Eraikiz* Think Tank

ANDONI EIZAGIRRE, *Mondragon Unibertsitatea*
MIREN LARREA, *Orkestra-Basque Institute of Competitiveness, University of Deusto*
FERNANDO TAPIA, *University of the Basque Country, UPV/EHU*

1.   Introduction

It has often been said by the political leadership of *Etorkizuna Eraikiz* that *how* things are done is as important as *what* is done. This stress on the *how* has raised the need to further explore the methodological dimension of the way in which a new political culture is constructed through collaborative governance. To meet this need, active experimentation has been included as a central part of *Etorkizuna Eraikiz*. This is evidenced not only in *Gipuzkoa Lab*, within which the experimental projects of *Etorkizuna Eraikiz* are framed, but in the initiative more widely.

The concept of active experimentation was popularised by Kolb (2015), who defined it as part of the experiential learning process. Kolb views experiential learning in terms of four-phase cycles that gradually overcome two dualities: 1) the action/reflection duality and 2) the duality of the experience and abstraction of that experience. In this approach, the process of apprehending an experience begins with living a phase linked to the experience itself. This is followed by the construction of its abstract conceptualisation. At the same time, in order to transform the experience, a reflective observation is first made, followed by active experimentation. Like a spiral, learning occurs when these four phases are repeated successively.

Etorkizuna Eraikiz has integrated active experimentation in different ways. One of these is action research, which Kolb (2015, p. 10) calls "a useful approach to planned-change interventions in small groups and large complex organisations and community systems".

Action research should be viewed not as a single methodology, but rather as an umbrella encompassing different approaches. Of these, *Etorkizuna Eraikiz* has used two. For the internal transformation of the Provincial Government of Gipuzkoa (PGG), it has applied action learning methodologies (Murphy & Canel, 2020), which are described in this book in relation to the *Ekinez Ikasi* ('Learning by Doing') initiative with staff from the PGG. In order to develop collaborative governance with other provincial stakeholders in Gipuzkoa, in 2009 the Provincial Government opted for *action research for territorial development* (ARTD). The term, coined by Karlsen & Larrea (2014), refers to a specific approach to action research that emerged between 2008 and 2011 through international collaboration on action research projects developed simultaneously in the Basque Country, Agder (Norway) and Rafaela (Santa Fe, Argentina). ARTD is one of the methodologies used to develop *Etorkizuna Eraikiz*. It is currently being applied in the Territorial Development Laboratory of *Etorkizuna Eraikiz* (TDLab), in the *Etorkizuna Eraikiz* Think Tank (EETT) and in the recently created Collaborative Governance Laboratory. This chapter begins by describing how the PGG has been integrating action research into its processes of constructing collaborative governance. It then goes on to present a series of lessons learned from the application of this methodology in EETT.

To this end, the second section of the chapter shares a series of initial definitions and basic principles of action research, a timeline describing how it has been integrated into *Etorkizuna Eraikiz* and a brief description of the context in which it is currently being applied in EETT. The third section shares three key lessons learned in EETT and the fourth and last section offers some closing reflections.

2.   Action research in the Provincial Government of Gipuzkoa

This second section describes the context in which the three lessons shared in the third section took place. In it, we set out: 1) a series of definitions and principles that will help explain what action research is; 2) the antecedents of action research at the PGG, to explain how it is currently being applied in EETT; and 3) the initial design of EETT, which enabled the methodology to be used in its workings.

2.1. Initial definitions and basic principles

Action research is "a participatory, democratic process concerned with developing practical knowing in the pursuit of worthwhile human purposes, grounded in a participatory worldview" (Reason & Bradbury, 2001, p. 1). Within this framework, action research for territorial development is a specific approach aimed at generating collaborative relationships between different actors within a territory, in this case, the province or territory of Gipuzkoa. Since 2009, the PGG has been working with the multi-local action research team that initially proposed and developed ARTD. This team is referred to throughout this chapter in abbreviated form as the *action research team*. It comprises researchers from Orkestra (the Basque Institute of Competitiveness) in the Basque Country; from Praxis (the Institute of Technological and Social Studies) in Rafaela, Santa Fe and the University of Tierra del Fuego, both in Argentina; and from the University of Agder in Norway. The PGG's ongoing partnership with this team dates from 2009.

ARTD consists of real-time processes of co-generation occurring at the intersection between research and territorial development and with participants who are immersed in processes of change. The research is developed through micro processes (involving a relatively small number of people), usually representing specific organisations, but the overall aim is to have a long-term structural impact on the territory (Karlsen & Larrea, 2014). Within this framework, 'territory' is defined as the set of actors living in a place, with their social, economic and political organisation, culture and institutions, as well as the physical environment of which they form part. 'Territorial development' is the process of mobilization and participation of different actors (public and private), whereby they discuss and agree on strategies to guide individual and collective behaviour (Alburquerque, 2012, pp. 3–4). ARTD is developed in spaces of dialogue in which researchers and local stakeholders address the problems of the territory in cycles of reflection and action.

In their analysis of the *Etorkizuna Eraikiz* case as a context for the application of ARTD, Fricke, Greenwood, Larrea & Streck (2022) argue that action research, as implemented by the action research team and the PGG, is based on three basic principles: 1) the development by a territory of its collective capabilities augments its possibilities of dealing with global challenges; 2) politics and policies can be the vehicle for developing such collective capabilities; and 3) action research can be the methodology for building collective capabilities through policy and politics.

To develop collective capabilities in the territory, ARTD proposes a series of processes of knowledge co-generation to be carried out by the territorial development actors (in the case of *Etorkizuna Eraikiz*, these are members of the ecosystems of PGG policies) and action research teams. The ecosystem of a given policy comprises stakeholders (organisations and individuals) linked to that policy at any of its phases (design, implementation, evaluation, etc.). One concrete example of an ecosystem is the one that has been developed in EETT between the PGG, companies, local *comarcal* development agencies, vocational training centres, business associations and the chamber of commerce in order, through PGG programmes, to help companies improve the quality of the work of the future.

Co-generation processes in ecosystems require a continuous dialogue, encompassing three types of knowledge: disciplinary knowledge (provided by the participants and invited experts), experiential knowledge (based on the experience of the participants), and process knowledge (methodological knowledge provided by the facilitators) (Karlsen & Larrea, 2014). This dialogue forms the basis for combining the action research team's relational role (through which it accompanies territorial actors in their efforts to achieve their established goals) and its critical role (through which it helps make the territorial stakeholders aware of habits embedded in their day-to-day operations that are hindering the desired transformations) (Arrona & Larrea, 2018).

2.2. Background on action research in the Provincial Government of Gipuzkoa

In order to understand how action research is currently being integrated into *Etorkizuna Eraikiz*, it is important to consider the process of methodological development initiated in 2009 in the project currently known as the *Etorkizuna Eraikiz* TDLab.

Table 5-1 shows the principal milestones in integrating ARTD at TDLab, from where, since 2017, it has been extended to *Etorkizuna Eraikiz*. For each period in the process, the table shows: 1) the aim of the action research process; 2) the concepts on which the reflection centred, in order both to discuss their significance and decide how to intervene in the territory in relation to these concepts; 3) the results in terms of the *what*s (i.e. results aimed at responding directly to the problem posed); and 4) the results in terms of the *how*s or methodological results (i.e. transformations linked to the ways of working). The lessons learned with regard to the *how*s were conceptualised to become part of the principles of ARTD. The last column shows some of the publications in which this conceptualisation is discussed.

Table 5-1: Implementation of action research at the PGG

Period	Aim	Main concepts	Results in terms of the *whats*	Results in terms of the hows integrated into the ARTD methodology
2009– 2011	Increase social capital to improve competitive- ness	Social capital, Competitive- ness, Values, Community	Analysis and measure- ment of social capital, the implications of which were discussed with representatives from organised society in each area	Dialogic forms of relationship were established between politicians and the action research team (Karlsen & Larrea, 2014)
2011– 2013	Propose a new territorial development model for Gipuzkoa	Territorial development, Strategy, Complexity, Participation	Proposal for a new territorial development model; the Directorate for Territorial Develop- ment was created within the Office of the Deputy Gen- eral (Provincial First Minister)	Emerging strategies of learning, negotiation and ideological debate were generated (Aranguren & Larrea, 2015)
2013– 2015	Implement a new model for relations between the government and other territorial actors	Governance, Strategy, Capabilities, Shared vision, Trust	Stable spaces for dialogue with regional agencies; two govern- ment programmes defined through participation	Facilitation was explicitly included as a relevant axis of transformation (Costamagna & Larrea, 2018)
2015– 2017	Institutionalise collaborative governance, which up to then had been experimental	Dialogue, Conflict Management, Learning, Negotiation, Institutionali- sation	Formal agreement between the PGG and the 11 *comarca* agencies on the col- laboration model	The complementa- rity of the critical and relational dimensions of the processes was extended (Arrona & Larrea, 2018)
2017– 2022	Increase efficiency in programmes for SMEs and people at risk of exclusion	Multi-level governance, Industry 4.0, Digitalisation, Networks for Employability	Collaborative pro- grammes of Industry 4.0, digitalisation and the *Elkar-Ekin Lanean* initiative.	A positive relationship was built up between democratisation and policy efficiency (Larrea, Estensoro & Sisti, 2018)

Source: adapted from Larrea (2019).

2.3.   ARTD at *Etorkizuna Eraikiz* Think Tank

The methodological bases of EETT, designed jointly by its policy-makers and the action research team, are based on ARTD and were published in the research diaries on the EETT website (see Appendix 4). Since then, consistent with Kolb (2015), there has been a move towards an abstraction of the experience through the concept of *action research think tanks* (Larrea & Karlsen, 2021). EETT currently has four spaces for dialogue, linked to the ecosystems addressed by the policies in four areas: the welfare state of the future, the green recovery, the work of the future and the new political culture. Each of these spaces has approximately five members from the PGG with responsibility for policies in these areas and between 15 and 20 representatives from the corresponding ecosystem. Each group is led by a political officer from the PGG, in three cases a deputy (*diputado* – member of the PGG Governing Council) and in another case a director (the next rank down). These policy-makers and their teams speak directly with the participants at EETT. In addition, with the action research team, they lead the experiential learning process (Kolb, 2015) of the group in question. The groups are stable, but not static, and have been gradually adapted to the needs of the processes. Following the cycles of reflection and continuous action proposed by ARTD, each group has: 1) agreed on the specific problem on which it wishes to focus its deliberations; 2) invited in experts to help it understand the problem; 3) established, through reflection, guidelines for action; and 4) defined mechanisms whereby it can continue learning from action.

One of the features of EETT is that these four dialogue spaces are not independent. EETT's overall activity is coordinated by the management team. This body comprises: one or two representatives from each dialogue space (one deputy, two directors and two political advisors); two policy-makers from *Etorkizuna Eraikiz*; the individuals responsible for studies/publications and dissemination of *Etorkizuna Eraikiz*; the representative of the technical secretariat of the Think Tank; and three people from the action research team. In all, there are 13 people learning from the processes of the four dialogue spaces and feeding back a series of operating criteria. Thus, EETT continues to be designed and built on an emergent basis, through the work of the approximately 100 people participating in it.

The authors of this chapter are members of the deliberation group on new political culture and one of them is also in charge of coordinating the action research team. On the basis of the documents reflecting this process of deliberation on new political culture (and, therefore, on the application of ARTD), and on the authors' own experience at EETT, three lessons have been identified on how action research has become a methodology for experimentation.

3. Action research applied to the construction of collaborative governance: three key lessons

The following are not only lessons *on* action research, but also lessons learned *through* action research.

3.1. ARTD builds non-linear relationships between theory and practice that aid in transformation

Praxis is a central plank of ARTD and consists of a continuous combination of reflection and action. Through praxis, the 20 participants in the deliberation group on new political culture (comprising representatives from the PGG, the three universities in the territory, several research institutes and two reference centres for experimentation) have gained awareness of their different approaches to knowledge generation, and how these can be combined more efficiently to build a new collaborative governance and transform the political culture in the ecosystem.

The lesson is that action research offers a relationship between reflection and action that helps overcome the expectation of a linear process from theory to practice. In ARTD, the action is no longer put off until the theoretical or conceptual dilemmas have been resolved. On the contrary, the action itself becomes the context in which answers to these dilemmas can be constructed.

This lesson helps ARTD practitioners to understand the effective importance of combining types of knowledge of a different nature, meaning and purpose in the process of building collaborative governance. It is not merely theoretical learning; it also entails a commitment to action.

The lesson has been learned through reflection on the contradictions raised in the deliberation group. The interpretation of praxis that emerged in the group at the beginning of the process was apparently quite simple: the aim was to create a plural and heterogeneous group with people involved in the PGG policy ecosystem in order to *transfer* to participants' organisations the ideas that were put forward and suggested by experts invited to join the process on an *ad hoc* basis.

The term *transfer* implies that knowledge is generated within a space (the academy or the EETT itself) and applied in another (the organisations of the ecosystem, including the PGG). However, this runs counter to the idea of praxis in ARTD, whereby action is not the result of applying knowledge brought in from outside, but rather, action acts as the starting point for reflection.

This coexistence of different frameworks in an ARTD process is commonplace. As was to be expected, certain differences of opinion arose at the outset. These were sometimes expressed in the form of incomprehension, demotivation or even ineffectiveness and a feeling that it would be difficult to channel the ideas expressed into practice. For instance, some people who said they tended to learn from practice felt that certain other members of the group ranked this type of knowledge below theoretical knowledge; others, in contrast, felt that the group did not value theoretical knowledge highly enough.

For such situations, the ARTD approach is to get these conflicts out in the open and seek agreed ways of overcoming them. The action research team assisted the group in this exercise. As a result, tasks were added to be carried out in smaller groups made up of people with similar ways of generating knowledge. One group took charge of making a theoretical contribution, while others undertook to intervene in three specific experiences (the PGG's *Aurrerabide* programme, and the *Arantzazulab* and *Badalab* reference centres) with a view to transforming governance of these experiences and bringing the lessons learned from this practice to the deliberation group. The theoretical results and these experiences are set out in *Etorkizuna Eraikiz* (2022). At a personal level, sharing these experiences has led several participants to change their judgements, deep-held beliefs and behavioural patterns in a quest for mutual understanding.

At the time of writing, the deliberation group continues to hold diverse views on how the knowledge required to transform the ecosystem should be generated. Nonetheless, progress has been made in overcoming a linear interpretation of knowledge transfer, in which it was assumed that acquiring and understanding abstract and disciplinary knowledge implies – if there is a desire and a willingness – transforming practical and organisational activity. By actively listening to the unease provoked by the dissociation of theory and practice, we have learned that theory, desire and willingness are not enough. Fertile knowledge is complex and the pace of transformation depends on a series of interests, routines, demands and resistances that tend to be undervalued or neglected in more theoretical reflections. ARTD offers ways in which these interests, routines, demands and resistances can be addressed.

From this position, by practising ARTD, the group has been able:

–   To identify the root problem that explains the low level of linkage perceived, felt and experienced between theory and practice: the group had very different frameworks on how to generate knowledge for transformation. We believe this is often the case in other contexts as well.

- To see the advisability of knowing how to address and combine theoretical knowledge with knowledge originating from daily experience and also with knowledge arising from processual interaction in the spaces for reflection. The deliberation group combined the *theoretical* knowledge provided by guest experts and some members of the ecosystem, the *experiential* knowledge linked to *Aurrerabide*, *Arantzazulab* and *Badalab* and the *process* knowledge integrated through facilitation, which has basically consisted of the ARTD principles.

- To learn that action research requires a willingness to assume personal and collective responsibilities based on cognitive, affective, emotional or strategic learning and that it generates trust in other people. For example, based on the awareness of different ways of generating knowledge, participants committed to contributing the type of knowledge that they believed they could best generate.

- To understand that action should be viewed not as a single area in which to apply theoretical knowledge, but as different spheres that are open to reflexivity and generate robust knowledge in so far as they are contextualised. Thus, *Aurrerabide*, *Arantzazulab* and *Badalab* have not been spaces in which the Think Tank's knowledge has been *applied*, but spaces whose reflexivity around the Think Tank's approaches has enabled new transformative knowledge to be generated.

3.2. ARTD helps to assume and manage the fears and suspicions generated by the participation of collaborative governance

Taking its inspiration from Greenwood & Levin (2007), ARTD includes participation as a third element that complements reflection and action, and serves as a link between them. Participation takes the form of processes of dialogue in which participants learn and negotiate action.

One of the important lessons learned at EETT is related to the ethical and political nature of the work of participating agents. Specifically, it has been seen that the participation involved in ARTD generates fears and suspicions that need to be addressed if real transformation processes are to be undertaken – or in other words, if we want to ensure that participants can "change their own practice" (Townsend, 2014, p. 7).

These fears and suspicions appear at the intersection between reflection and action, i.e. when the co-generated knowledge is likely to have an impact on the political agenda and, therefore, on the PGG's public policies.

Participation in EETT involves a collaborative or cooperative conception of power entailing a recognition that the plurality and complexity of our societies requires the cooperation of 'political' stakeholders (policy-makers *stricto sensu*, experts from various fields, researchers from the academic field, etc.), at different levels, using various instruments of collaboration. Participants in this process understood that ARTD's links with the transformation of power relations towards cooperative or collaborative forms were related to a political dimension of ARTD, which involved seeking the democratisation of processes through participation.

This type of process, in the initial stage of building collaborative governance as a cooperative model for the exercise of political power, requires a basic moral structure that sets the limits of participation and defines the mutual commitments among the agents and their levels of responsibility. Without such a structure, fears and suspicions can arise. In the case of the *Etorkizuna Eraikiz* Think Tank, these fears and suspicions were stated explicitly at the beginning of 2022, two years after the Think Tank's activities began, when there was little more than a year remaining before the end of the government's term of office and the 2023 elections.

Fears and suspicions were initially raised in one of the four focus groups. Some of its participants expressed their concern that the government might somehow attribute responsibility for governmental decisions to the group of people participating in the Think Tank. The proximity of the elections only served to heighten this feeling. This gave rise to a concern that might at first sight appear contradictory. The Think Tank was created precisely in order that its reflections would impact PGG policies, and this characteristic was accepted by the people from the ecosystem who participated in it. However, when, in 2022, this impact on policy began to be realised, some participants expressed their worry. This raised the following question: who would be responsible for an unwise decision made by the government based on the Think Tank's reflections?

In order to answer this question, between March and May 2022 the action research team facilitated a process based on ARTD guidelines for stating conflict explicitly and building agreements for action. By means of this process, a structure was constructed for collective action. This was set out in a 'Code of Good Governance'. The purpose of this code is to clarify the commitments and the degree of responsibility of the people involved, with a view to boosting their trust in the process. Starting from the contributions made at the deliberation group that initially raised the problem in early 2022, a proposal for a code was developed and taken to the EETT management team. It was subsequently discussed in each of the dialogue spaces.

The code explicitly sets out the ethical commitment of the participants in the Think Tank, their position *vis-à-vis* the diversity of interests represented in the deliberation groups, and the obligations and commitments they are willing to take on. The fundamental principle agreed upon among the participants is that the PGG has sole responsibility for its own decisions and actions. This means applying to the PGG the general principle adopted on the use of knowledge co-generated in the EETT, which is set out below:

> People participating in deliberative processes, who are part of policy ecosystems, can use the co-generated knowledge for decision-making and actions in their own organisations. The responsibility for each participant's use of such knowledge rests with that person, or to the extent to which it is assumed by his or her organisation, with each organisation.
>
> Application of this principle to the specific case of the Provincial Government of Gipuzkoa, which proposes and leads the Think Tank, means that in cases in which the individuals or teams from the Provincial Government consider integrating the knowledge co-generated in the Think Tank in their decision-making processes and actions, the remaining participants do not directly assume any commitment in said decision-making process or in relation to said actions.
>
> (Excerpt from EETT's Code of Good Governance)

It is important to note that one of the promoters of *Etorkizuna Eraikiz* raised the concern that this principle did not favour the construction of co-responsibility of all participants in the public policy ecosystem. Consequently, the management team added another heading to set out the dynamic nature of EETT, thus contemplating the possibility that some of the principles contained in the code could be adapted at a later date:

> The code responds to the initial stage of building collaborative governance, in which the PGG has opened some of its decisions and actions to deliberation with the ecosystem. It is in this context that the PGG's exclusive responsibility for decisions and actions is framed. However, processes are beginning to emerge within the Think Tank oriented towards deliberating on decisions and actions shared by the entire ecosystem, thus further extending collaborative governance. As the Think Tank moves in this direction, this code will be adapted also to accommodate forms of shared responsibility for the ecosystem transformation process.
>
> (Excerpt from EETT's Code of Good Governance)

The lesson learned from the experience of developing the code is that, in the transition from reflection to action, materialised through participation, the participants' contributions impact not only on their own actions, but also on those of other participants. An awareness of this impact may generate fears. In the short term, EETT has addressed these fears by delimiting each participant's areas of responsibility (see first excerpt from the code). However, the EETT management team hope that, going forward, conditions will be generated in EETT for co-responsibility to emerge (see second excerpt from the code), for example through shared projects in which members of the ecosystem not only contribute knowledge to PGG decisions and actions, but undertake shared projects in which everyone decides and acts together.

3.3.   ARTD makes it possible to address the emotional dimension of building collaborative governance

Another of the lessons learned in EETT in relation to action research is the relevance of the emotional dimension. The critical role described in section 2.1 of this chapter, as articulated by both researchers and ecosystem members, can lead to emotional exhaustion among participants.

Action research has contributed to an explicit consideration of emotions in the Think Tank, within the framework of first-person action research. One of the most recent proposals in this field is *action research for transformations* (ART) (Bradbury, 2022). *Etorkizuna Eraikiz*, and more specifically the deliberation group for the construction of a new political culture, have examined this framework (Diputación Foral de Gipuzkoa, 2020a). Consequently, some of its principles (adapted to the territorial context) have been integrated into ARTD.

The main result of this experimentation has been to propose integrating the concept of *reflexive co-agency* as part of ARTD. This form of cooperation "aims to transform the very mindset and relational interactions that hold our political systems captive in either/or thinking that is largely unresponsive to the growing complexity of modern democracies" (Larrea, Bradbury & Barandiarán, 2021, p. 44).

Reflexive co-agency in ARTD requires an appreciation of subjectivity, and in practising it, policy-makers and researchers turn the camera simultaneously on themselves and on each other, discovering different subjective interpretations of their own actions, relationships and the structures within which these operate. By looking at themselves, politicians and researchers discover not only their own rationality, but also their emotions; they are so closely linked to one another that it is difficult to view them as separate entities.

To explain this idea better, we would like to conclude this section with an excerpt from the dialogue generated in one of the experiments conducted at *Etorkizuna Eraikiz*, which serves as an example of a process of reflexive co-agency (Larrea, Bradbury & Barandiarán, 2021, p. 51):

> Xabier: In politics, up to now we consider the political objects and the rules that regulate them. But we do not consider this intangible feature that we can name as love, affection, admiration. But it exists and it is not anecdotal. The most transformative political relationships that I know have been based on the love that certain people felt for each other.
>
> Hilary: I'm surprised that you, that we, say love in our conversation. I don't think we normally say love. Which is actually really interesting. 'Cause we are talking about love, yet somehow, we cannot use the word. This says something about the normative discourse that prevents this conversation.
>
> Xabier: I think this intangible factor, OK, let's call it love, is an element to relearn politics in the context of the actual transformation worldwide. The political system will not be able to face complexity unless it becomes more horizontal, democratic and flexible.

The processes for talking about emotions, not just about rational thought, are not often found in processes linked to politics. However, they can help to integrate the emotional dimension of the processes in a healthier way, improving not only the wellbeing of the people involved, but also the long-term consolidation of the processes. By incorporating reflexive co-agency, ARTD can help achieve these objectives.

4.   Final reflections

The three lessons shared in this chapter were made within the framework of transformation processes framed within *Etorkizuna Eraikiz*. However, it would be naïve to think that the transformation sought by this initiative has already taken place. We (all participants in *Etorkizuna Eraikiz*) will need to sustain this effort over time, using this and other methodologies, going further and deeper at every step. What the lessons learned in this chapter show us is that action research – and specifically ARTD – can be a valid methodology for making progress along the road towards collaborative governance, overcoming the dichotomies that often block it.

5.   Lessons for practitioners

–   Policy-makers can use action research as a strategy to construct col-
    laborative governance.
–   To integrate action research into policy-making, policy-makers and
    action researchers need to work as a team; this approach differs from the
    traditional relationship between policy-makers and researchers, which
    is based on reports and other types of deliverables.
–   When constructing collaborative governance, action research can help:
    •   to overcome excessive reliance by collaborative governance processes
        on planning or, alternatively, to explore emergent strategies;
    •   to express and manage participants' fears that the process of col-
        laborative governance might be misused; and
    •   to address the emotional dimensions of the process.

Chapter 6
Communicating for collaborative governance

Ion Muñoa Errasti, University of Deusto, San Sebastián, Spain

1. Introduction

Given that this chapter focuses on the role played by communication in *Etorkizuna Eraikiz*'s development, one might start by saying that since 2016, over 275 actions have been launched, representing over 275 opportunities for communication by the Provincial Government of Gipuzkoa. Some of the questions we might analyse are these: How have these opportunities been used? How has each of the communicable objects been managed? How have the different channels been used? What have the main actions been? What audiences have been reached? What have been the main messages? How has the *Etorkizuna Eraikiz* brand been addressed? How has the narrative been built? What has the organisation learned? To what extent and in what way has the institution's way of communicating changed? What have been the main obstacles that have needed to be overcome?

There are certainly many questions that can be raised, and many points of view from which they can be answered in any analysis of the case of *Etorkizuna Eraikiz* from the perspective of communication. However, above all other concerns there is one central question that I believe should guide our reflection in this chapter: What does communication contribute to collaborative governance at *Etorkizuna Eraikiz*?

To answer this central question, this chapter first describes how communication is conceived in the *Etorkizuna Eraikiz* model of collaborative governance. Taking this conceptual framework, I then analyse the specific practical approach taken in three areas of communication: institutional relations, media relations and digital communication. In each of these areas, I describe what was done and how any problems that arose were dealt with. Finally, by way of a conclusion, I offer some final reflections, with a view to drawing lessons from the *Etorkizuna Eraikiz* case with regard to the role played by communication in collaborative governance.

2.   The main pillars of the vision of communication in *Etorkizuna Eraikiz*

This section will attempt to set out the principles on which the conception of *Etorkizuna Eraikiz*'s communication is based. The purpose is to provide some context for its practical development, as described in the third section. This conception has been formally analysed for this chapter, and is based on: a review of the basic literature; the background in sociology and communication of several of the people involved in the design and development of the programme; the Provincial Government's interaction with professionals and agencies specialising in communication, public relations and advertising; and conversations and joint reflection between political leaders, civil servants and communication professionals at a number of workshops and reflection processes undertaken over these years.

There is one phrase that clearly reflects how communication is viewed in the collaborative governance model of *Etorkizuna Eraikiz* by those working in it: "Collaborative governance is not communicated; collaborative governance is *in itself* communication". This means accepting that communication is an intrinsic element of the model itself and getting away from the idea of communication as a function for telling, staging, relating or 'selling' what the Provincial Government does through *Etorkizuna Eraikiz*. In other words, communication does not come after collaborative governance. Rather, it is an integral part of all the spaces and processes of the collaborative governance model *Etorkizuna Eraikiz* embraces.

I believe that this view of communication eschews an approach that some have described as 'marketinian', focusing instead on the relational and integral dimension of communication. Communication at *Etorkizuna Eraikiz* is viewed as a social interaction with which to build trust. With this goal in mind, we do not consider that it is enough merely to improve intermediation processes and techniques. Rather, the interaction of communication must be placed at the heart of any political action, transforming governance in the ways described in the following subheadings.

2.1.   Communication is relationship and social interaction

In categorising the communication of EE, it may be helpful to turn to the distinction made by Martín Algarra (2010), who said that all possible definitions of communication can be grouped into two major perspectives: the relational perspective and the symbolic perspective. It has to be clarified that the 'relational perspective of communication' as this author understands it

differs from that of 'relational communication', which refers to the management of organisational communication and has to do with the relationship
with different stakeholders. For Martín Algarra, the relational perspective is
broader, in that it views communication as existing whenever there is contact
or any other form of relationship. That is to say, for example, communication
exists whenever two objects or two animals relate to one another. In the
symbolic approach, on the other hand, communication is restricted to relationships in which some cognitive content is conveyed. Of the two, political
communication belongs more properly to the symbolic perspective, since it
views communication as an action whose purpose is to signify something.

Martín Algarra (2010) explores this conceptualisation using Schütz's
theories on the knowledge of reality, and argues that in communicating,
"conscious contents are shared: knowledge, feelings, etc." (p. 39), and what
is shared with someone is not lost. In this regard, communication is a 'social
reality'. In order to share with someone there has to be someone. And in turn,
to be able to share, one must be able to "transform the world into meaningful
knowledge" (p. 39) through the ability to produce symbols. Based on Martín
Algarra's (2010) broad review of the different communication theories, one
can conclude that communication is a process of social interaction, involving
at least two subjects (one who manifests and the other who interprets) who
share knowledge about reality with an intentionality.

The idea of 'social interaction' is a key feature to bear in mind to understand
the wider perspective of the form of political communication that best suits
EE. As Martín Algarra explains, different sociological schools and theories,
from the constructivists (interactionism or phenomenology) to the structural-
ists, all view communication as the element that enables social action and
interaction. There are differences when it comes to explaining this interaction,
but all interpretations recognise the importance of communication (and its
social dimension) in any society. It is this idea of social interaction that lies
at the heart of EE's conception of communication, and which goes beyond
simply conveying messages or intermediation.

2.2. Institutional communication to build trust

A second feature of EE's communication is that it was designed to express
a model of collaborative governance that builds trust. Trust as one of the
goals of communication has been a recurrent object of study. According to
Gutiérrez García (2013), "one of the fundamental variables in cultivating
trust is the communicative relationship with the public; hence effective
communication is essential" (p. 13). Nonetheless, it is important to bear

in mind that many different variables may be involved in the processes of both communication and trust-building. Gutiérrez García (2013) notes that "restoring the crisis of credibility and trust depends on multiple factors, among which communication can play a relevant role, although not an essential one if other problems have not previously been corrected" (p. 52). In other words, trust is multi-causal. In this regard, Gaber (2009) argues that in complex democratic societies, an increase in public communication and the possibility of accessing more information does not always appear to result in greater levels of trust.

Trust facilitates collective action among people and among institutions by promoting cooperation and the construction of common norms and values. Luhmann (1988), Putman (2000) or Giddens (1990), among others, stress the importance of this intangible value in the proper functioning of any social system. Trust is an essential and intrinsic element of communication processes, and indispensable to any democratic society. As Gutiérrez García (2013) puts it, "[t]rust is a highly valuable intangible in a democratic and social system, since it nourishes the social legitimacy of institutions and makes it easier for citizens to make decisions without the laborious work of verifying the reliability of the person who is the depositary of it, especially in complex societies" (p. 51).

Precisely in complex societies with democratic systems, visions and definitions of political communication have evolved from a perspective in which communication is viewed as an addition to politics, to one in which communication is seen as standing at the very centre of politics. The first authors to discuss this subject, such as Fagen (1966), Blake & Haroldsen (1975) and Meadow (1980), viewed political communication as being all those actions that can influence the political system now or in the future. The prevailing notion was of two separate worlds, the communicative and the political, mutually influencing one another.

Subsequent scholars, such as Wolton (1992), Shudson (1997) and Canel (1999), stressed the interrelationships and interactions between all the agents influencing the political system and public decisions, as constituents of the processes of political communication. In this view, political communication is seen as encompassing all communicative actions and actors that in some way intervene in the public space, and thus in the political system. Along similar lines, Canel (1999) identifies at least three main functions of political communication: to provide the information and communication necessary for any decision-making; to legitimise the decision-making and execution processes; and to enable the necessary debate for the collective organisation of societies. In this vision, political communication is a fundamental pillar of political action.

Institutional communication is one of the principal areas within the broad field of political communication. All public institutions in democratic systems, regardless of their powers, their geographical scope or their size, have certain communication needs in their relationship with citizens and other organisations that contain common features. The discipline of institutional communication encompasses all these communication processes, which in addition to covering the practical needs deriving from everyday functions, have the central need of responding to the very existence of the institution. As Canel (2010) puts it, the identity of the institution is not only built through the law; it is also related to other issues such as the way in which the institution defines itself, the way it sets out its objectives or justifies its actions, its ability to involve others in its own actions, etc. From this perspective, institutional communication is linked to the strategic dimension of the organisation itself. Communication must therefore be aligned with the institution's project and identity and cannot be restricted to providing information about what it does, since it is a constituent element of the institution's very existence. Therefore, communication strategies and planning must lie at the core of the institution, in order to make it credible and coherent.

Similarly, Canel & Sanders (2013) draw on the work of Botan & Taylor (2004) to conclude that the way in which institutional communication is viewed has evolved from a "functional perspective to a co-creative perspective. While the former sees the public and communication as a tool or means of achieving organisational goal, the latter sees the public as a co-creator of the organisation's meaning and communication" (p. 35). This co-creative perspective is entirely in consonance with the relational notion of organisational communication in general and institutional communication in particular (Canel & Sanders, 2013; Gutiérrez García, 2013).

In the case of institutional communication, bearing in mind the tendency to view and implement institutional communication integrally and strategically in the multi-level relationship with the institution's environment, dialogue is essential. In order for a true communicative relationship to exist, the public – i.e. the citizen – must be viewed as an interlocutor and not as the passive target of the communication.

In developing the concept of communication used to advance the *Etorkizuna Eraikiz* initiative, we took into account the prevailing trends in institutional communication, and more specifically the development of its strategic dimension, the vocation to respond to the current needs of complex societies, and the objective of generating trust.

However, how and in what form has this view of communication been manifested in *Etorkizuna Eraikiz*? How has the theoretical approach to social interaction actually been applied? Does communication of *Etorkizuna Eraikiz* actually fulfil the guidelines on trust-building? I will examine this question in the following sections.

3.   Communication management at *Etorkizuna Eraikiz*: from conceptual approach to everyday reality

The features that characterise the *Etorkizuna Eraikiz* approach are comprehensive, relational and trust-building communication. However, putting this concept into practice entails challenges, since it requires changing work processes, overcoming existing inertia and achieving consensus on the goals. This became clear with the different actors participating in *Etorkizuna Eraikiz*: policy-makers, technical staff (civil servants) from the Provincial Government of Gipuzkoa, political leaders, communication managers, stakeholders and the media.

Generally speaking, experience has shown that changes cannot be implemented overnight or in their entirety. In the case of *Etorkizuna Eraikiz* there has been an evolutionary process over the last five years (2017–2022). This was to some extent conditioned by the timing of the initiative itself (it was launched during the run-up to an election); by the political, economic and social context of Gipuzkoa; and by the cultural change experienced by the different agents involved. In general terms, for example, the approach to communication was not the same at the launch of EE, when the programme had to be presented and given visibility, as it has been in recent years, when the real material evidence of the initiative's spaces, processes and projects are already in place. This process of evolution has highlighted the existence of dynamic levers, and also of tensions, contradictions and gaps between conceptualisation and practical development.

I will now analyse what has been done so far, focusing on three areas of *Etorkizuna Eraikiz*'s communication: institutional relations, media relations and digital communication. I address these areas in particular, because they have shown to be especially significant in the development of *Etorkizuna Eraikiz*. Indeed, these were the areas identified in the organisation chart when the communication area was reorganised at the beginning of the 2019 term of government. In the previous term (2014–2019) the Provincial Government's communication was concentrated in a single department, answering directly to the communication bureau of the Office of the Deputy General. In the current term (2019–2023), it has been reorganised: there is a communication department with three sub-areas (institutional relations, digital communication and media communication), each with its own officer in charge. Communication from *Etorkizuna Eraikiz* has been based on this distribution of areas and tasks.

There follows a brief short description of what has been done in each of these areas, with particular emphasis on the gap between concept and practice and the challenges I believe lie ahead.

3.1. Institutional relations

Because collaboration with civil society is, by definition, the cornerstone of the *Etorkizuna Eraikiz* model, relations with other institutions and organisations in society form the central plank of *Etorkizuna Eraikiz*'s collaborative governance model and thus of its communication.

Here it is important to note that the Provincial Government basically has two types of relationship with the organisations within the framework of *Etorkizuna Eraikiz*:

1. Formal institutional relations: i.e. actions aimed at establishing, maintaining and strengthening the Provincial Government's relations with other agents in the province. These include official visits, collaboration agreements, public events, presentations, etc. They are 'formal' in the sense that they have a certain structure and formalisation.

2. Informal institutional relationships deriving from the different initiatives that make up *Etorkizuna Eraikiz* (spaces, projects, processes). Such relations give rise to continuous interaction, since there are many different spaces for meeting, debate, shared reflection and dialogue, as described in the first chapter of this book.

One might say that the actions and staging of formal relations follow a more classical line, since they are based on a logic of institutional representation that has been developed over several decades. However, *Etorkizuna Eraikiz* has made it possible to introduce new contents into some existing relations by incorporating new projects and forms of collaboration and establishing new relations with other agents. An example can be seen in the case of relations with the business world. By launching new collaborative projects for the future, EE modifies the existing institutional relation, creating more shared ways of viewing the reality of the province, and enables new economic agents to be included who begin to relate exclusively through content. In keeping with the *Etorkizuna Eraikiz* philosophy, even in the most formal relationships, we have sought to reinforce trust and provide collaborations and public events with content that is in line with the model.

It is the second type of relations, the informal ones, which might be said to be the most innovative. Here, new opportunities have emerged for relations and interaction between the Provincial Government of Gipuzkoa and very diverse agents, including other public institutions, social organisations, companies, universities, development agencies, etc. These relations have been instituted and developed at very different levels: in private and in public, in informal relationships linked to projects or spaces such as the Think Tank, face-to-face and online, at the level of institutional representation and at the level of personal representation, etc.

These institutional relations have been communicated through a variety of actions: initial presentations (throughout 2017) of *Etorkizuna Eraikiz* to universities, the principal economic and social agents in the province, the local (*comarca*) agencies, and Provincial Government employees; discussions with economic, social and cultural agents, etc. from the province to extend align-ment on the strategic themes in the EE agenda; meetings with international ex-perts; meetings with drivers of the pilot projects; presentations of experimental projects; signing of cooperation agreements with universities, development agencies, etc.; *Etorkizuna Eraikids* (initiative developed in conjunction with schools to discuss the future with schoolchildren); conferences and summer courses; events to mark the setting-up of each of the reference centres; webinars and themed seminars on the new political agenda of EE; meetings of the 'political panel' attended by the different political parties; the plenary meeting of *Etorkizuna Eraikiz*, which (as discussed in previous chapters) combines public- and private-sector entities; the forum, a space for reflection led by the Public University of the Basque Country, where citizens have an opportunity to debate different topics through intergenerational dialogue, etc. In short, the different spaces and processes within *Etorkizuna Eraikiz* offer a host of opportunities for relations between agents. In the ecosystem of institutional and organisational relationships thus created, the Provincial Government has been the central organisation, but not the only one (nor indeed has it always been essential). In this way, the interaction arising out of *Etorkizuna Eraikiz* has not only qualitatively and quantitatively strengthened the Provincial Government's institutional relations; it has also fostered relations between the different agents taking part in different initiatives.

However, although relations have certainly been enriched, we have yet to reach the point in the model we would have liked when it comes to institutional relations. A number of challenges have been identified:

- Many institutional events are still viewed by different economic, social and cultural actors as mere box-ticking, elements of protocol, which they have to attend simply for the sake of institutional representation.

Given the culture of institutional relations that has been developed over the years (and decades), some of the participants and agents involved (especially those who have been around for some time) have difficulty accepting the philosophy that lies behind the events organised in the context of *Etorkizuna Eraikiz*. Some groups and citizens have tended to view such events as acts of political marketing. In other words, there is evidence of some scepticism among the target audiences of such events as to their authenticity. We therefore need to continue working to create the right conditions at the events, acts and meetings organised to strengthen collaborative relationships and gain credibility and trust.

– The current formats do not yet enable people to contribute and participate as much as the *Etorkizuna Eraikiz* communication model requires. We therefore need to make an effort to find the formats that will best facilitate this participation.

– Not all those participating in the different initiatives, and thus in the relationship system, feel themselves to be part of *Etorkizuna Eraikiz* as a whole. One of the clear challenges is to foster a sense of belonging to the project.

– It is difficult to attract ordinary citizens (i.e. those who do not belong to the organisations with which EE works) to the various events that are staged. The challenge, therefore, is to create attractive spaces for ordinary citizens, with particular emphasis on listening to them (to learn about their interests and concerns) and opting for innovative formats and ways of approaching the public.

3.2. Media relations

Communication from the Provincial Government of Gipuzkoa has tended to prioritise relationships with the media, to the detriment of other communication tasks. The media are at the epicentre of the communication strategy. Simplifying greatly, one might say that the most common way of viewing political communication among people who have worked on it has been based on the idea that: "anything that works well in the media has been a communication success". This has led to the development of certain initiatives, forms of inertias and ways of doing things which, according to our internal reflections, are not entirely in line with *Etorkizuna Eraikiz*'s concept of communication.

It is also important to bear in mind that Gipuzkoa has a relatively small media ecosystem, in which everyone knows each other. This further affects the Provincial Government's relations with the media.

Etorkizuna Eraikiz does need media coverage, for two reasons (among others): first, to legitimise the initiative among its stakeholders, among whom there are a certain number for whom EE's media visibility is important; and second, to promote knowledge among citizens. The media has therefore been at the centre of *Etorkizuna Eraikiz*'s communication strategy from the outset and staff have been aware of the need for coverage.

Initially, we worked with an advertising agency on the communication strategy. We held press conferences, gave interviews and planned communication campaigns. However, this approach proved difficult. Most of the journalists saw *Etorkizuna Eraikiz* as part of a new political marketing strategy, because these communication activities did not provide them with the amount and type of information they wanted. It was almost impossible to discuss collaborative governance with journalists who were covering six press conferences a day and hold their attention. They wanted details, tangible facts, dates, millions of euros, etc. It was very difficult to come up with a newsworthy hook. And so, between 2018 and 2019 (during the second half of the term of government), we decided to implement a more generic form of communication, evoking the future and trying to link the Provincial Government to themes that might be of general interest, such as population ageing and care, the future of work, climate change and ecological transition, digitisation, etc.

According to a reflection by people involved in *Etorkizuna Eraikiz*, these initial difficulties were overcome when the reference centres began to gestate, from 2019 on. They offered the possibility of moving from idea to reality, of giving some material substance to the project. Judging from conversations with journalists and the coverage received in the media, it was from that moment that the project began to gain credibility: the foundations underpinning the reference centres began to operate; the people in charge of these centres occupied media space and the media were more receptive. They asked for more information about *Etorkizuna Eraikiz*, began to attend more press calls, and gave more coverage to the topics and the leaders of this governmental project.

At the same time, most of the Provincial Government's communication capacity was focused on *Etorkizuna Eraikiz*, i.e. EE was prioritised as its central strategy of communication and public and social positioning. A number of advertising campaigns were launched, with considerable investment in the media. All this increased the visibility of *Etorkizuna Eraikiz*, although it tended to be associated above all with a general idea of the future and less with collaborative governance.

The May 2019 elections were an important milestone. Given the electoral contest, there was pressure to provide sufficient visibility. At the same time, however, there were some who believed that excessive visibility might further a suspicion among the public that *Etorkizuna Eraikiz* had electoral interests.

With the start of the new term of government (July 2019), and with the tension of the elections out of the way, those in charge of directing the provincial government's strategy decided that the time had come to consolidate and advance the initiative, a process they referred to as 'qualifying' *Etorkizuna Eraikiz*. They felt that with the advertising campaigns and institutional events, the goal of extending the brand, i.e. giving visibility to the project, had been achieved (this was reflected in the *Sociometer* (regular surveys of the population), which showed a ten-point increase in suggested recognition between October 2018 and October 2019). They therefore felt that the time had come to gain credibility. The idea was to cease any communicative actions that the public might negatively associate with 'marketing' and focus on disseminating what was really being done in *Etorkizuna Eraikiz* in the media and among the public. Significant tangible and material achievements had already been made: think tanks, reference centres, calls for pilot projects, grants for citizen-based social innovation projects, a network of municipal councils to extend the model, etc. A change of course could then be made that would make it possible to gain in seriousness and credibility not only with the stakeholders, but also with people in the media. Those of us working on this issue felt that there were signs of change in the media. They were beginning to see that they were receiving weekly accounts of the progress of the different projects; they were provided with the new policies and achievements; and they were being given access to see the actual real gains made, for example through visits to reference centres. In short, they could see that we were talking about real, tangible elements.

As discussed here, there has been an evolution in the relationship with the media that we consider positive, insofar as *Etorkizuna Eraikiz* has been growing and making tangible advances in areas that had initially been only promises that sounded more like self-promoting political marketing. Nonetheless, some concerns still remain with regard to our communication with the media.

- Our investment in content production has been disproportionate to the media coverage actually achieved. This poses a double challenge: on the one hand, we need to be more selective about the content to be disseminated and on the other hand, we need to focus on topics that have a greater news appeal.
- The collaborative governance model *per se*, and most of the content, processes and complex realities being promoted by *Etorkizuna Eraikiz*, are not entirely media-attractive. It remains to be seen whether, with

time and a change in culture, as these approaches mature and develop, they will gradually be given greater coverage in the media.

– The media require tangible realities and, more often than not, the public and political innovation that is associated with collaborative governance is based on intangibles rather than tangibles. This challenge raises at least two issues: How can we make the intangible visible and easy to understand? And how can we make media managers aware of the social, political, economic and cultural importance of providing space for this type of content?

– The main subject of communication of *Etorkizuna Eraikiz* when it comes to the media is the public institution, as embodied in its principal policy-makers. This qualifies and limits both the scope and impact of what is reported. The challenge is to give greater prominence to the stakeholders without distorting the identity of EE and maintaining the narrative relationship with the Provincial Government of Gipuzkoa.

3.3.   Digital communication

The digital strategy has also sought to improve the quality of communication between citizens and the institution. On the one hand, social media offers a range of interesting possibilities for communication and dialogue of an initiative based on collaborative governance. On the other, the initiative itself, *Etorkizuna Eraikiz*, offers new options for content, branding and interaction that can go beyond the limits encountered in the Provincial Government's digital communication, which by its nature tends to spawn very institutional content, with little appeal to the average online user. We have therefore tried to use this opportunity to make some qualitative leaps in the field of digital communication.

Our aim is to ensure that *Etorkizuna Eraikiz*'s digital communication operates in both directions. On the one hand, we want to inform people about the initiative and the projects being developed from it. On the other, digital channels offer more possibilities for getting direct and immediate feedback from society at large. In keeping with the *Etorkizuna Eraikiz* philosophy, we want the whole of online Gipuzkoan society to become digital stakeholders in the initiative. However, given the complexity of the project, the distance required for citizens to connect with a government initiative and the difficulty in ensuring truly two-way communications between the institution and society, for the time being, we can only engage in digital communication with certain specific target audiences.

The target audience can be divided into two levels. On the one hand, there is the *Etorkizuna Eraikiz* ecosystem – i.e. organisations related to public policies, a qualified audience that is familiar with the project. This audience shows more knowledge and interest in the initiative, since they have, in one way or another, participated in it. They are also more active and participatory, and thanks to them, a greater reach and impact is being achieved in digital communications, since they then disseminate EE content on their own networks. On the other hand, there is the wider society, which constitutes a less well-informed audience that shows less interest in *Etorkizuna Eraikiz*. With this audience, our communication ends up being more one-way; users do not participate much and do not show an interest in being informed.

These are some of the defining features of *Etorkizuna Eraikiz*'s digital communication:

–   The institutional web page provides information on the general features of the initiative and offers the latest news, while also offering access to the different spaces for user participation and interaction.
–   We have a presence on Twitter, Facebook, Instagram and LinkedIn. All channels are regularly updated and active.
–   These channels are treated differently according to the needs of each segment and the opportunities each one offers.

In general, communication has been strengthened on all these channels, but with differentiated strategies. We have stepped up information updating; the content has been adapted to encourage user participation, and the initiative has been 'humanised' (with faces) to make *Etorkizuna Eraikiz* more approachable. We try to use each channel to create a bond and to bring legitimacy to the initiative among the different segments in a more direct and effective way. Each medium is used to receive input from users and to interact with them in an instantaneous, individual and personalised way. For example, questions, data, examples, etc. are posed which, as well as offering information on EE-related topics, serve as an 'excuse' for a more 'natural' interaction between the different users. Along the same lines, we steer away from more institutional-type staging that would spark greater online rejection and instead try to find images that better engage with the tastes of the digital target audiences.

Clearly, digital media offer great potential for bringing *Etorkizuna Eraikiz* closer to citizens and to establish a closer, more human and direct relationship with them, through digital dialogue. This is why collaborative governance can also be built and developed in the digital arena. The digital communication strategy is designed with this in mind, but there are still a number of challenges to be addressed:

–   The necessary conditions have not yet been established to develop collaborative governance in the digital space. A stronger and more stable digital community needs to be created to allow for more interactions and possibilities for better-quality dialogue.

- We are concerned about how we can expand and improve the interaction between the Provincial Government and the citizens in the digital environment through *Etorkizuna Eraikiz*. We have tested out and experimented with new methods and channels, but there are still limits and the reality is still a long way from what we would like.
- We have not been entirely successful in generating or adapting the content of the networks to make them appealing to the general public. For example, the Think Tank – which is a central space within EE – generates some very important and profound documents and reflections on the future of public policies in the territory; however, by their very nature it is extremely difficult to turn these contents into the subject of intermediation with digital audiences. The challenge is to 'translate' this type of content into readily 'consumable' online content.
- There are still many cultural and political barriers to be overcome before users in Gipuzkoa can interact normally with a public institution like the Provincial Government.

4.   Some conclusions about communication and *Etorkizuna Eraikiz*

Having explained the conception of communication in the *Etorkizuna Eraikiz* model and analysed real practice from different approaches and areas of communication, I would now like to set out a series of conclusions for consideration.

First of all, it is important to note that in the *Etorkizuna Eraikiz* model, communication is designed from and for collaborative governance. Experience has shown that communication is an integral part of the model, and that it can be used to seek and reinforce interactions, which means putting into practice a relational approach to communication. However, this way of approaching communication has to coexist with the intrinsic needs and functions of institutional communication, which can sometimes generate certain tensions, as well as developing practices that run counter to the model. In this regard, experience has shown that it is helpful to consider a progressive development in the relational approach, without disturbing the balance in the forms of communication that enable day-to-day legitimisation of the institution.

Secondly, it is evident that there are still important gaps between the concept and actual practice in the three dimensions analysed (institutional relations, relations with the media and digital media). While there has been significant progress in all three areas, and the reality of communication is now closer to the ideal than when *Etorkizuna Eraikiz* was initially launched, it is still far from achieving its ultimate goal.

Thirdly, taking a closer look at this evolution, we note that the drive of *Etorkizuna Eraikiz* has brought about changes in the different levels and processes of communication – in many of the actions, in the way events are designed, in some aspects of the way communication managers work, and in the communication processes. Above all, there has been a transformation (albeit not total) in the way communications from the Provincial Government of Gipuzkoa are viewed and exercised. *Etorkizuna Eraikiz* has therefore constituted a great collective learning process on communication for the organisation as a whole.

Fourthly, we can identify a number of achievements of *Etorkizuna Eraikiz* in the area of communication.

– New spaces and opportunities have opened up for collaboration, and by extension, for interaction and dialogue. In many cases the conditions have been established to develop a form of communication that generates shared contents and meanings.
– In all communication spaces and channels, there has been a transition from a one-way to a two-way approach. The Provincial Government's digital communication space has been innovated, strengthened and improved from this approach.
– Progress has been made in trust-building communication, gaining in credibility and reliability (at least among stakeholders and the most qualified audiences).
– We have demonstrated that it is possible to implement (at least partially) another way of viewing and practising institutional communication.

Fifthly, we should not ignore the fact that there are still serious difficulties in advancing towards the model of communication proposed by *Etorkizuna Eraikiz*.

– Within the organisation itself, amongst other agents and in the media, there is still a degree of inertia at an operational level, which runs counter to the proposed approach to communication. Specifically, even today we still see many classic 'stagings' that prioritise the 'photo' of the visit, rather than actual spaces for dialogue.
– There is still reticence among the public towards possible elements that are identified with the instrumental and political use of *Etorkizuna Eraikiz*.
– Difficulties remain in communicating intangible elements.

- There are still difficulties in establishing new relationships (e.g. with important players in the business world and a major portion of the general public) and continuing to grow with the relational model.
- There are doubts about the extent to which the different actors participating in *Etorkizuna Eraikiz* feel themselves to be an integral part of the initiative. Here, one might consider whether there is an *Etorkizuna Eraikiz* community that can continue to grow beyond the central nucleus of the most active people who participate in the different initiatives and projects.

Sixth, at the beginning of this chapter, I posed the following central question: What does communication bring to collaborative governance? Based on the above analysis, I conclude that communication is not just necessary for informing and legitimising any action of collaborative governance; it is essential for the very existence of collaborative governance. In this regard, it would be of interest to explore further the elements and features that optimal communication of collaborative governance requires.

Finally, and to turn the initial question on its head, one could say that in the case of *Etorkizuna Eraikiz* collaborative governance has contributed a great deal to communication. It has been the lever which has brought about the transformation that was needed in the Provincial Government's institutional communication. We can therefore conclude that collaborative governance processes are also processes for transforming the communication of public institutions.

5.   Lessons for practitioners

- Collaborative governance requires thinking about communication from collaborative governance itself. In the case of *Etorkizuna Eraikiz*, it is understood that "collaborative governance is not communicated; collaborative governance is in itself communication". That means that communication does not come after collaborative governance, but it is an integral part of all the spaces and processes of the collaborative governance model *Etorkizuna Eraikiz* embraces.
- The features that characterise the *Etorkizuna Eraikiz* approach are comprehensive, relational and trust-building communication. However, putting this concept into practice entails challenges, since it requires changing work processes, overcoming existing inertia and achieving consensus on the goals. This became clear with the different actors participating in *Etorkizuna Eraikiz*: policy-makers, technical staff (civil servants) from the

Provincial Government of Gipuzkoa, political leaders, communication managers, stakeholders and the media.

–   It is essential, but not enough, to have a clear and well-defined communication model for collaborative governance. Taking into account the experience of *Etorkizuna Eraikiz*, it would also be advisable to foresee the roadmap to implement this model, considering the main changes that it implies.

–   The collaborative governance model *per se*, and most of the content, processes and realities promoted by *Etorkizuna Eraikiz* are complex in themselves. This makes it difficult to attract media and citizens (both physically and virtually). In general, tangible realities are required; and more often than not, the public and political innovation that is associated with collaborative governance is based on intangibles rather than on tangibles.

–   In the experience of *Etorkizuna Eraikiz*, we have learned that managing communication properly can improve collaborative governance; and *vice versa*, a process of political innovation such as *Etorkizuna Eraikiz*, based on collaborative governance, can also improve the communication processes of a public institution.

Chapter 7
Listening and learning together: Using action learning for collaborative governance

ANNE MURPHY, *Lancaster University, United Kingdom*
MARÍA JOSÉ CANEL, *University Complutense of Madrid, Spain*
OLATZ ERRAZQUIN, *Diputación Foral de Gipuzkoa*
ANDER ARZELUS, *Diputación Foral de Gipuzkoa*
ELENA OYÓN, *Learning advisor, United Kingdom*

1. Introduction

Action learning is a pragmatic approach to engaging participants "in learning from their attempts to improve things" (Pedler & Brook, 2017, p. 217) and has been applied in a wide range of organisational contexts, including collaborative governance (Hale *et al.*, 2018; Murphy *et al.*, 2020; Pedler, 2002, 2020). Associated with the pioneering work of Reg Revans (1971, 1982, 1998), the approach offers a discipline for action-orientated learning which is focused explicitly on problems "that matter to those who are charged with addressing them" (Brook, 2022, p. 7). The classical model of action learning (for example, Pedler, 2008) works with small groups, often referred to as sets, in which participants help each other to tackle their pressing organisational problems and to learn from their attempts to change things. Revans never provided a single definition of action learning. Instead he maintained that, while the idea is simple, it cannot be applied or replicated in a formulaic 'best practice' way, because, as he is at pains to point out, "[a]ction cannot be taken in general terms; it's always was, is, and always will be dependent on its conditions and on those who take it" (Revans, 1971, p. 98). In practice, as Pedler (2008) reminds us, this is one of the strengths of action learning because:

> Being both profound and simple it is never in danger, as mere techniques are, of being here today and gone tomorrow. We always need to re-invent our own ways of putting the basic ideas into practice. This inventing element is what maintains the life in action learning. (2008, p. 6)

In Gipuzkoa, small groups of colleagues have adapted and reinvented the simplicity of this idea and made it their own. The story begins with a small but influential pilot carried out in 2018 towards the end of the electoral cycle in which eight elected politicians (and two senior public officials) decided to try the action learning approach in order to 'listen to society'. Led by the President of the Provincial Council (the *Diputado General*) and his chief of staff, this pioneer group took enthusiastically to the task of learning (and listening) by taking action, then reflecting on and sharing the results with the members of the group who supported, challenged and, above all, listened to each other. Personal challenges, always treated in confidence, resulted in steps being taken to address the gulf between what the politicians said they were doing, what they actually did and what the electorate heard and understood. The results of this learning experience have been reported elsewhere in the context of citizen engagement (Canel *et al.*, 2022), social capital (Barandiarán *et al.*, 2022) and leadership learning (Murphy *et al.*, 2020). It was during this first pilot that 'action learning' became *Ekinez Ikasi*. In rejecting the verb 'to do' (*egin*) in favour of the verb meaning 'to initiate action' (*ekin*), the translation into Basque adds a sense of dynamism to the original English.

Since this first pilot edition of the programme, people from the PCG have been 'accoucheurs' (i.e. the person or persons who, according to Revans, create the conditions for learning to take place, and take root) to no less than 11 groups of action learners and, at the time of writing, stand ready for the next edition which will gather another six groups to the collective learning process. Before we briefly describe the different editions in the following section, it is important to reflect on possible reasons why the approach has proved so timely. We identify three key reasons. First, the approach has given some hope that the day-to-day working relationships which produce collaborative governance may be accomplished differently. Participants are, of course, aware of previous unsatisfactory attempts to 'manage change' and consequently treat the positive energy around the programme with respect and care, but most share a sense of excitement that this time, they can make a different sort of difference. Secondly, while action learning is premised on taking action on problems in which "I am part of the problem and the problem is part of me" (Pedler, 2008, p. 11), this is not traditional learning with a focus on individual skills and knowledge, but a shared, collective process of meaning-making which involves contexts, materialities and bodies as well as human minds and motivations (Elkjaer, 2022). Human beings are part of complex 'situations' (Dewey, 1939 [1988]), so other factors, including power, emotion, other voices, history and economic matters, are equally important for learning (Carroll & Smolović Jones, 2018; Easterby-Smith *et al.* 1999;

Vince, 2019; Pedler, 2020). Realised through learning encounters across and between groups, this collective aspect of action learning meant that shared analyses sharpened participants' understanding of institution-wide problems. Finally, *Ekinez Ikasi* is inspired by a version of action learning which eschews reliance on external experts in favour of insights born of a shared commitment to action and learning between equals or 'comrades in adversity' as Revans called them (Revans, 1998). Participants know that however they choose to proceed, they are making progress on important organisational problems by themselves – and their own diagnosis is much more precise that any external expert intervention might hope to be.

The chapter describes the application of action learning methodology that has been used in the *Etorkizuna Eraikiz* initiative with the express objective of developing the listening and learning skills and competencies needed for collaborative governance. The chapter begins with a description of the four completed editions of the programme before going on to outline the role played by the *bidelagunak*, or 'travelling companions' who took on the task of advising and supporting their own *Ekinez Ikasi* groups. Next, we address the future by looking at how the initiative might develop in continued support of *Etorkizuna Eraikiz*, including the fifth edition of the programme, which is in progress at the time of writing. We conclude with reflections about our collective learning and lessons for practitioners.

2.   *Ekinez Ikasi*: the story so far

This section briefly summarises the way the programme has been developed by its participants, including the institutional steps taken to evaluate and learn from the experience as it evolved.

2.1.   First edition: the *políticos* (elected politicians), 2018

The ten-strong *políticos* group of action learners met off-site five times over a six-month period, each time for an uninterrupted five-hour session. Problems brought to the group included how to: reach out better to citizens; involve civil servants more; align different departments with the goals of *Etorkizuna Eraikiz*; show the authenticity of one's willingness to count on stakeholders; increase the transformational capacity of one's departmental policies; and allocate functions and tasks to make departments ready for change. The process of support and challenge required by action learning helped members of the group to develop important questions focused on learning and action.

These included: What do citizens think about this project and how do you know? What do you think matters for citizens? Do you think the PCG is not attracting good talent, and if so why? Is your willingness to involve civil servants sincere? What do you mean exactly by 'listening to society'? Are you ready to hear criticism from citizens? Do you believe we really want to share power with citizens? Actions agreed included to: involve the top leader (*Diputado General*) in cross-departmental meetings; make changes to the format of public encounters with citizens; invite new and different people to public encounters; collect data about petitions people are making through participatory budgeting and reflect on readiness to adequately respond; arrange a meeting with a hospital and use good practices of listening and then reflect on how to extend them to other departments; and explore the list of voluntary organisations to analyse better how society is evolving in their engagement with volunteer work (see Murphy *et al.*, 2020, p. 6 for further details). At the end of every session the group reflected on the usual questions in action learning (see Pedler & Abbott, 2013), their learning about themselves, their group, the Diputación and *Etorkizuna Eraikiz*; questions about their learning about listening and about society were also added.

The (written) reflections were analysed, synthesised and presented back to the group who then identified important gaps and challenges for the future. Decisions were taken to continue to develop and adapt *Ekinez Ikasi* to requirements of the institution by extending the experience to council employees and by setting up of an oversight group with a remit for making sure actions decided upon in the groups received full support from the top. An important consequence of this first edition was that the participants so appreciated the renewed cohesion that the action learning programme gave them, they decided to invite employees (technicians and civil servants) to join action learning sets as they took steps to improve the way they worked.

2.2.   Second edition: the *funcionarios* (career civil servants), 2019

Two groups of eight senior civil servants were formed by approaching those people usually willing to commit additional time and effort to improvement activities, especially *Etorkizuna Eraikiz*. The groups had backing from the chief of staff, whose genuine commitment to personally see that organisational blockages were removed left participants feeling able to tackle problems with organisation-wide consequences. Like the *políticos* they also met five times for five hours every five or six weeks. Coordinators were appointed to liaise between participants, the steering group and the two 'outside' facilitators (the first and second authors). Different kinds of problems were identified, actions undertaken, and individual and organisational outcomes achieved. At the end of the programme a joint session was arranged for participants to compare and contrast their experiences and learning. Conclusions drew attention to the difficulties of collaborating within the government and its institutions, and also to the need to open up deliberative processes in such a way that the voices of technical teams could also be heard.

Again gaps and challenges for the future (*brechas*) were identified. Two specific challenges stood out: first, the enormous gulf between the politicians (including political appointees in management positions) and local government officers and staff; and second, the gap in understanding and administrative coherence between directors, managers and employees of the county council and those working in other public service bodies under direct control of the council. As a result, the steering group was re-positioned as the *grupo de escucha interna* (vehicle for internal listening) and given a broad remit for ensuring continuity of the programme after the elections scheduled just before the end of the *funcionarios* edition. The first important decision taken at this time by the internal listening group was to steer *Ekinez Ikasi* towards the organisational problem of collaboration that had been identified in the form of two specific gaps: 1) across the public sector and 2) among elected politicians and government employees. In other words, *Ekinez Ikasi* began to be seen as a vehicle for learning about how collaborative governance might be achieved in practice. Hence, the second influential decision taken by the internal listening group was to form two new *mixed* groups which focused on these organisational problems and which were made up of both political appointees and government employees. Undertaking this step was considered to be a big shift since so far it had never happened that politicians participated together with technicians in a learning experience that put all sides on a level. At this point, the programme broke for what the steering group thought was for the summer (2019), to be resumed once the new government was in place.

2.3. Third edition: the *grupos mixtos* (political and administrative roles), 2020–2021

The newly elected government needed to negotiate and agree the details of its coalition. Until decisions had been taken about which party would lead which department, and which departmental directors were therefore to be appointed, *Ekinez Ikasi* was held in waiting. It is important to understand that political appointees hold the influential roles in the organisational hierarchy, and without them, little of consequence can be undertaken. The autumn progressed and the decision was taken that it was in everyone's interests to launch the third edition in January 2020. Bringing together political appointees and civil servants was seen as nigh impossible and, given the high profile of the two focal issues, no one wanted to take any unnecessary risks. Then the onset of the COVID-19 pandemic further complicated everyone's workload and availability. Furthermore, *Ekinez Ikasi* had so far been a face-to-face experience and no one was really sure if this still delicate seedling would survive the online environment. Several months passed before the steering group took the bold step of setting dates for the third edition face-to-face, hybrid or online depending on the public health regulations. As soon as circumstances allowed, the second author was given special permission to travel and the groups met face-to-face. The first author attended online throughout.

Bringing the mixed groups together to work on problems of shared concern lent new energy and drive to the process, exceeding expectations of how people across party and professional divides would be willing and able to work together. Actions, which were taken individually and in collaboration, made breakthrough progress against stubborn organisational blockages – particularly in the work regarding the relationship between the government and the wider public sector, as well as building trust between the directors (i.e. political appointees of differing colours) and the employees (career civil servants). At the end of the cycle, the groups were again invited to come together to reflect on their achievements and learning, and to identify any further gaps or challenges that they considered *Ekinez Ikasi* to be a suitable vehicle for action and learning. As well as concrete outcomes from the actions undertaken, there was widespread agreement that the slow and incremental process of seeing one's colleagues in a new and generally more favourable light, developing trust and even friendships, and seeing the traces of positivity in places that had previously seen only tension were slowly opening up possibilities for thinking and behaving in new ways. At the final meeting of the internal listening group, members harnessed this cautious optimism and decided to make a step-change in the way the programme was to run. No longer seen as a pilot, and also having the full backing of the authorities responsible for the management of the staff (the county councillor for governance), the decision was taken to train up internal people, both political appointees and local government officers, to support this approach to learning, including setting up and facilitating their own action learning sets. These sets advisors were to form a new kind of group established in order to learn how to support their own *Ekinez Ikasi* groups. Two further mixed groups were also agreed, which, in order to distinguish them from the facilitator training, became known as the 'ordinary' groups.

2.4.   Fourth edition: the step-change, 2021–2022

The development of the fourth edition took a number of twists and turns. Some key action leaners from previous editions left the groups to become facilitators. And while there had always been a careful balance between new members and 'old hands', there had been enough continuity of membership to build up a level of group competence. Setting up the facilitator group was a hugely important step which in the end proved to be the most important decision the internal listening group had taken, but the 'ordinary' groups stumbled: attendance became a little more patchy, at times new members were puzzled by the unfamiliar process, and 'old hands' wondered if they were not just going round in circles. This was a critical moment for the programme and one only the action learners themselves were in a position to make sense of and address. It was at the mid-point – session three of five – that the groups took charge by naming the issues that were hampering their progress and 'grasping the nettle' of what their groups were actually for and what they wanted to do in them. The group of facilitators on the other hand, although at first unsteady on their feet as action learning facilitators, were united by a strong sense of shared purpose. Their *Ekinez Ikasi* meetings were designed as a forum where issues related to establishing, supporting and best serving their own *Ekinez Ikasi* groups could be shared. We worked on the principle that while *teaching* the skills of running an action learning set would be inconsistent with the values and practice of action learning, these skills could nonetheless be *learnt.* Furthermore, given that the group of facilitators also led four other new groups, a total of 41 participants, the end-of-cycle learning exchange became an important forum for collective learning. Before going on to address facilitator training and learning exchange in more detail in the next section, we close this section by drawing attention to the organic development of the initiative. In four editions, the emphasis has moved from the political elites to diverse groups of learners, from individual 'problems' to high-stakes organisational issues, and from looking to external facilitators to trusting the power of their own expertise. We believe that the critical success factor has been the enormously strong commitment of the people to living, breathing and owning their own *Ekinez Ikasi.*

3.   The *bidelagunak* travelling companions

Revans (1998) understood the critical, and oft under-appreciated, task of enabling action learning to be the most difficult challenge of all. The facilitators' learning journey began in exactly this spot. The eight-strong group – still a mix of directors (political appointees) and government officers – chose to work in pairs, starting with the task of gathering a group together for them to work with so that they were able to learn first-hand about facilitating *Ekinez Ikasi*. We struggled to find a word in either or Basque or Spanish which captured the essence of this task and the particular way the members of the group wanted to engage with it. 'Training' was too formal and deficit orientated, 'animator' suggested 'entertraining' and 'facilitator' evoked the consultant-led change programmes the group so wished to avoid. Finally, in an echo of the naming of *Ekinez Ikasi* itself, a member of the group suggested *bidelagun* (plural *bidelagunak*), which translates as 'travelling companion'. This captured the egalitarian spirit of a jointly undertaken endeavour that the group so wished to preserve. Each pair engaged with possible participants, discussed the scope and values of *Ekinez Ikasi*, recruited new action learners, set the timetable of meetings and launched themselves into the unknown. Guided by the first author, the *bidelagunak* met seven times in total, first to prepare themselves for the first meetings, and later to prepare and share materials, to share successes and challenges of guiding their own groups and to learn how best to develop the programme overall.

The early action learning meetings of the *bidelagunak* concentrated on getting their groups established and engaged in both action and learning. This was by no means an easy task. *Ekinez Ikasi* had previously been experienced positively but the number of participants was modest and, to an extent, still under the radar. By engaging with a new set of participants whose roles and work challenges were highly visible, the development raised the profile and the stakes of *Ekinez Ikasi*. The professionalism and dedication of the *bidelagunak* meant that by the mid-point all their groups had gained their own sense of purpose and cohesion. At this point the issue of continuity was raised. The group wanted a resource they could use with new groups as they formed and as new *bidelagunak* stepped up to the challenge. This resource needed to be concrete so as to be a support to those taking on the role, yet flexible to adapt to evolving practice and new organisational learning from action. A design workshop was held to harvest lessons learned and these formed the basis of a draft, updatable resource which drew together local adaptations based on published materials (Chivers & Pedler, 2004; Pedler & Abbott, 2013; Pedler, 2008; Murphy & Canel, 2020; Nesta, 2022), worksheets that had been prepared for reflection between sessions, and a synthesis of the 'what works' conversations held during the design workshop. This ongoing, updatable resource for the *bidelagunak* belongs to the group and the current plan is to update it every year.

The practice of joint reflection at the end of each group session (Pedler & Abbott, 2013, p. 80) became a habit, and the more experience they gained, the more the participants learnt to make these sessions meaningful. For this reason, the end-of-cycle 'learning exchanges' which brought groups together were found to be rich and stimulating, and this was particularly the case with the learning exchange at the end of the fifth edition. The two-hour session, which brought together 35 participants, was co-designed and run by the *bidelagunak* along 'World Café' lines (Brown & Isaacs, 2005). Groups worked around tables, jotting down ideas on the make-shift paper table-cloths and moving between tables from time to time. They addressed two principal questions:
1) What have we done/achieved/learned so far?
2) What do we want to do now?

The table notes, which were analysed, synthesised and transcribed by the third author, formed the basis of the end-of-cycle meeting of the internal listening group. Some of the issues highlighted in the session went beyond the individual learning generated by *Ekinez Ikasi*, such as: "*Ekinez Ikasi* has made it possible to generate spaces for dialogue; it has enabled to the participants to break out of their usual patterns and inertia; it has been possible to activate skills such as: listening, empathy, engagement" and so on. On the top of that, *Ekinez Ikasi* has generated important intangibles such as trust between people in the organisation, knowledge of people and realities in other services and departments, and a sense of belonging to a group and to the organisation, all of which are essential in order to work on organisational problems.

Outcomes for the meeting were synthesised into a series of learning points and distributed to everyone involved. It was clear from these results that problems being identified were no longer limited to individual or even departmental issues but could only be addressed by tackling significant institution-wide structural questions. Therefore, a subtle shift of balance took place as a result of this meeting. First, the 'ordinary group' were recast as 'extraordinary groups' in recognition of their now critical (but time limited) corporate remit of addressing the quality of leadership and decision-making across the institution. The change in name had another effect. The *bidelagunak* who had previously seen themselves as learners in an experiment, could now see themselves as the more permanent players. What was experimental became more 'ordinary' with the realisation that the ball was firmly in their court.

4.   What is next?

At the time of writing, we have just launched the fifth edition. This is made up of two 'extraordinary groups' comprising old hands, previous *bidelagunak* and also a small but influential number of participants who are new to the process, and a group of *bidelagunak* who have welcomed new members to their number. The first, most important task is to make sure that all these groups are gathered together well, that they understand the values and purpose of *Ekinez Ikasi* and that they identify important problems or opportunities to work on in action. The story of *Ekinez Ikasi* in the PCG is one of a series of incremental changes: the positive results with the *políticos* group led to establishing the groups of *funcionarios* which in turn enabled the creation of the *grupos mixtos* and *bidelagunak*. This next phase calls for consolidation around issues of more collective and institutional significance, in other words *grupos corporativos*. Other issues, secondary for the time being but being put forward with increasing urgency, include making best use of the flexible learning resource and exactly what it means in strategic and operational terms for the *bidelagunak* to take over the running of the programme. How, for example, might a repeatable pattern be established? How is the process to be kept fresh and appealing to people inside the PCG and more widely across the territory? How can those involved make connections with others who take this approach so that they are inspired to keep learning and so that others can also learn from them? And lastly, we face the challenge of consolidating the dynamic and ensuring the continuity so the change of legislature is not a rupture. That said, the link between *Etorkizuna Eraikiz* and *Ekinez Ikasi* is increasingly direct. An important *Etorkizuna Eraikiz* challenge is extending the approach across the governmental institutions. Specifically, the model demands that new and wide-ranging deliberative spaces are configured. Innovative ideas about managing knowledge and collective intelligence can only work if actors external and internal to government are involved. By engaging organisational members who deal with and care about the problems in question, *Ekinez Ikasi* has shifted away from a reliance on external experts and, as a result, this has meant a step-change in working practices aligned to the philosophy of *Etorkizuna Eraikiz*. The *Ekinez Ikasi* and *bidelagunak* experiences have, above all, demonstrated the usefulness of a forum where people listen to each other, take action and learn from the results of that action individually and together – the very engine of collaborative governance.

5.   Learning

In particular, we reflect on our own learning in order to consider the role action learning has played, and might play in the future, in the development and practice of collaborative governance. We draw attention to three important aspects:

1. Action learning helps to establish spaces for critical listening and learning. The existence of these spaces is fundamental in developing the collaborative skills needed to make a collaborative governance model work in practice.

2. Regarding skills, we specifically draw attention to the ability to listen with humility, to be reflexive and positively self-critical, to open up new angles on problems, and to look at individual problems in an organisational context. For collaboration to work, it is crucial to establish bridges between individual and personal development and an organisation-wide perspective on collective learning.

3. Action learning helps to locate positive energy for change among members of an organisation and/or system, channel this energy into concrete steps and actions, and connect the people who are committed to making change happen.

6.   Lessons for practitioners

Finally, in our lessons for practitioners we highlight the following:

–   It is important to involve the most senior political and managerial teams from the start. That they are engaged and open to learning in this way *themselves* is critical for success.

–   Listening, learning and acting in this way has to be voluntary for it to impact change from within. The overall direction of the work may, of course, be guided 'from the top' to ensure alignment with the overall governance strategy, but the final responsibility and accountability for learning and success lies with each and every one of the action learners.

–   Action learning takes time and effort – but in practice this is not an extra burden for already extremely busy people. This is because the approach involves the identification and subsequent resolution (in action) of real problems involving real people in real time, including finding ways to address challenges thrown up by the global pandemic.

Workshop 2
Synthesis of interactions between scholars and practitioners

What follows is a synthesis of the discussions, including major ideas, comments, further questions and challenges, that emerged from the interaction between the local/international scholars and the practitioners (politicians, civil servants, stakeholders) embedded in *Etorkizuna Eraikiz*.

1. Analysis of stakeholders: Who is in, who is still out? Issues of democracy

Initial response and reactions

Etorkizuna Eraikiz is a living project that actively tries to involve its stakeholders, including a wide variety of actors and spaces to foster collaborative governance: citizens, reference centres, political actors (including the opposition), municipalities, researchers, business and societal organisations.

Thematic debates

The following comments and suggestions emerge from the discussion:
- Criteria for inclusion: Who is to be involved? Those affected by the problem? Those interested? Those with the abilities, resources and power to influence the solution of the problem? The criterion being used by EE is "organised society", those who have responsibility and therefore make decisions and deploy resources for addressing specific issues; people with practical experience. Innovation is also a criterion.
- Knowledge is a criterion for including actors: knowledge provides causality for intervening. EE appears to be an open and inclusive initiative, but with contradictions. There is tacit knowledge and explicit knowledge. Most citizens are those with tacit knowledge. And those with tacit knowledge know more than what they are able to express, but express less than those with explicit knowledge (business people, academics and

politicians). A collaborative governance project has to lend a voice and empower those with tacit knowledge.

Diversity is beneficial for the development of CG, for it brings new perspectives. Listening to stakeholders is not enough; they have to participate.

– A stakeholder map (drawn up by the EE Think Tank) has shown that inclusion is not a dichotomic issue (who is in and who is out). Instead, what needs to be looked at is how a specific actor is represented, and how relations are established between different actors. EE shows changes in relationships between the Provincial Government and the universities, 'county' (*comarca*) agencies and the media.
– Some specifics about who is in and out:
   Municipalities (and county agencies) have been involved not from the start, but from the last two years. It is clarified that this relationship has been institutionalised after a long and tough process of negotiation. Interinstitutional relationships are not easy: each institutional actor tends to worry about its own interest, and in this sense it is difficult to promote collaborative governance processes. The topic that triggered agreement was fostering competitiveness between SMEs and medium-sized business though collaborative processes (principles, procedures, dialogue for co-creation of public policies). Topics now on the agenda: employability, circular economy, digital transformation, inclusivity of people in employment.
   Unions: they were voluntarily excluded from the start, because it was thought that, if included, processes would be slowed down.

Further questions, critical issues and challenges

– Registering participation appears to be needed. Projects look for ample representation from the different sectors of civil society, but there is not a rate of participation. If looked at by sector, most important actors are included, yet certain parts of society are being missed.
– Inclusion might entail some exclusion. Is inclusion always good? Contradiction: contrasting with the normal assumption that inclusion is good for collaborative governance, the reality shows that including everyone is difficult. There are limitations which cannot be overlooked. Exclusion is also needed when there is lack of reputation, history of corruption, lack of credibility.

- Self-exclusion is being shown. People who lack listening skills (and do not accept criticism) self-exclude from collaborating. Some self-exclusion is being seen at EE amongst the following groups: a) *politicians*: some of them tend to see collaboration as a weakness, and do not get involved; b) *civil servants*: some departments prefer to stick to a traditional culture rather than following collaborative governance culture; c) *Large companies* who think they do not need to interact collaboratively; d) *Young people*: not many young people are participating in EE projects. Why? Digital global technologies are changing the way young people interact with public institutions. Experimental projects are being conducted among youth movements. The intention is to develop an EE programme led by young people. Looking at the self-excluded, it appears that collaborative governance necessarily brings together stakeholders with different logics, rules and roles. Therefore, different means have to be developed to achieve an inclusive approach.
- Conflict plays a role. EE has a history of conflict management. Conflict with politicians (because of their resistance to change), with external bodies (because of their ambitions), with the conceptual design of the model (different understandings between politicians and academics), with some societal actors (because of a lack of common understanding about the intangible value of collaborative governance).
- The process is an ingredient in itself. Collaborative governance is done by interacting.
- Is collaborative governance the solution? We do not know. What we can state is that it is at least a learning strategy. There is no magic recipe, and we learn by doing. We need to keep learning about collaborative governance.
- Guaranteeing the sustainability of the initiative is a challenge. You want to involve many, but you also need to retain them. Looking for causality of involvement is good for making the initiative sustainable. EE appears to be a brilliant initiative, but one that requires great efforts to make it sustainable.

2.   The role of culture in interaction management: What worked and what did not in aligning different stakeholders around common goals? Why do people engage in collaborative governance (efficiency, equality, social and economic growth)?

Initial response and reactions

Three major drivers for involvement in EE:
–   An explicit declaration from the Provincial Government that the initiative will not be instrumentalised: cameras away!
–   There is mutual acknowledgement of both sides' authority.
–   The Provincial Government makes a commitment to stakeholders on the assumption that the invitation is not only to deliberate, but also to provide input for public policies. Stakeholders have evidence that their input is being taken into account; they interact directly with politicians (i.e. at the Think Tank).

Thematic debates

The following comments and suggestions emerge from the discussion:
–   The project is inspired, launched and driven by politicians (as compared to other initiatives, which are launched by technicians and to which politicians react reluctantly). Could this be because some of the leaders of EE are former civil servants? It appears to be that those pushing EE already know how things work. This suggests that the future of EE requires technicians as well as politicians to own the initiative.
–   The goal is not only to solve problems that are relevant for the local community, but also to build trust and to change political culture. Changes in culture take time. As compared to many initiatives of this kind, EE is undertaking this long-term goal.
–   "The glory of hybrid democracy": the attempt is to link representative democracy with direct democracy, and also at the same time bureaucracy with democracy. This is a hybrid beast. A lot is being written about hybrid democracy, and EE may be a good example of it.

Further questions, critical issues and challenges

- To avoid incoherencies: when the message is given that collaborative governance is the goal, you have to behave accordingly on an everyday basis. If not, the Provincial Government will become the target of all protests.
- To differentiate political management from administrative management. This means that politicians have the function of keeping a constant dialogue with citizens, to know and represent them; and afterwards, with them, to establish criteria for political action. This is different from institutional management. At the same time, co-creation between politicians and technicians is needed. EE has been late in involving technicians.

3. The role of leadership: How to organise leadership? What skills are needed for leading collaborative governance?

Initial response and reactions

According to people from the Provincial Government, EE has shown that the kind of leadership that is needed for collaborative governance is as follows:
- An inspiring leadership that looks for commitment and the involvement of politicians, technicians and agents from the territory.
- A collective and distributed leadership.
- A deliberate form of decision-making that includes all the agents from a specific sector.
- A leadership that is co-created by a set of shared values. The values which they are attempting to develop are: collaboration, anticipation, experimentation, openness.

From the discussion, the following ideas emerge:
- EE shows some kind of collective leadership: there is personal leadership, but also collective leadership by the Provincial Government, which works as an umbrella; within it, different personal individual leaderships are being developed.
  More specifically, different understandings/sources of leadership have been shown in the development of EE: based on traditional hierarchy, collectively built by different actors, professional (scholars have had an influence), visionary (a single actor strongly portraying a view), social (e.g.

Mondragon). Communicating vessels between the different leaderships have operated at EE.

– EE is showing that collaborative governance builds collaborative leadership which generates energy around a view. Along with the spaces of reflection and of experimentation, collaborative governance builds spaces of strong cohesion which include vital as well as informal factors. Room for different types of leadership has to be allowed for in order to make collaborative governance happen.

Thematic debates

The following comments and suggestions emerge from the discussion:

– In collaborative governance, leadership has to be conceived more as a function than as a position. There are many people in leadership positions who do not lead, and people who are not in leadership positions but who do actually lead.

– EE shows that collaborative governance entails leading people with a strong political influence. For collaborative governance to succeed, and since time is needed for visible results and outcomes, there has to be somebody who is able to go through tough and conflictual situations.

– The paradox is that for collective leadership to happen, you need to develop a strong individual leadership which rests on collective interest. That helps individual leadership to move to collective. This is happening in EE, but it is necessary to explicitly set out how it is being done.

– Several aspects of leadership can be looked at, and one is the effort to achieve goals through others. If so defined, collaborative governance challenges leadership. We need a revolution in leadership, because we have been exerting a typical leadership for many years, and now we are demanding leadership to be developed not only within the organisation but outside it as well. EE is a laboratory for this kind of leadership.

Further questions, critical issues and challenges

– Is there only one type of leadership that makes EE work? If so, there would be failure.

– There are three types of leadership: traditional (the leader person steps forward and gathers the whole group, leading them in the right direction), the opposite (everyone is a leader), and the network leader (several agents are recruited to form a selected group). There is also distributed leadership (across different places). Where does EE's leadership stand in this categorisation?

- Where does leadership reside? With individuals? In the processes? The different form of leadership that have been developed in the implementation of collaborative governance of EE have to be identified. Does EE leadership derive just from EE leaders? In other words, does leadership have to come from the person designated as the leader? Hypothesis: leadership comes from the person who has the ideas to pull people in one direction.
- What will happen when the structural leading person goes? Will EE keep going?
- Can CG change leaders, and if so, how? The leader can change governance, but the opposite can also happen: a strong culture of collaboration will change the leader.

4. How has EE approached communication? What can be learned from it about the role communication plays in collaborative governance?

Initial response and reactions

Understanding of communication in EE rests on the assumption that collaborative governance is not communicated but it is rather communication in itself. Communication is hence an intrinsic factor of the EE model, and is located at the core of the relational spaces that are developed; thus, communication is not a function to 'sell' what the government does. The communication activities developed in three areas (institutional communication, media relations, and digital communication) have been oriented to establish relationships with stakeholders of the different spaces and projects. Implementing this conceptualisation has faced opposition and given rise to internal and external tensions, and still problems emerge. Current formats do not yet enable people to contribute and participate as much as the *Etorkizuna Eraikiz* communication model requires.

Thematic debates

The following comments and suggestions emerge from the discussion:
- Segmenting publics and looking for feedback is key when building collaborative governance. Feedback is looked for via quality assessments, meetings, surveys, interviews, and the interactions with stakeholders in the projects. There is not yet a clear approach to process all this information in order to make sense of the data and interpret stakeholders' reactions.

- What is the role of communication? Communicating collaborative governance leads to placing emphasis on actions, facts and actual performance over the narratives. The core of the conceptualisation of EE's communication is about performance, achievements and acting, and hence communicating EE is more about interacting with stakeholders than about advertising it. The role of communication at EE is thus understood as inviting people to act together, to undertake joint action. By acting together you are communicating.
- Collaborative governance puts into practice a relational approach to communication.
- Gaps emerge between facts and messages, between the theory of collaboration and its practice. Collaborative governance undertakes the risk of a rebounding effect: credibility is lost when behaviours do not correspond to the promise of collaboration.

Further questions, critical issues and challenges

- The extent to which awareness of a government initiative on collaborative governance should be taken as an indicator of good communication performance is debatable. It might be the case that while awareness of the whole project is low, audiences are aware of the impact of the public policies that collaborative governance develops.
- How is communication to be controlled in a collaborative governance initiative? Should it be? Coordinating communication and messages is particularly challenging since collaboration entails including different entities from different levels and sectors. Each side may pursue its own interests. What does power sharing imply for communication coordination? This challenge becomes particularly evident when municipalities from different political parties are involved.
- In election years, the risk of instrumentalising communication is larger. Politicians tend to pursue media visibility, and this may raise citizens' suspicions about the authenticity of collaborative policies.
- Communicating for building collaborative governance faces challenges related to media coverage. The media require tangible realities, and the innovation that is associated with collaborative governance is based on intangibles rather than tangibles. Collaborative governance appears not to get media attention until there are newsworthy outcomes.
- Communicating for collaborative governance becomes more challenging in social networks, where young people are used to short, quick and gimmicky communication.

Comments from scholars

Comment 5
Collaborative governance, accountability and leadership in *Etorkizuna Eraikiz*

Sonia M. Ospina, *R.F. Wagner Graduate School of Public Service, New York University, US*

1.   Introduction

Accountability and leadership are core drivers of performance and legitimacy in effective public collaborative arrangements, particularly if they are anchored in robust internal systems of governance and a purpose articulated collectively. In this essay I use my understanding of *Etorkizuna Eraikiz* to reflect on the role of accountability and leadership in collaborative governance.

I draw on received knowledge and conversations with selected Gipuzkoa leaders, some site visits and selected documents. My view is incomplete absent conversations with civil society participants. Focused on the public administration side of the story, my impressions are filtered through my conviction of the promise of participation for democracy, and my expertise in three domains: organisation and management studies, social innovation and leadership studies.

The essay has four parts. Against the backdrop of received knowledge from these literatures, I start by exploring *Etorkizuna Eraikiz*'s architecture, then reflect on its accountability and leadership dynamics, and finally characterise it as a social innovation in government.

2.   What is seen from the outside: a parallel networked architecture

Created by the Gipuzkoa Provincial Council to transform "politics and the public agenda" (O&E, 2022, p. 5), *Etorkizuna Eraikiz* (EE) implements a model of collaborative governance that has transformed the region's political culture, public administration and approach to public policy.

Organisational structures are institutionalised paths coordinating collective action toward a goal. EE adds a parallel networked structure to the provincial public administration (PA), affording flexibility and boundary-spanning capacity to face complex contemporary challenges. It is a network of networks, operating within governmental authority, and thus bounded by the rule of law and democratic principles.

EE's basic unit of action is the project – more precisely, collaborative projects on the ground. Three social spaces form EE's architecture: *Gipuzkoa Taldean* fosters deliberation, dialogue and reflection; *Gipuzkoa Lab* fosters experimentation and demonstration projects; and the *reference centres* foster specialised policy design via partnership with independent non-governmental organisations that advance strategic areas for the territory. Local collaborative projects are 'seeded' in these spaces, where participants deliberate, negotiate and implement solutions.

Anchored in this architecture, multiple stakeholders in hundreds of local projects foster and create innovation on the ground. Projects in *Gipuzkoa Taldean* illustrate this. A Think Tank invites action-oriented deliberation across diverse participants who propose projects around four strategic areas (green recovery; new political culture; possible futures of the welfare state; future employment). Other citizen projects emerge from community responses to government RFPs around local challenges, like youth participation, intergenerational cooperation or community development. Other citizens engage in dialogue around funding priorities in the Open Budget initiative, where community proposals selected by participants' votes receive grants (e.g. to support first job searches for young people, or to increase civic awareness of climate change). And representatives from Gipuzkoa municipalities discuss implementing their own collaborative projects.

These projects are embedded in a polycentric system with simultaneous authority centres, each working in a domain with their own stakeholders and place-based challenges. For example, *Gipuzkoa Lab* experiments with local solutions that show future promise outside policy priorities. Public administrators, civil society, the university and international experts collaborate and, if successful, solutions are incorporated into policy. These experimental projects probe, among others, arts and cultural activities for adolescents, women experiencing domestic violence, and person-centred care models for the elderly.

Projects (and their organisational hosts) differ in content, design and implementation. For example, the reference centres are independent entities partnering with provincial ministries to pursue strategic policy goals (e.g. aging, sustainable mobility, industrial cybersecurity, climate change, language revitalisation, gastronomy, inclusive employment reinsertion). Other partnerships and local projects emerge within each strategic area.

Independent initiatives and projects connect via their structural location in the integrated system and EE's overall collective purpose. A formal Office of Projects – a Council (*Comisión*) staffed by government and external members – oversees (and somewhat regulates) EE projects, while ensuring they respond to local realities.

In sum, as the basic unit of action in EE, collaborative projects are configurations of actors (or organisations) using network arrangements. Featuring varied internal governing systems, they drive accountabilities to ensure commitment to the collaborative process and its goals, led by *Etorkizuna Eraikiz*'s purpose. Absent a single chain of command, horizontal accountability mechanisms guide participants' reciprocal expectations, given their contributions to achieving the collaboration's goals.

3.   A hybrid accountability structure

Public accountability assumptions have changed historically from the early 20th-century bureaucratic paradigm to the new public management paradigm of the late 20th century, and again with the emergent new governance paradigm of the 21st century (Lee & Ospina, 2022). Accountability dynamics are complex in hierarchical organisations, and even more in collaborative governance arrangements: *who accounts, for what, to whom and how* happens within "a tangled web of accountability relations" (Lee, 2022).

Accountability refers in public administration to a relationship between an actor with the obligation to explain behaviours/actions (giving accounts) and an inquiring body (forum) passing judgement with consequences for the actor. Account-giving and account-holding rest on explicit standards and implicit norms. Accountability mechanisms clarify work relationships and the standards that regulate them, generating information flows about expectations and actions, how these are discussed and judged and the consequent rewards or sanctions (Lee, 2022).

The primary accountability relations in networks are horizontal and informal. Network collaboration is not bounded by legal authority but by the common purpose participants cannot achieve alone. Commitment to work together around the unifying mission depends on reciprocal and trustworthy interactions developed over time. But vertical accountability is also present. Organisational representatives in networks are also bounded by antecedent accountability relations with their superiors and peers. Furthermore, the publicness of collaborative governance also bounds its members to formal bureaucratic and political authority. Collaborative governance efforts do not replace hierarchies with networks, they add networks to hierarchical arrangements. EE reflects this tangled, hybrid accountability structure.

At EE, a cascading system of accountability mechanisms progressively involves more actors, as follows:

1) at the top, political leaders (e.g. the Deputy General and the Director of EE) and civil servants from assigned offices (e.g. the Projects Office and pertinent ministries) are responsible for this experiment in Gipuzkoa's public administration. They are accountable to democratic institutions and to the public;

2) in the middle are the three social spaces crystallising EE's architecture (*Gipuzkoa Taldean, Gipuzkoa Lab* and the reference centres); here various network configurations with diverse degrees of formalisation (foundations, coalitions, cross-sector partnerships, service delivery networks and programmes) are accountable to EE leadership, to the public administration and to political leaders. They are also accountable to their external formal partners;

3) on the ground are multiple projects embedded in each EE social space (e.g. Think Tank projects, citizen projects, Open Budget projects in *Gipuzkoa Taldean*; experimentation projects in *Gipuzkoa Lab*; and spin-off projects in the reference centres). Projects are accountable to EE (via the Projects Office or ministries) but are equally and reciprocally accountable to partners and participating citizens. Horizontal accountabilities seem to be primarily managed via localised dialogue and deliberation around project issues.

Considered the basic unit of action, EE's collaborative projects resemble mini partnerships: multi-sector "projects formed explicitly to address social issues and causes that actively engage the partners on an ongoing basis" (Selsky & Parker, 2010, p. 849). At a minimum, the literature on partnerships suggests that their internal governance systems must create accountability and leadership mechanisms to drive collaboration toward success. Whether this is happening in EE requires more research. Based on limited information, the table below briefly sketches impressions for the whole EE system (similar exercises may apply to the other levels described).

Table 1. Accountability preconditions for partnership success applied to EE

Requisites	Evidence based on *Etorkizuna Eraikiz's* governance structure
Achieving strategic goals based on agreed measures	EE communicates to stakeholders the strategic goals and their implications for the lower project levels, where discretion is afforded, while ensuring measures and targets. The Office of Projects acts as a control mechanism to oversee the management of units where projects are embedded; some projects (e.g. funded citizen projects) are embedded in regular public administration units, with their own budgetary rules and monitoring; conceived as public–private partnerships, the reference centres develop jointly goals and measures. Monitoring and evaluation at the system level is not clearly defined; important conversations are happening around specific measures for the overall EE; there is now urgency to crystallise these more formally, which seems late in the lifecycle of the effort.
Enabling the partnership to resolve disputes and concerns within the system	Intentional degree of autonomy and discretion allows this to happen at the organisational level and its embedded projects, with ample opportunity for dialogue.
Solving resourcing challenges	Since most projects are partially or totally funded by the public administration, traditional accountability measures may exist for each, but not for the whole effort.
Ensuring continuous learning, improvement and system innovation	Constant feedback loops exist at EE, the organisational units and projects, within a strong culture guided by action learning and action research practice; dialogue and deliberations are embedded in the projects.
Embedding systems of downward accountability and voice	The polycentric structure generates cascading mechanisms of downward accountability and citizen participation affords voice. Some vulnerable populations are hard to reach.

Source: author's own elaboration based on Rochlin, Zadek & Forstater (2008).

Summing up, Gipuzkoa's political leaders and public administrators have made explicit commitments to support networks of outside participants in the projects that give life to the *Etorkizuna Eraikiz* system. As a network of networks, EE relies on cascading mechanisms of accountability that, following traditional public administration rules, regulate and monitor collective action at the various levels of the system. Its network structure simultaneously ensures the discretion needed on the ground to foster strong horizontal relationships of accountability with partners and citizens, generating a unique version of local social innovation, as will be further described below (Parés, Ospina & Subirats, 2017). As a civil servant asserted, EE leadership has managed to promote social innovation at the lower levels of the system while ensuring that this innovation remains within the confines of the rule of law and best practices demanded in public administration.

4. Collective leadership in action

Profound changes in post-industrial, globalised, digital societies require reframing leadership. In the workplace, new organisational forms reduce traditional managerial authority, and turbulent environments augment complexity, volatility and diversity, while working groups and permeable boundaries demand a relational understanding of leadership: collaborative, contextual and fully embedded in a system of relationships that must be viewed as a collective.

Networks for knowledge, information sharing, service delivery and policy reform, multi-stakeholder coalitions and cross-sector partnerships reflect this reality in the public sector. Understanding public leadership today means considering more actors, processes, arenas and levels of analysis, and an expanded awareness of interdependency, complexity and shared authority (Ospina, 2017).

Shared/distributed and relational/network leadership models reflect collective approaches, grounded on new assumptions and leadership practices. The source of leadership expands beyond leaders and roles to include other system properties such as decision-making rules, accountability mechanisms or participation spaces. The object of leadership moves beyond influencing followers or groups to develop conditions to ensure collective responsibility for the results. The outcome of leadership work now includes generating human capacity to co-produce a valued purpose, as much as achieving it (Ospina, 2017)

Shared/distributed models emphasise the horizontal relationships of accountability and shared responsibility over joint work and its outcomes, given the diminished relevance of command and control. Collaborative governance scholars advocate the contingent distribution of facilitative leadership roles outside formal positions, in different locations and at different times. Relational/network models further push the relational lens, moving the epicentre of leadership to the practices that make leadership happen. Leadership is emergent, interactive 'work' around local members' capacity and adaptability to navigate complexity at the collective level.

Leadership in nested collaborative contexts enacts these assumptions and practices to foster collaboration. Yet research also shows that bureaucratic and network logics operate simultaneously in collaborative governance, and that formal leaders make use of directive leadership to foster more relational approaches. To engage interdependent, yet diverse stakeholders around a collective purpose, formal leaders build conditions where capacity, safety and readiness afford participants down the line opportunities to make meaningful contributions through collaboration. Following the cascading lines of accountability, formal leaders intentionally expand leadership in the system by cultivating emergent leadership at different levels. This in turn authorises participants to lead upward and sideward, that is, to become collaborative leaders themselves within their sphere of influence. This is collaborative leadership at its best. The experience of EE suggests that developing this type of leadership at all levels of the collaborative governance system requires, indeed, visible, strong formal leaders with political and moral authority.

In addition to strong collaborative leaders at the top, work in *Etorkizuna Eraikiz* reflects features that collective leadership studies have documented showing how, absent recurrent interventions of an appointed leader, other mechanisms help diverse members engage in leadership work (e.g. project-related collective tasks, participatory problem-solving, and meaningful stories and narratives around EE's compelling purpose). All these help participants at the project level to do the leadership work of connecting and making meaning to articulate a direction, align their contributions and make collaborative commitments toward their shared purpose (Drath *et al.*, 2008).

My research colleagues and I identified recurrent practices of leadership work in community-based organisations trying to transform systems. We found that successful groups practised recurrent leadership work resulting in reframing discourse, bridging difference and unleashing human energies to leverage power and produce change. We argue that this leadership work is applicable to public-sector contexts and has great potential if used more intentionally (Ospina & Foldy, 2015).

Etorkizuna Eraikiz offers evidence of successful leadership work, and more research could draw important lessons for collaborative governance. To illustrate, the table below defines these leadership practices and offers a glimpse of their emergence in EE.

Table 2. Signs of (collective) leadership work in *Etorkizuna Eraikiz*

Collective leadership practices	Evidence in EE
Reframing discourse happens when established social frames that reinforce problems are challenged and new frames, narratives and vocabulary (more congruent with the group's vision of the future) are articulated and enacted	Naming traditional political culture as part of the problem/articulating an alternative way of being and doing policy and public administration Revalorising the role of Basque cultural values (self-government and territorial sovereignty; language, community and cooperation; strong social tissue) to interrupt growing individualism and to motivate citizen participation Reframing institutional leadership as collaborative, and collaboration as a public-sector strength Valuing co-produced knowledge's multiple ways of knowing beyond expertise Pushing authority and leadership downward and out into society (via projects) Other reframed core ideas: representation (engaging with electors, political leaders as active participants); power (as a shareable resource); political imagination (to reinvent action); diversity (a strength and a political value)
Bridging difference happens when diverse actors understand each other's perspectives and recognise their potential contributions to the common purpose, despite their differences	Intentionally connecting government with each: academics; private sector; civil society; citizens; parties in the opposition Connecting public administration actors: political leaders, public administrators/civil servants and front-line employees; municipalities within Gipuzkoa; and the latter with other Basque Country provinces Aligning EU and Gipuzkoa strategic goals Cultivating networks of actors within service or policy ecosystems Organising dialogue among diverse actors
Unleashing human energies happens when the group members' potential for transformational learning is tapped, yielding self-efficacy and liberating passion and motivation to gain capabilities that contribute to the common purpose	Inviting stakeholder participation Offering spaces for varying degrees of engagement/participation (meetings, workshops, agoras, citizen assemblies, formal partnerships, youth neighbourhood engagement) Experimenting deeply (failure is culturally acceptable) Celebrating the messiness of co-creation and collaborative leadership Inviting intentional dialogue, problem-solving and meaning-making about collaborative governance and the new political culture Using action research and action learning to build spaces that foster innovation, create feedback learning loops, co-produce knowledge and conduct collective problem-solving Using action learning/action research to build collective leadership capabilities and align diverse perspectives

Source: author's own elaboration.

In sum, collaborative governance arrangements demand a different way of doing public leadership. Attention shifts from position, authority or charisma to the processes by which the group co-creates results that are valued by its members; and there is a cultural shift around participant mobilisation, from relying on control to cultivating purpose. Leadership is the group's work – performed both by formal and emergent leaders – to find the direction, alignment and commitment they need to achieve this purpose. This understanding of public leadership seems appropriate to interpret leadership in EE, but more research is needed to understand how it happens.

5. A systemic social innovation

Contemporary scholars have championed a socio-political and systemic approach to social innovation conceptualised as "a complex process of introducing alternative solutions that produce systemic changes" (Parés, Ospina & Subirats, 2017, p. 5). Three basic features characterise it: 1) satisfying alienated human needs; 2) transforming social relations; and 3) empowering citizens. The first feature conceptualises social innovation as public value creation; the second and third introduce ethical and political dimensions: power relations are transformed by placing instrumental goals (like technology or economic development) within a broader human purpose; and by acknowledging the role of a community's cultural assets in reconfiguring social relations, governance arrangements and social learning.

Rather than a mere public tool that incorporates outside capacity to respond efficiently to social problems, the ontology of this approach posits innovation as a social change process. In other words, innovation fosters agency and collective capacity to challenge existing social frames that hinder human development and equity, and thus change "the basic routines, resources, beliefs and power relationships of the social system in which it occurs" (Parés et al., 2017, p. 10, citing Moulart et al., 2005).

This resonates with EE's strategy and ethos. EE uses the most innovative approach to contemporary public administration to create public value – collaborative governance. In doing so, it is changing Gipuzkoa's political culture, and creating new ways of doing public administration and policy implementation. Experimentation and citizen participation generate change from the ground up, reasserting and reframing for a contemporary context the Basque Country's deepest cultural values.

EE does not just foster innovation; it is a governmental social innovation. Political leaders intentionally designed EE as a top-down strategy that engages the public administration of Gipuzkoa. They did so to foster bottom-up citizen participation, which in turn requires affording relative autonomy to place-based projects. This successful strategy contributes insights that link debates in three literatures.

In the policy implementation literature, references to bottom-up and top-down are about control and discretion over implementation: should policy-makers or street-level bureaucrats lead? In the collaborative governance literature, the question shifts: should public administrators or external actors lead? For social innovation scholars, the question is about where social innovation emerges, from within government (top-down) or from within civil society (bottom-up). Research finds that bottom-up initiatives are more effective and scalable when they are linked to public institutions through collaboration in a "bottom-linked" approach (Pares et al., 2017, citing Eizaguirre et al., 2012). Bottom-linked scholars study efforts initiated by those experiencing the problem and recognise the role of institutions in strengthening these initiatives by supporting agency and guaranteeing citizen rights (Parés et al., 2017). They highlight the benefits of multi-scalar strategies for solving complex social problems, like those featured in EE.

Enacting this 'both-and' alternative, the experience of EE as a social innovation challenges the 'either-or' conundrum featured in the implementation and collaborative governance literatures. The case of *Etorkizuna Eraikiz* suggests that bottom-linked approaches can happen in reverse: a top-down responsible strategy aiming to support social innovation at the bottom. This unique approach has emerged through iterations of reflective experimentation, aiming to advance policy through a collaborative governance strategy and collaborative leadership. While fostering bottom-up social innovation, EE's formal leaders maintain some control over an innovation that aspires to create a more democratic and participatory way of governing. In fact, EE draws legitimacy from the top via the political authority of representative democracy, and from the bottom via the social authority granted by articulating purpose around community felt needs.

6.   Concluding remarks

Gipuzkoa's *Etorkizuna Eraikiz* is an extraordinary experiment of public value creation that weaves together an integrated participatory system mobilising multiple and diverse stakeholders, and changing Gipuzkoa's political culture. It is also shaping how political leaders, public administrators and citizens imagine and craft together a different future.

As its leaders acknowledge, six years of implementation have afforded shortcomings, gaps, contradictions and exclusions. Yet the achievements in its short existence show promise for the future. As an example of bottom-linked innovation, EE's architecture, accountability systems and collaborative leadership practices have evolved into a dynamic network of networks. In this architecture, strong, top-down formal authority is used to foster bottom-up frontline discretion and citizen participation; oversight is ensured via formal cascading accountability mechanisms that prioritise vertical relations at the system and organisational levels, and horizontal relations at the project level; and directive leadership is used to promote collaborative leadership. In this system, recurrent reflective/dialogic spaces are cultivated intentionally, where all actors – political leaders, public servants, frontline employees, partners and project participants (including citizens) – can explore the contradictions and tensions of collaborative governance, and, as a participant said, "make meaning of the mess". *Etorkizuna Eraikiz* is a vital asset of the public administration of Gipuzkoa, the Basque Country and Spain. It represents a source of deep wisdom as well, for those interested in the theory and practice of collaborative governance in democratic contexts.

Comment 6
Etorkizuna Eraikiz: A case of interactive political leadership

EVA SØRENSEN, *Department of Social Sciences and Business, Roskilde University, Denmark*

1.   Introduction

As extensively documented in research, collaborative forms of governance hold considerable potential for promoting effective and legitimate govern-ance by engaging relevant and affected public and private actors in a shared effort to create something of value for society and the citizenry (Agger *et al.*, 2015). In most cases, however, collaborative governance processes do not involve politicians, and the implications of the arm's-length distance between politicians and collaborative processes can ultimately exacerbate the current democratic crisis rather than solving it (Rosanvallon & Goldhammer, 2008). *Etorkizuna Eraikiz* represents a noteworthy exception to this general tendency, as the politicians are the main initiators of the collaborative governance processes and participate actively in them. In so doing, they find opportunity to establish stronger ties to local stakeholders and citizens than the standard political institutions in representative democracies are typically able to do, voice their ideas and perspectives to members of the community, and harvest input from stakeholders that enhance their capacity to make well-informed and innovative strategic decisions about how to make society better. The project stands out as an intriguing case of interactive political leadership and opens a much needed alternative pathway for politicians who are looking for alternatives to meeting public discontent and rising levels of distrust in government and politics with authoritative forms of populist political leadership (Sørensen, 2020).

2.   The missing link in collaborative governance

Public officials in liberal democracies are increasingly turning to collaborative forms of governance in their efforts to solve complex governance problems and to develop society in a desired direction (Ansell & Gash, 2008; Morse, 2011; Bianchi *et al.*, 2021; Peters *et al.*, 2022). What renders collaborative governance so attractive is that it not only mobilises the many ideas, visons and knowhow that actors within the public sector possess, but also the invaluable insights, skills and experiences of private businesses, civil society organisations and citizens. In unison, these resources can all enhance the problem-solving capacity of a society and its ability to meet its goals and aspirations, as well as to build social capital. When policy strategies and practical projects are developed and implemented in collaboration between all of the relevant and affected actors in society, they tend to become more successful, partly because they are better informed and more innovative, and partly because more people are committed to carrying them out (Emerson & Nabatchi, 2015a; Doberstein, 2016; Torfing, 2016).

As a general trend in the research and practice of collaborative govern-ance, the public actors involved are mainly public administrators, whereas politicians are positioned at arm's length from the collaborations (Sørensen *et al.* 2020). If politicians play a role, it is usually to commission public ad-ministrators to participate, to allocate resources or to endorse governance outputs. Consequently, democratically elected representatives often end up with two options. First, they can accept decisions made in collaborative governance arenas, thereby ending up as 'policy-takers' who rubberstamp decisions made by non-elected actors. Or, second, they can insist on their sovereign position as authoritative policy-makers and disregard what the collaborative governance actors have decided. Both options are problematic for politicians and representative democracy alike, as they tend to trigger distrust in politicians and the political institutions. When politicians pick the first option and become policy-takers, questions are raised regarding the relevance of elections and the willingness and ability of political elites to take action when needed to solve problems and move society forward. But when the politicians choose the second option and disregard or even reject the work done in collaborative governance arenas, the actors who invested time and energy in participating are left discontent. Both cases risk nourishing authoritative populism (Mudde, 2016; Rooduijn, 2018).

3.   The promise of *Etorkizuna Eraikiz*

New strands of democratic theory and research propose a third strategy: that politicians engage in close and continuous formal as well as informal dialogue with relevant and affected publics (see e.g. Hendriks, 2016). This is exactly what happens in the huge collaborative endeavour to 'shape the future together' in the Basque province of Gipuzkoa, where politicians play an active role in all phases in the collaboration processes. Politicians initiated the *Etorkizuna Eraikiz* project, and they have focused on securing broad support among public administrators and public employees. Moreover, the politicians have supported the hiring and training of staff with competencies to design and facilitate the collaboration processes. Finally, they are taking active part in developing and governing the different sub-projects. The role that politicians play as both leaders and participants in the collaborative governance processes allows them to make decisions in ongoing dialogue with the local community members rather than being either policy-takers *or* sovereign policy-makers. Collaborative policy-making between politicians and citizens is important for several reasons. Firstly, it can strengthen the ability of politicians to provide well-informed, innovative political leadership. Hence, input from societal actors is likely to enhance the effectiveness and innovativeness of government responses to complex and turbulent governance problems, such as global warming, pandemics and migration, as well as strategies for promoting economic growth and prosperity (Torfing, 2016). Moreover, continuous dialogue between politicians and members of the local political community enhances the mutual understanding and trust between them, and can potentially reduce the polarisation between different groups in society (Hendriks & Lees-Marshment, 2019; Sørensen & Torfing, 2019a). Those benefits do not depend on whether the collaborative process produces consensus between the involved actors. Negotiations that result in a balanced decision that take all the different voices into account are a cornerstone in democratic decision-making, and collaborative governance is a productive tool for making this happen. In a nutshell, successful collaborative governance promotes and thrives on a certain kind of collective political intelligence, defined as "a realistic and deep understanding of what the disagreements are, what it would require to make decisions that satisfy several views, and what the costs would be of making decisions that produce losers" (Sørensen & Torfing, 2022). The collaborative governance processes in *Etorkizuna Eraikiz* hold the potential to nourish the collective political intelligence in the province.

Comment 7
The need to systematise relationships with stakeholders to make collaborative governance work

JACOB TORFING, *Roskilde University, Denmark and Nord University, Norway*

1.   Introduction

Democratic governments are facing two pressing challenges: they are confronting a growing number of complex societal problems that call for new and innovative governance solutions, and their populations have become more competent, critical and assertive and want to participate more directly and actively in the making of the decisions affecting their daily lives than the institutions of representative democracy allow. Failing to deal with these challenges might be fatal, as the accumulation of unsolved societal problems and the persistent ignorance of the new demands for enhanced democratic participation may deepen the distrust in elected governments and nurture the rise of authoritarian populism that will undermine liberal democracy.

By introducing collaborative governance into the heart of government, the *Etorkizuna Eraikiz* project ('Building the Future' in English) aims to kill two birds with one stone. The involvement of elected politicians, civil servants, policy entrepreneurs, researchers, organised stakeholders and citizens in collaborative governance tends to facilitate creative problem-solving while creating new opportunities for effective participation in public governance. When a diverse set of actors interact, they will tend to disturb each other's views and ideas, and this disturbance will tend to stimulate mutual learning and the creation of innovative solutions that outperform the existing ones. The manifold actors participating in the collaborative innovation process will most likely develop shared ownership over the new solutions, and they will feel empowered by their ability to influence key decisions. In short, bridging the widening gulf between government and citizens by expanding collaborative governance may enhance both input legitimacy through more inclusive participation and output legitimacy through the construction of better-quality governance solutions that hit the target.

What is remarkable about *Etorkizuna Eraikiz* is that collaborative governance is not merely introduced as an *ad hoc* tool that is used sporadically when other hierarchical or market-based forms of governance have been tried and found wanting. Rather, the Provincial Council of Gipuzkoa is in the process of transforming itself into a platform organisation that, instead of aiming to solve all public tasks and problems by itself, creates participatory and collaborative governance arenas to mobilise a broad range of societal ideas and resources in order to boost policy innovation and deepen democracy. In essence, *Etorkizuna Eraikiz* is a platform supporting the formation and adaptation of different arenas, including arenas for reflection on problems and needs and thematic agenda setting (e.g. think tanks, citizen projects, open budgeting), arenas for future-oriented design, experimentation and learning (*Gipuzkoa Lab* and experimental projects), and arenas for strategic development and knowledge production (reference centres and strategies organised as consortiums, foundations or partnerships). The collaborative governance platforms and multiple arenas are meta-governed by the Project Office and the Provincial Council of Gipuzkoa.

The scale and sincerity of the organisational investment in collaborative governance is considerable, and continuous attempts are made at advancing the collaborative governance model to local municipalities and other provinces, governments and countries. The consistent, long-term political commitment to the expansion and deepening of the collaborative governance model is strong, as is the willingness to learn and adapt. Hence, *Etorkizuna Eraikiz* has a real potential for developing a new type of interactive political leadership (Sørensen, 2020; Sørensen & Torfing, 2019b) whereby elected politicians receive valuable inputs from relevant and affected actors to better understand the problems at hand, design innovative solutions that work in practice, and to test and implement new and bold solutions through a combination of top-down and bottom-up experiments.

Whether the potentials of *Etorkizuna Eraikiz* are realised depends on the systematic efforts to ensure the inclusion and alignment of a diverse groups of public and private actors and to lead the co-creation of new and better governance solutions. To that end, this text reflects on the need to systematise relationships with stakeholders. The discussion draws on state-of-the-art literature on collaborative governance and public innovation (Peters *et al.*, 2022; Torfing, 2016) as well as experiences from a three-day workshop with people from *Etorkizuna Eraikiz*.

2.   Inclusion and empowerment of the participants in collaborative governance

The basic idea of collaborative governance is to involve a group of interdependent actors in collaborative processes based on open deliberation that lead to better outcomes due to the possibility to exchange and pool experiences, ideas and resources (Ansell & Gash, 2008). Research points to the importance of involving actors with a strong interest in getting the problem at hand solved and actors with the power, authority and expertise to solve the problem (Ansell, Sørensen & Torfing, 2022). Here, stakeholder analysis is important to identify the relevant as well as the affected actors and motivate them to participate (see Bryson, Cunningham & Lokkesmoe, 2002). *Etorkizuna Eraikiz* uses stakeholder analysis to map relevant and affected actors and to aim to represent different sectors in the collaborative arenas to be able to draw on their different inputs. Sometimes existing networks in the public, private and civic sectors are asked to select representatives. However, an unresolved problem is that some citizens are not represented by existing networks and organisations and must therefore be reached in other ways.

Stakeholder type tends to vary with the goal and ambition of the collaborative arena. The broad inclusion of different communities and citizens is important for enhancing democratic legitimacy, the involvement of competent and knowledgeable actors is crucial for enhancing governance effectiveness, and diversity is important for producing innovative solutions (Sørensen and Torfing 2017). Hence, depending on the purpose, conveners must ask openly who can help them to solve a particular problem or task in accordance with the stipulated goals and ambitions. Posing and answering this question helps conveners to identify relevant and affected actors and build a dream team around the problems and task that needs to be defined, solved and/or explored.

The inclusion of societal stakeholders in collaborative governance arenas is important because they have crucial experience with problems and possible solutions. More than 200 organisations, associations and groups have participated, but some continue to go it alone without benefitting from cross-boundary collaboration. The participation of elected politicians is also important because they require input to understand problems and design-wise solutions and because they have the authority to secure the implementation of new and bold solutions. Here, the picture is mixed; some are actively participating in collaborative governance while others are not, either because they have a traditional view of political leadership or because they see themselves as a kind of civil servant. Lastly but importantly, civil servants and administrative personnel must be included in collaborative governance because they possess valuable professional knowledge and expertise that is strictly necessary for collaborative governance to produce legal, effective and feasible solutions. Many civil servants initially thought that the collaborative governance initiative was a political communication stunt and that it limited their support and involvement in the project. However, middle managers are frequently involved in the collaborative governance arenas, either as participants or facilitators, and the administrative personnel is gradually won over, although there is still some way to go before the administration adopts collaborative governance as a core governance principle.

Collaborative governance thrives on inclusion, but including all relevant and affected actors is often impossible as there are simply too many of them. Hence, some actors must be excluded. *Etorkizuna Eraikiz* sometimes decides to exclude actors such as trade unions that will tend to act as veto-actors, preventing or blocking joint decisions. Some actors exclude themselves because they do not want to participate or have limited resources and capacities. The external exclusion of potential participants is supplemented by an internal exclusion (Young, 2000), which happens when actors join a collaborative arena but never voice their opinion. Broad-based inclusion is a key goal for *Etorkizuna Eraikiz* and sought to be obtained by operating with different degrees of inclusion in collaborative management, joint workshops, hearings or newsletters. Hence, actors are not either 'in' or 'out', but may participate in different ways.

While relevant actors are often quite powerful, affected actors may not have the knowledge and resources required to ensure effective participation. This calls for the empowerment of weaker actors, and perhaps also disempowerment of the stronger actors, who need to understand that steamrolling the weaker actors may undermine the collaborative endeavour. Like all other similar initiatives, *Etorkizuna Eraikiz* struggles to involve young people and does not reach citizens on the fringes of society. However, there is a continuous effort to use new tools for stimulating participation, including digital tools, action groups, citizen assemblies and bridge-building within local ecosystems. The experience is that participation itself has an empowerment effect, but there are also special efforts to empower participants. External consultants are sometimes brought in to empower young people.

3.   Alignment and conflict mediation in collaborative arenas engaged in learning and experimentation

The Provincial Council has considerable convening power, as societal actors are keen to participate when invited. The prospect of having a real impact on public governance by participating in collaboration on a relatively neutral platform is also conducive for generating participation. A final factor is the recognition of the mutual dependence between the invited actors in the sense that they are able to achieve things together that none of them would otherwise be able to do on their own (Huxham & Vangen, 2013).

Now, when relevant and affected actors are brought together in collaborative governance arenas, the alignment of their expectations, ideas and interests is crucial to be able to construct a common ground for joint problem-solving. Mapping the motivation and discourse of the participating actors may help to construct a storyline that aligns the actors (Bryson, Cunningham & Lokkesmoe, 2002), perhaps through multivocality, whereby different actors agree on a certain formulation of common goals but interpret the key terms in different ways (Padgett & Ansell, 1993). In *Etorkizuna Eraikiz*, stakeholders sometimes come to the table to get money, but proactive efforts to frame the collaborative process often help to change expectations and facilitate alignment. It has also proven helpful to spend time explaining goals, ideas and arguments, as well as exploring overlaps between the participants.

Since some actors come to the table with different interests, ideas and proposals, collaboration is rarely easy and conflict may eventually arise. Here, it is important to understand that conflict and collaboration are not necessarily antithetical. Much depends on how we define collaboration. Some define collaboration as an effort to obtain unanimous consent, but collaboration may also be defined as a constructive management of differences (Gray, 1989). The latter definition facilitates collaboration between a diversity of actors who may sometimes disagree on key issues, but facilitation and conflict mediation is required to prevent small and productive conflicts from growing and becoming destructive. In *Etorkizuna Eraikiz*, conflicts sometimes prevent the actors from moving forward and making effective governance decisions. Facilitators aim to prevent or mediate emerging conflicts by making the conflicting views and ideas explicit in order to explore whether the conflict is founded on misinformation, misunderstanding, prejudice or a lack of trust. Other helpful tools for conflict mediation include the use of boundary objects, joint fact-finding missions, attempts to depersonalise conflicts and taking the money out of the equation and focusing on goals.

Collaborative governance between a diverse set of aligned actors may enhance effective and democratic governance, but it may also stimulate innovation. When actors come together in collaborative governance, they tend to disturb each other's way of thinking about problems and solutions, and out of this disturbance comes learning and ultimately innovation. Stimulating learning and innovation, for example through brainstorming, scenario building, design thinking and role games with exchange of perspectives, is of utmost importance. *Etorkizuna Eraikiz* aims to stimulate learning and catalyse innovation by allocating resources to co-creation processes, linking collaborative arenas to external sources of inspiration and by creating an open and safe space for thinking aloud and testing new ideas in joint discussions.

The experimental approach of the *Etorkizuna Eraikiz* project also stimulates learning and innovation. Developing and testing prototypes through joint action facilitates rapid learning, and the iterative rounds of design, testing and revision of new solutions facilitate the scaling of what works in practice and helps to break down the boundary between design and implementation. Experimentation may be assisted by some more or less well-defined procedures and templates that can be tailored to specific projects. In *Etorkizuna Eraikiz*, there are several competing templates for conducting real-life experiments with new governance solutions. The evaluation and integration of the different templates is needed to further support the experimental strategy.

4.   Leading collaborative governance processes for innovation and democracy

People who believe that collaborative governance processes are spontaneous, self-organised and bound to succeed are wrong. Like all other governance processes, collaborative governance requires the exercise of leadership. Strategic leadership can help to design organisations amenable for collaborative governance. Political leadership can set the overall policy goals and collaborative leadership can convene actors, build trust, facilitate collaboration and catalyse innovation (Torfing, 2016).

Collaborative governance presents challenges to leadership, as we lack a clear understanding of what it entails. In recent decades, we have trained leaders to focus on achieving a particular set of goals and pre-determined performance targets by mobilising their own organisation, budget and employees and securing compliance with administrative rules. Now, public leaders and managers face the formidable challenge of learning how to lead cross-boundary collaboration and foster new and innovative solutions (Hofstad *et al.*, 2021). Instead of leading inward and downward, they must learn to lead outward and focus on relations, which is an entirely different ballgame. *Etorkizuna Eraikiz* focuses on collective and distributed leadership. Collective leadership bids farewell to heroic leadership exercised by a single individual in charge of mobilising other actors, instead perceiving leadership as an effort to create spaces where participants can enact their joint leadership for the common good (Ospina, 2017). Similarly, distributed leadership decentres leadership by involving participants in collaborative governance in performing different leadership tasks (Bolden, 2011). At a more concrete level, this means that leaders in the collaborative governance arenas in the *Etorkizuna Eraikiz* project are looking for answers together with the participants rather than presenting answers to them.

The horizontal and decentred character of leadership in collaborative settings raises the question of who leads and what leadership model is chosen. While leadership might be shared among a large group of participating actors, some actors will play a bigger leadership role than others. This begs the question of who is exercising leadership and how the exercise of leadership in collaborative arenas is organised. Research shows that an empirical distinction can be drawn between three models of collaborative leadership: 1) leadership might be shared by all actors and exercised in and through joint decisions made in plenary meetings; 2) leadership is exercised by a small group of key actors from different organisations who form an inter-organisational steering group; and 3) leadership is exercised by a lead organisation where one or two leaders are supported by a small secretariat or a secretary (Milward & Provan, 2006). The three models are sometimes combined into a hybrid leadership model. The formation of an inter-organisational steering group otherwise tends to be the preferred solution, as it combines inclusion with speed and competence. That said, in reality, the lead actor model is found fairly often in collaborative settings, which also applies in *Etorkizuna Eraikiz*, where lead actors tend to be accepted as collaborative leaders because they can offer strong ideas, good facilitation skills and much needed professional expertise.

A key challenge for *Etorkizuna Eraikiz*, which has been spearheaded by politicians, is that elected politicians often have little time to participate in and to lead collaborative governance processes. They may delegate the day-to-day collaborative leadership to their administrative aides, who over time become adept meta-governors (Sørensen & Torfing, 2009). However, there is a limit to this delegation. Not only are meta-governing administrators gaining a lot of power vis-à-vis the elected politicians through their role as gatekeepers vis-à-vis the collaborative governance arenas, there are also many political issues about inclusion and exclusion, goal setting, budget frames and the endorsement of final decisions that call for political rather than administrative meta-governance (Sørensen & Torfing, 2016). A solution to the problem of the politicians' time pressure may be the formation of leadership teams with the participation of both politicians and administrators who combine administrative and political meta-governance.

5.   Learning from *Etorkizuna Eraikiz*

There is much to learn from studying the *Etorkizuna Eraikiz* project. Strong and persistent political commitment is important to launch such a visionary and large-scale collaborative governance initiative, and a supportive context in the shape of a well-organised civil society and a tradition of collaboration must be in place. However, this text has shown that political vision and the commitment to solve complex problems and to deepen democracy through collaboration with citizens and organised societal stakeholders is not enough. What is also needed to get off the ground and produce concrete and tangible results is an effort to systematise the relationships to the many different stakeholders through attention to inclusion, alignment and leadership, without which *Etorkizuna Eraikiz* will be nothing but good intentions and will have nothing to show. Hence, the lesson to learn for other governments that want to improve the quality of public governance and representative democracy by replicating the ideas and practices of *Etorkizuna Eraikiz* is that the day-to-day effort to meta-govern the collaborative governance arenas while supporting the entire endeavour through strategic leadership is paramount to success.

On a larger scale, the efforts in Gipuzkoa to reform democratic governance by promoting the collaboration between politicians, public administrators and local community members, including businesses, civil society organisations and citizens, is noteworthy because it envisages a remedy against the mushrooming examples of authoritarian populist political leadership in Europe and other representative democracies. This remedy is a turn to interactive political leadership. Populist political leaders such as former US President Donald Trump claim to represent the people against a corrupt political elite consisting of some kind of united political establishment of elected politicians (Mudde, 2016). Moreover, they treat those who disagree with their standpoints as enemies of the people, whether they be opposition politicians or citizens with diverging views and opinions. The antagonist approach to political opponents and the disrespect for political pluralism among populist political leaders foster political distrust and question key democratic values and the very institutions of representative democracy.

In contrast, interactive forms of political leadership employ collaborative forms of governance as a platform for politicians and citizens with different views and ideas to come together in an effort to find a way forward for society that takes all the different views and perspectives among politicians and stakeholders into account. Moreover, interactive political leaders seek collaboration with other societies rather than turning their backs on the outside world (Sørensen, 2020). Interactive political leaders assume responsibility for guiding and participating in the negotiations that lead to decisions and activities that effectively address challenging problems and exploit emerging opportunities because they are well informed and enjoy broad support. A key objective for interactive political leaders is to convene the right actors, that is, actors who can not only contribute to making well-informed and innovative strategies and projects but who also secure the commitment needed to implement the decisions made. Although these are still early days, *Etorkizuna Eraikiz* stands out as a highly interesting experiment that deserves keen attention from researchers and decision-makers interested in finding a pathway forward for democracy.

Comment 8
Public-sector communication to engage citizens in collaborative governance

VILMA LUOMA-AHO, *School of Business and Economics, University of Jyväskylä, Finland*

The challenge facing *Etorkizuna Eraikiz* and almost all public-sector organisations globally is the challenge of involving and engaging those who are served, and it has been established as vital for a blooming society (Delli Carpini, Cook & Jacobs, 2004). The operation environment within which public-sector entities function has changed, and citizens in their own self-selected communication bubbles (Sloterdijk, 2011) tailor their communication according to their needs, recommendations, interests, preferences and life choices.

Scholars suggest that an urgent shift has occurred from a 'culture of controls' towards citizen-centred engagement (Bourgon, 2011), and there much relies on communication (Johnston & Taylor, 2018). For public-sector organisations this poses the challenge of moving from organisation-optimised communication to citizen-optimised communication (Canel & Luoma-aho, 2019): how to answer citizen questions while keeping the organisational agenda of public good in mind?

Digitalisation of communication has altered the way in which citizens seek to interact and engage with public administrations (Lovari & Parisi, 2015). Citizens are expecting a more dynamic, interactive and co-creative experience when collaborating with authorities and public-sector organisations (Canel & Luoma-aho, 2019). Arranging for citizens to provide feedback is not enough to meet this need; as stated by Muñoa (a workshop participant from the Gipuzkoa Provincial Council), and in the words of the public servants (2022): "Collaborative governance is not communicated; collaborative governance is *in itself* communication". Hence many common mass-produced, one-way sources of information have become unable to reach and engage citizens, and hence become outdated (Canel & Luoma-aho, 2019).

During the COVID-19 crisis, authority communication became very central for most societies in their survival (Chen *et al.*, 2020). Descriptive of this new environment are the "heightened citizen expectations regarding dialogue, influence, and the heavy reliance on real-time and social media" (Luoma-aho *et al.*, 2021, p. 20). Despite these visible new needs, 'networked publics' (Papacharissi, 2014, p. 154) are not all created equal and do not react the same, but range from highly engaged (cognitively, emotionally and behaviourally) producers of content to individuals who are unengaged, unable to engage or remain in a state of engaged passivity (van Dijk & Van Dick, 2009), making the task of *Etorkizuna Eraikiz* more central than ever. Public managers need to update their understanding of what now counts as citizen engagement and re-architect the citizen experience of engagement to also consider the more negative relationships that may form while citizens engage.

So, what should future citizen engagement contain? If engagement is central for democracy (Bourgon, 2011; Delli Carpini *et al.*, 2004), then ensuring it also in the future becomes important. As summarised well by Muñoa, engagement as a construct actually brings the relationship between citizens and organisations to a more equal level. Subsequently, this will affect the development and maintenance of organisational legitimacy and other intangible assets such as trust or positive reputation, which again strengthen the relationship further.

If public-sector communication is defined as "strategically planned communication between organisations and their stakeholders, enabling public sector functions, within their specific cultural/political settings, with the purpose of building and maintaining the public good" (Canel & Luoma-aho, 2019, p. 33), to help *Etorkizuna Eraikiz* move forward to the future of citizen engagement, and keep all the valuable lessons learned, the following seven Future Citizen Engagement propositions are suggested (see Luoma-aho *et al.*, 2021):

1) *Etorkizuna Eraikiz* must ensure that the willingness and empowerment to engage in the future is apparent on both sides: citizens and authorities. These can take the form of ensuring sufficient time and resources are dedicated it, as well as providing a safe emotional climate to operate and develop it.

2) There is always the potential for either positive or negative manifestations of engagement, hence preparation is needed to address and receive both. While negative engagement may burden both authorities as well as citizens experiencing problems, ways to work through these in dialogue are needed, and sometimes also support structures such as therapy and work counselling for authorities on the front lines.

3) The expectations for outcomes of citizen engagement should be maintained at a realistic level. This is not so often due to individual aims but rather to the project nature of development: many applications, projects and plans simply aim too high in relation to the resources available. Keeping in mind the available resources and potential will ensure future citizen engagement stays sustainable for all involved.

4) Citizen engagement is a process; there is no clear start or end. This may be a challenge for those authorities hoping to report back on successful cases and developments, as there are no clear outcomes of this. In fact, citizen engagement that fails may be easier to distinguish than a good, continuous dialogue.

5) The ultimate aim of improving society should always be kept in mid by those involved. Despite this, both citizens and public-sector organisations have their own personal targets to meet and reach. Sometimes society is improved by enabling dialogue and disagreement, and these should be valued as highly as agreements and decisions.

6) All engagement is increasingly global, so collaboration across borders and cultural division lines are necessary. This was a surprise lesson learned by many governments during the COVID-19 pandemic, as foreign governments were able to reach and target their citizens unexpectedly, and citizen networks shared information in real time across cultural and country borders. Understanding how citizens are connected globally will help make more lasting results.

7) Citizen engagement is a team sport, enforced by others in society, not just related to individual citizens and their experiences. Understanding which stakeholders to collaborate with and who they can connect with and engage in dialogue, even unexpectedly, are future skills for all public authorities.

PART III

LOOKING AT RESULTS
AND CONCLUSIONS

Workshop 3
Synthesis of interactions between scholars and practitioners

What follows is a synthesis of the discussions, including major ideas, comments, further questions and challenges that emerged from the interaction between the local/international scholars and the practitioners (politicians, civil servants, stakeholders) embedded in *Etorkizuna Eraikiz*.

1. What indicators are there about *Etorkizuna Eraikiz*?

Initial response and reactions

The DFG presents quantitative and qualitative data (included in Chapter 1): satisfaction of the participants, political commitment, changes in relationships (with the media, universities, business organisations and societal organisations), changes in politicians-technicians interactions, changes in stakeholders' assessments about the DFG's role (from money-giver to partner), changes in the scope of relationships with municipalities, and new actors contacted (particularly people in risk of social exclusion). On the whole, 150 projects, 50,000 people.

Thematic debates

The following comments and suggestions emerge from the discussion:
- In measuring innovation, an attempt is usually made to assess direct effects. But what about indirect effects? It could happen that there are beneficiaries with no awareness of either the DFG or EE. Indirect effects are therefore to be also taken into account.
- Government programmes usually include traditional structures and projects. EE shows that the reform is being expanded and institutionalised; it has a higher volume than usual reforms. The system is changing and being rebalanced. To measure this, beyond looking at figures (i.e. percentage of people participating) it is also necessary to look at the why: Why is the system changing?

- Trust is something that happens at the end, but also at the beginning. Trust should also be taken as a precondition of CG interventions.
- Trust implies lowering oneself to vulnerability. Measuring trust then includes looking at the extent to which honest talks are being undertaken.

Further questions, critical issues and challenges

- CG could lead to a vacuum in politics. Intermediary organisations become central, to the detriment of parliaments. Complexities emerge about the role parties play in parliamentary representation: Are parties blocking parliamentary deliberation?
- Politicians versus technicians: Is CG just about managing better? What is the role of politicians? Is it just to manage or to represent better?

2.   How do we jump from results to trust? How is the collaborative governance of *Etorkizuna Eraikiz* building and keeping trust?

Initial response and reactions

The following data and evidence are referred to:
1) Some quantitative data (survey among Gipuzkoan general population) are presented showing: that those who show awareness of EE assess the DFG's performance as being better than those who do not; that they are more politically active; and that they show higher social trust.
2) Some qualitative data (interviews with EE's stakeholders) are presented showing: a predominantly relational trust source over rules and structures; and a strongly shared (among politicians, technicians and societal organisations) normative framework about the benefit of collaboration and participation.

Thematic debates

The following comments and suggestions emerge from the discussion:
- From a learning perspective, it is suggested to look at the role of difference: How are perceived differences valued? How are differences managed? The DFG makes it explicit that they take differences as something good, but they recognise that they do not know how to manage them.
- The predominance of relationships (EE is seen as a relational model) indicates that assessing EE is very much about assessing relationships.

Further questions, critical issues and challenges

- Differences are shown between trust in politics and politicians and trust in public institutions. Political trust seems to be not well correlated with institutional trust.
- The relation between communication and trust. Does communication lead to trust or the opposite? Internal debates within the DFG are shared about the use of marketing and advertising for the promotion of EE. On the one hand, there is awareness of the need for the brand to have visibility; on the other, there is also the assumption that high visibility may hamper the purpose of EE. The goal of EE's communication is not that people remember the name *Etorkizuna Eraikiz*, but that EE's activities lead people to think differently about politics and the public.

3. How to further analyse outputs and impact of collaborative governance?

Initial response and reactions

The DFG has collected evaluation data from different projects, but now it feels the need to properly conduct an overall evaluation of EE, which is being tendered. According to the major characteristics of EE, the following elements are to be included in the evaluation framework: Listening, Deliberation, Experimentation and Analysis, as well as actual consequences in public policies. Changes in the following will be looked at: in collaboration (ways of doing), in the processes, in the traction capacity. An impact map is pursued, including mapping the problem, resources, changes and, ultimately, trust.

Thematic debates

The following comments and suggestions emerge from the discussion:
- Who will be the end users of the evaluation? Who are those who want to learn? a) Those who are at the top of EE, in order to have an overall view of what has been done; b) external actors and society in general, in order to account for the deployed resources.
- Different forms of evaluation are needed. There is evaluation for acknowledging what has happened, and there is strategic evaluation for redefining the future.

- Evaluation should be able to grasp learning. This suggests that a way of evaluating is by asking what has been learned.
- Evaluating helps self-understanding. Things have developed intuitively, without much reflexivity. What is pursued in assessing is not only to acknowledge impact, but also to understand what has been done. Evaluating thus helps asking the right questions, and even reflecting about the new questions that should be asked.
- New ways of evaluating are needed. EE has used traditional indicators, but if the reality is being transformed, new indicators are needed.
- Trust evaluation requires looking at behaviours. Evaluating trust entails looking at passive trust (attitudes) and active trust (behaviours). How have behaviours changed in relation to participation as a result of EE initiatives?
- Workshop participants jointly list questions for evaluation, among which the following are mentioned: Will you come back? What did we do right and what wrong? Was your problem solved? How did your willingness to collaborate change? Who is missing? Would you have achieved the same by yourself? Did you learn something new? Has your motivation to be involved improved? Do you have a better understanding about why things do not work?

Each one of these questions could serve to start a conversation for learning. Would you come back? No. Why not? What is missing? These questions are instrumental for the purposes of collaborative governance.

Further questions, critical issues and challenges

- To combine the emotional with the rational dimension, subjective indicators with objective ones. Subjectivity shapes evaluation. Evaluation should register tangible changes in public policies, but also trust, and trust is subjective.
- To account for intangible outcomes. There is the need to make tangible the intangible. Legitimacy has a value which is difficult to visualise.
- How to measure intangible outcomes with objective indicators? Evaluating intangible outcomes requires registering gaps between real achievements and perceived achievements. For intangible resources to exist, both real achievements and activating acknowledgement of the latter are needed. What is needed is to register how intangible resources transform reality. Validating narratives without factual support is risky.

Comments from scholars

Comment 9
Notes on the evaluation of *Etorkizuna Eraikiz*

GREGG G. VAN RYZIN, *Rutgers University, New Jersey, US*

Etorkizuna Eraikiz is a collaborative governance initiative of Gipuzkoa Province, which is in Spain's Basque County and home to a little over 700,000 people. Reflecting the province's long history of self-governance and cooperative production, the initiative aims to involve citizens in a variety of projects aimed at pressing issues, such as balancing work and family life, protecting the environment, developing high-technology industry, and preserving the Basque language and culture. Citizens and civil society organisations work with public officials and project staff to identify issues and design solutions. Thus, it is a policy initiative with not only multiple activities, involving a variety of stakeholders, but one with a wide range of substantive goals and outcomes.

How can such an initiative be evaluated? Some tentative answers to this question are presented in this essay, which is based on ideas discussed in, or inspired by, a workshop with Gipuzkoa government leaders and affiliated experts who gathered to consider how to measure and evaluate *Etorkizuna Eraikiz*. Hopefully, the ideas and suggestion that follow will be helpful to the leaders and staff of *Etorkizuna Eraikiz* as well as to those involved in similar collaborative governance initiatives around the world.

One key suggestion from the workshop was that concentrating on trust of government might help focus the evaluation. Indeed, in an important sense, *Etorkizuna Eraikiz* was launched to demonstrate that the provincial government was making an effort to listen to the public and to address some of their most pressing concerns. The effect of *Etorkizuna Eraikiz* on trust is likely not only direct, shaping the views of those who directly participate in its activities, but also indirect to the extent the broader public becomes aware of *Etorkizuna Eraikiz* and views its themes and activities positively. In fact, *Etorkizuna Eraikiz* promotes itself through branding and social marketing across the province. And, importantly, the provincial government measures awareness of *Etorkizuna Eraikiz* and trust of government through regular annual telephone surveys of the population. Survey results shared at the workshop suggest that awareness of *Etorkizuna Eraikiz* is increasing and that those who have heard of the initiative report higher levels of trust of the provincial government. This certainly represents a promising start to the task of evaluating the effects of *Etorkizuna Eraikiz* on trust.

A few comments and suggestions, however, can be offered to build on what has been done. To begin with, although awareness of *Etorkizuna Eraikiz* is associated with trust, we remain unsure of which way the causal arrow goes: it could well be that more trusting citizens simply have more interest in (and thus awareness of) a government initiative like EE. To better get at causation, the province could run some survey experiments in which a treatment group is randomly assigned to receive information about *Etorkizuna Eraikiz* (such as a brief description), the trust questions are asked after this treatment, and results compared with a control group that receives no information about EE. This could be done in the context of a future annual telephone survey or, less expensively, with an online market research panel. Although online panels are not as statically representative, randomised experiments still provide solid causal evidence with non-probability samples. (Think about randomised clinical trials in medicine, for example, which are done mostly with volunteers and not a random sample of the population.) Having experimental evidence that awareness of *Etorkizuna Eraikiz* actually causes higher trust of government would add support to the suggestive patterns observed in the annual telephone surveys (mentioned above). For more on experimental approaches to public management research, including survey experiments, see James, Jilke & Van Ryzin (2017).

Another strategy, if survey data exist for nearby provinces such as Bizkaia, is to do what is termed a difference-in-differences analysis of trust before and after the implementation of *Etorkizuna Eraikiz* in Gipuzkoa. The method is simple and straightforward: if trust is increasing in Gipuzkoa after the implementation of *Etorkizuna Eraikiz* but stagnant or declining in Bizkaia, over the same years, then we have more reason to believe *Etorkizuna Eraikiz* may be causing the increased trust observed in Gipuzkoa. In other words, we have better evidence to rule out the possibility that the trust trends in Gipuzkoa merely reflect broader trends across Basque society in how people view government. Of course, this method depends on having survey measures of trust (or related attitudes toward government) asked in the same years in both provinces. For general introductions to the difference-in-differences strategy, see Remler & Van Ryzin (2022) and Angrist & Pischke (2014).

Although trust is a foundational motivation as well as general aim of EE, some in the workshop worried that survey measures of trust would be considered too subjective and intangible to justify government spending on *Etorkizuna Eraikiz* to sceptical stakeholders. Thus, some additional approaches could be considered to generate metrics that capture more concrete outcomes. Because *Etorkizuna Eraikiz* contains multiple reference centres focused on diverse policy areas, each could be required to come up with a detailed list of tangible goals (or targets) in consultation with citizens, centre staff, civic organisations and public officials. Undoubtedly, this would take some effort and would be complicated by the usual difficulties of defining outcomes, setting goals and developing indicators. But it would help to encourage reference centres to make their targets fairly simple, concrete and measurable. Once agreed upon, the targets could be the objects of regular (perhaps quarterly) reporting by each reference centre. The results could be compiled and a report on the *percentage of targets achieved* – for each reference centre as well as for *Etorkizuna Eraikiz* as a whole – could be presented to the provincial government and related stakeholders.

A final suggestion, somewhat outside the box, is to set up an independent panel of judges to assess the success of *Etorkizuna Eraikiz*. With such a varied package of activities and aims, a comprehensive evaluation may simply be beyond the scope of social science measurement and analysis. Moreover, many complex objects in society are evaluated by judges and not by measurement methods: gymnastic events, boxing matches, legal cases, book prizes and dog shows, to name a few. But, curiously, using judges is not an approach used to evaluate public policies or programmes – although it could be. The judges would have to be selected carefully to reflect a relevant range of perspectives and expertise. They would need to be independent and shielded from the influence of public officials, programme staff or other actors with a vested interest in a given outcome (which is what happens with trial jurors or financial auditors). They would need to be able to request information, conduct site visits, observe meetings and gather other facts about the programme as needed. They could then deliberate and render a judgement, much as an appellate court issues a ruling. But in this case, they would be rendering an evaluation of the programme: What are its strengths, and weaknesses? Is it effective? Is it efficient? Does it appear to be accomplishing its goals? Admittedly, this would remain a subjective judgement – but one that is independent, careful and considered. In the end, such a judgement may come closer to what government and the public really need from a policy evaluation than does a report on the inevitably limited and ambiguous quantitative indicators that make up the usual social science approach.

Evaluation of a complex, multifaceted collaborative governance initiative like *Etorkizuna Eraikiz* is challenging – but necessary. A focus on trust provides a broad focus, and various strategies to estimate the initiative's impacts on trust are possible (as discussed above). But more concrete evidence may be needed, and it might be necessary to think outside the box about alternatives to traditional social measurement and analysis – such as the use of independent, expert judges – that could help render a useful and credible evaluation of *Etorkizuna Eraikiz*.

Comment 10
Looking at the impact of collaborative policies on intangibles and outcomes through dynamic performance governance

CARMINE BIANCHI, *Professor in Public Management & Governance at the University of Palermo, Italy*

1.   Managing sustainable growth in collaborative networks through learning-oriented performance governance

The *Etorkizuna Eraikiz* (EE) case study provides thought-provoking insights on the role of intangibles as driving forces for a collaborative network governance primarily lead by the civil society. Among such factors are: 1) social cohesion around core values rooted in cultural traditions (e.g. language and gastronomy); 2) natural and historical assets; 3) human and social capital; and 4) policy innovation. All of them are at the same time framed in an ideal continuity with history, and consistently transposed into the future (Bianchi *et al.*, 2019, p. 104).

The fast and intensive growth in both the collaborative network and the achieved outcomes experienced since the inception of the EE 'model' suggests how intangibles (e.g. leadership, active citizenship and stakeholders' aptitude to leverage natural and historical assets) can make a difference for generating community value. In the EE case, the intangibles profiling the civil society have been the main trigger for successfully deploying the endowment of available shared strategic resources (most of which are intangible too) to generate community outcomes.

The involvement of local government and other stakeholders in the collaborative network, and the adoption of formal institutional structures and coordinating mechanisms (e.g. the reference centres) have certainly contributed to foster consistency among the different network initiatives inside a holistic – though multifaceted – political entity and organisational ecosystem. However, the efforts at which the local grassroots organisations and volunteers have pursued new ventures in various collaborative domains may look even more intensive and pervasive than the pace at which the network governance has perhaps been able to cope with such growth. This condition is a potential factor of unsustainable network performance in the long run, which requires proper methods to plan the future growth of EE, with a focus on capacity building and network legitimacy, to attract, involve and retain stakeholders. Though the final outcomes for EE are undoubtedly associated with community value creation, relevant intermediate outcomes are related to the network leaders' capability to pursue growth in the network governance capacity and legitimacy that may sustain the growth in the volume and scope of the projects carried out.

Network capacity not only refers to the number of people working in the projects and to their skills, but also to the number and mix of stakeholders involved and the consistency of their profile with the initiatives carried out. Governance legitimacy is another strategic resource to consider for assessing collaborative network growth sustainability. It is related to the level of trust and mutual accountability among network members and from the external stakeholders towards the network itself. This asset provides a fundamental performance driver affecting the acquisition and retention of stakeholders, which in turn may allow further network growth to be sustained.

Both network capacity and legitimacy sustain policy-makers' ability to consistently leverage and deploy social cohesion around core values, natural and historical assets, and human/social capital. An expression of such ability is policy innovation, to position EE in an ideal continuity with history towards a future that may gradually incorporate new values, consistently with those transmitted by past generations.

Obviously, such strategic resources cannot be procured in the market (Bianchi, 2016, p. 73). Their acquisition and retention are outcomes of value generation processes for which policy-makers should be able to detect and affect the driving factors. Hence, enabling EE leaders through proper planning methods to enhance their learning processes in the implementation of policy innovation for leveraging local intangible assets may prevent growth crises and foster enduring performance outcomes.

There is a relative paucity in the public policy literature on collaborative network lifecycle and growth crises. Among the few studies in the field, Ulibarri et al. (2020) and Imperial (2022) identify four main lifecycle stages describing what they define as the "useful life of collaborative network governance", i.e.: 1) activation; 2) collectivity; 3) institutionalisation and stability; and 4) decline or reorientation. Each stage underlies specific challenges and opportunities for collaborative network growth and sustainability. In this regard, two insightful issues of debate have been raised by Ulibarri et al. (2020, p. 634), i.e.: "How do collaborative leaders or participants identify the need for reorientations or recreations, and how can they successfully manage these changes? Is decline inevitable, or could adjustments in leadership, accountability, and process dynamics stave off premature endings?" Two more debating issues can be added, i.e.: What kinds of crises can be encountered through collaborative network lifecycles? How could learning-oriented performance governance help in preventing or counteracting them?

Greiner (1972) distinguished four main organisational growth crises. In the early stages of growth, a *leadership crisis* can be generated by the unaddressed need of a formal professional management (organisational structures, budgets, incentives, etc.) to deal with an increasing number of employees. In the next growth stage, an *autonomy crisis* can be generated by the unaddressed need to delegate power. In a further stage, a *control crisis* can happen due to lack of coordination between autonomous field managers. In a later stage, a *red tape crisis* can be caused by a lack of collaboration to counteract an excess of departmentalisation. To prevent these crises, for each phase Greiner suggested adopting tailored organisational responses through the management focus, the organisation structure, the top management style, and the control and management reward systems. The implicit idea behind this conceptualisation is that organisational growth generates more complexity, requiring an increasing resort to formal and informal structures and processes with a different nature and focus, as business maturity advances.

Conversely, framing and addressing the risks of unsustainable growth in public governance networks is perhaps a more complex and less predictable issue than for single organisations. This is primarily due to the intrinsic wickedness of network governance and community value generation processes in today's public service ecosystems (Osborne, 2021), and to the complexity of pursuing coordination and collaboration at an inter-organisational level, consistently with the level of the individual networked organisations (Bianchi, 2021; 2022).

In collaborative network governance, different potential kinds of crisis may converge together to affect the growth and survival of the projects undertaken. For instance, a *red tape crisis* may jeopardise the take-off of the collaboration, because of prevailing cultural systems on the basis of which an excessive emphasis is given to the formal structure and features forging governance agreements. At the same time, a *leadership crisis* can be a potential challenge for collaborative networks in their start-up and early growth stages, because of poor or ineffective efforts towards enhancing individual leadership in a blurred setting where roles, decisions and accountabilities are carried out outside of formal institutional boundaries.

Fostering leadership cannot only refer to an individual dimension, which initiates change, provides vision, instils values, and fosters trust and commitment. Enhancing *collective leadership* (Mintzberg, 2009, pp. 152–154) by leveraging individual leadership is also needed in the medium term. This is to keep direction, to adapt to internal or environmental change, to gather support and to manage relationships not only within a single field or project (e.g. a reference centre), but also with other stakeholders, both in and outside a network.

At societal level, collective leadership entails a pervasive tension by people towards the common good, inspired to a deep feel of belonging to a community. In this regard, Crosby & Bryson (2010, p. 211) refer to *integrative public leadership* as "bringing diverse groups and organizations together in semi-permanent ways, and typically across sector boundaries, to remedy complex public problems and achieve the common good". As noted by Cooper *et al.* (2006, p. 84), "high ethical citizenship conceives of citizenship as a responsibility […] Low ethical citizenship, on the other hand, conceives of authority as hierarchically distributed".

Therefore, particularly in the described governance context, the concepts of leadership, trust and active citizenship are nested in one another. Detecting the performance drivers triggering each of such intangibles and those through which collaborative policies deploying them may foster local area attractiveness and community wellbeing is vital for effective performance governance (Bouckaert & Halligan, 2007). Sustainable performance at local area level shows, in the medium to long run, a stabilised aptitude of collaborative policy outcomes to build up and retain a balanced set of shared strategic resources, such as common goods. Common goods are natural, social or historical assets which are rooted in a region so as to profile its intimate identity. Examples are ecosystem attributes (e.g. quality, preservation and enjoyability), availability of green spaces, respect for the environment, usability of cultural heritage usability and social awareness of it, safety, financial stability, and active citizenship (Bianchi, 2021, p. 340). Common goods provide a suitable basis for improving (or ensuring stability of) the quality of life that can be achieved and the attractiveness of the local area.

A learning-oriented approach to planning may enhance individual leaders' aptitudes to frame and share with other stakeholders their values and visions, as well as the necessary actions for attaining community outcomes. It can also enhance building leadership, legitimacy, trust, and conflict management (Bryson *et al.*, 2006). There is a need for innovative governance methods based on facilitated modelling for performance dialogue among the stakeholders involved to enable them to explore the cause-and-effect relationships between the policies adopted, intangible assets and community outcomes. Embodying such a learning-oriented approach in performance governance may substantially help stakeholders enrich the planning process. Through this view, facilitated modelling can support stakeholders in outlining sustainable policies and identifying a set of performance drivers affecting the accumulation and retention of the intangible shared strategic resources in which the EE 'model' is rooted, and their impact on community value generation.

Just such an innovative framework can be provided by 'dynamic performance governance' (DPG). The next section will illustrate the logics and potential benefits of DPG for managing sustainable growth and detecting/counteracting early signs of crisis in implementing the EE model.

2. Dynamic performance governance as a learning-oriented approach to policy analysis for pursuing sustainable outcomes in collaborative networks

DPG aims at fostering performance dialogue in boundary-crossing settings by bridging three scientific domains, i.e. System Dynamics, Performance Management, and Collaborative Governance. It adopts a selective approach to foster stakeholder learning by modelling policy sustainability across three interconnected stages, i.e.: 1) outlining the targeted end-results; 2) exploring performance drivers affecting them; and 3) setting policies to build up and deploy strategic resources for affecting performance drivers (Bianchi, 2021, 2022; Bianchi *et al.*, 2019).

Strategic resources are stocks of available – tangible and intangible – assets (e.g. natural resources, cultural heritage, image, skills, leadership, trust, population, quality of life) shared in a context by different stakeholders.

The level of such assets changes over time through flows, as the end-result of network governance policies, through which stakeholders affect community outcomes by leveraging shared strategic resources consistently with organisational resources. Different levels of intermediate outcomes are identified through DPG as the end-results which impact final outcomes. For instance, an increase in local area attractiveness can be affected by a plurality of intermediate outcomes, which gauge a change in more specific strategic resources on which such attractiveness depends (e.g. human capital, infrastructures, green areas, services to households and businesses).

Performance drivers refer to the critical success factors for attaining community outcomes. To allow policy-makers to promptly perceive and counteract the effects of discontinuity on performance, they should be continuously monitored for 'weak signals' of change.

Performance drivers are gauged as ratios comparing a strategic resource endowment to a benchmark. A performance driver numerator may refer to different categories, such as: 1) allocated capacity (time; skills; scope, pervasiveness and inclusiveness of collaboration; authority; incentives); 2) shared organisational/individual capacity (e.g. information, contacts); 3) community capacity (e.g. common goods, refurbishment sites); 4) legitimacy (e.g. trust, mutual accountability); 5) service delivery (e.g. percentage of population reached by community services, percentage of enforced policy interventions); or 6) financial (e.g. lien-to-market-value, tax arrears, public funding). All these categories underlie possible effects on agents' behaviour, which impact on the change in other shared strategic resources. For instance, allocated time, shared information and contacts may affect change in trust. Modelling such relationships requires a selective approach.

While most performance management and governance is focused on financial and tangible measures through a static perspective, DPG adopts a feedback view through which policy-makers are engaged in framing the causes behind the observed patterns of behaviour showing system performance over time. Given the dynamic complexity of framing causation in outcome-based performance governance, the adopted approach is descriptive – rather than prescriptive. To avoid the risk of modelling turning into an illusion of control, DPG helps stakeholders in framing the system's structure and behaviour, and learning from a continuous comparison between the real world and the model (Lane 1994). This requires that stakeholders actively participate in model building: their explicit and tacit knowledge, together with coded data from formal information systems, are prerequisites for learning (Forrester, 1994).

DPG may help stakeholders to detect lack of performance sustainability and policy resistance, which occurs when "policy actions trigger feedback from the environment that undermines the policy and at times even exacerbates the original problem" (Ghaffarzadegan et al., 2011, p. 24). For instance, promoting the image of a place to attract tourists, in order to counteract a financial crisis, without also making investments in infrastructure, may generate an improvement in a bounded set of shared strategic resources (e.g. tourist visits, image, business investments, available jobs) in the short run. However, in the long run, it would deplete other shared strategic resources (e.g. cultural heritage usability, quality of air, sanitation, public space saturation and safety), which would cause the place's image, attractiveness and quality of life to deteriorate, leading tourist visits to drop.

Through learning forums (Ansell & Gash, 2018; Douglas & Ansell, 2021), DPG enables performance dialogue (Rajala et al., 2018). It provides 'boundary objects' for implementing collaborative platforms (Bianchi, 2022), which supports change processes in decision-makers' attitudes and mental models (Moynihan, 2008, p. 111).

3.   Conclusions

This paper has illustrated the potential problems that static planning or emotional collaborative networking may generate in the medium to long run, in pursuing community outcomes. We suggested DPG as a learning-oriented framework for performance governance to deal with sustainable network growth and to foster stakeholders' ability to frame the cause-and-effect relationships behind the outcomes from implemented collaborative policies.

The described approach can strengthen the quality of policy analysis by addressing a number of unsolved issues in outcome-based performance governance, such as: enhancing performance dialogue and policy alignment, managing conflict, fostering trust and legitimacy, building up and deploying shared strategic resources, framing policy trade-offs, dealing with intangibles and non-monetary performance measures, and turning collaborative governance from a discrete event to a continuous process (Bianchi *et al.*, 2021).

In the EE case, DPG could be useful to outline how sustainable collaborative policies may affect intangibles like trust, leadership, active citizenship and culture, in which key policy ideas are rooted. It can also be helpful in supporting stakeholders in outlining policies that, by leveraging such intangibles, may affect performance drivers leading to sustainable community value creation.

Comment 11
Looking about achievements and results: Further steps to evaluate *Etorkizuna Eraikiz*

STEPHEN ANSOLABEHERE, *Frank G. Thompson Professor of Government, Harvard University, Boston, US*

Collaborative governance, once an ideal, is becoming a reality. A wide range of ways of organising public decision-making fall under the umbrella of collaborative governance. Broadly speaking, it is any process of public decision-making in which a wide set of stakeholders, including the members of the general public, participate directly in decisions guiding the planning, design, enactment and implementation of a public activity, project or policy.

This notion of broad engagement in governance decisions grows out of many different traditions of economic, political and social thought. The projects examined in this volume most clearly flow out of two lines of thought. The first, originating with Joseph Schumpeter and Karl Polanyi, asks how can democracy and capitalism coexist? The need to regulate the economy and the constant effort by economic stakeholders to influence democracy pushes for an external authority to solve problems of governing. That external authority is, by its nature, undemocratic. The second line of thinking, of which Elinor Ostrom is the central figure, grapples with vexing problems involving the management of common pool resources, such as fisheries, water and land. Ostrom shows that a practical approach to decision-making that is incremental and sequential and involves all affected parties in direct discussion and negation can solve common pool problems. In this 'bottom-up' approach to problem-solving communications is the key. These two important streams of thinking have fuelled efforts at collaborative governance, deliberative democracy and polyarchic governance throughout the world.

The Schumpeter–Polanyi perspective and the Ostrom perspective each point to different approaches for evaluating the performance of collaborative governance. The former perspective is concerned with the health of democratic processes, and the latter is concerned more with outcomes, especially the ability of people to overcome the limits on collective action and the provision of public goods.

At this point in the evolution of these new modes of governing what is most needed are systematic, empirically grounded evaluations. Much of the academic literature on these new modes offers theorising and advocacy, but practical, hard-nosed empirics are lacking. What is happening in these many experiments in Europe and around the world? Are people arriving at better decisions? Is the legitimacy of government improving? This volume offers just such a rich examination of the experiments in collaborative governance undertaken by the government of Gipuzkoa Province in the Basque Autonomous Community of Spain. *Etorkizuna Eraikiz* – 'Building the Future' in English – launched 125 experiments in deliberative democracy, participatory budgeting and other forms of collaborative governance. The very important task now is to assess what we can learn from these experiments about building the future.

First, I encourage the readers of this volume and of any other work on the proper design of policy and government to think like a structural engineer: focus on the failures. If we want to make a structure, such as a bridge, stronger we must stress the model to the point of breaking and understand where and why it failed. In her classic study *Governing the Commons*, Elinor Ostrom emphasised the instances of failures of deliberation, negotiation and problem-solving in order understand what forms of governance can and cannot solve. Ostrom emphasised the incremental and sequential nature of problem-solving about collective goods. Solving difficult problems, such as public goods provision, is especially hard. People must understand and accept each other; they must adjust rules of decision-making to the particular problem; and they must communicate with each other. It takes time to build trust, to make appropriate rules and to communicate.

The failures are important for both internal and external learning. Evaluation, after all, is ultimately important because any project, or, in this case, many projects, offers us an opportunity to learn. Internal learning is the gathering and use of information by those involved in a project to improve the project as it evolves. During the fourth workshop, the participants in the seminar undertook an exercise of writing ten simple questions that could aid in the evaluation of a project. These included "Would you come back?", "Was your problem solved?" and "Were all of the people who should be here, here?" The answers to these and other questions can help those involved in a project improve what they are doing. They are not the end point of evaluation, but the opening of a dialogue with participants in a project (such as those who use the programme's services) to find out what happened and how the project can be improved.

External learning is the gathering of information about a project by those outside the project in order to ascertain whether the project should continue to receive support and what aspects of the project might be useful elsewhere. External learning is essential for ensuring the accountability of the project management. It is also the vector through which the lessons of *Etorkizuna Eraikiz* will carry to other places in Euskadi, in Europe and around the globe.

How far can experiments in collaborative governance go before trust breaks down or before a project cannot be managed practically?

Second, follow (and document) the flow of communication. Elinor Ostrom emphasised that the advantage of polyarchic governance (or collaborative governance) grows out of improvement in communication. Better and faster communication helps solves three essential problems: (i) collective action, (ii) monitoring, and (iii) commitment (trust). It is critical to solve problems of *collective action* in order to arrive at optimal outcomes – outcomes that benefit all of us collectively, but that can only be accomplished if the group works together. Monitoring is of obvious importance in order to ensure that all parties comply with an agreement. And commitment, which is rooted in mutual trust, ensures that deals do not break down, and that the participants will continue to work on the problem in the future.

The 150 distinct projects under the *Etorkizua Eraikiz* umbrella have compiled extensive amounts of text associated with their activities, including minutes of meetings among stakeholders. This is a rare opportunity to analyse the communications within collaborative governance projects, as a wide range of different sorts of projects have been conducted simultaneously. Some surely have fared better than others in building communication flows and trust among stakeholders. An intensive evaluation of that text offers an extremely valuable resource for those outside of these projects to examine how collaborative governance actually happens. In addition, this body of text is also an interesting opportunity for the further development of text analysis and natural language processing tools that have been developed over the past two decades.

Third, understand the alternatives to what is put forth. Often, the alternative to collaborative governance is 1) a hierarchy or top-down decision-making, 2) a market, or 3) an external authority. Participatory budgeting, for example, is proposed as a novel way to set budgets in ways that reflect the preferences and information of the public broadly. Budget requests reflect the needs and observations of citizens. The alternative is that administrative agencies make budget requests that are approved or amended by an elected council. A different form of expertise and knowledge is involved in each of these two sorts of budgeting. There may be advantages to each, and trade-offs from relying on one of these approaches versus the other.

In evaluating collaborative governance, it is essential to understand the alternatives. It is widely argued by advocates that collaborative governance is 'better', but better than what, and in what ways?

1) What is the counter-factual form of government against which collaborative governance is to be compared? What form of decision-making

would occur in the absence of the collaborative governance programme? We could compare the experiment to what government organisations did before the implementation of a collaborative approach, or to the decisions, activities and performance of other government agencies in other municipalities or provinces with similar responsibilities.

2) What is the standard for improvement (not success, but improvement)? Was the outcome different than results that occur with an alternative form of decision-making? Was the implementation more expedient with collaborative governance? Was there wider uptake and acceptance?

Fourth, understand the process. Collaborative governance changes the basic process of citizen involvement, from one of a principal (a voter) holding an agent (elected official) accountable to one in which the citizen has agency. It will be helpful in evaluating the *Etorkizuna Eraikiz* projects to map the different points in the process and ways in which people are involved.

In my thinking about collaborative governance and related innovations, what is distinctive is the point in the decision-making process at which people are engaged. In polyarchic forms of government, stakeholders and even the broader public are engaged throughout the process, especially early on. In other forms of government decision-making, the people are engaged in the end. For example, in siting an electric powerline, collaborative governance would engage people in planning and design decisions. In common practice, public hearings are held late in the process, and then only to allow people to vent their frustration. As a result, all that the public can do is acquiesce or complain. The public is made out to be the bad guy because people end up opposing many projects. Collaborative governance reverses this process. The public and stakeholders are engaged early in deliberations, and throughout the decision-making process. How does this shift in the process improve either relational outcomes, such as trust, or objective factors, such as time to completion, project costs or distribution of benefits from the project?

One important challenge of collaborative governance is the tendency for participation to be low and highly skewed toward higher-educated and higher-income citizens when a participatory project makes high demands on people's time and attention. Participatory budgeting in Scotland, for instance, generated relatively low numbers of proposals, and almost all of them came from people with college degrees. In this regard, collaborative governance may only magnify inequities that arise in traditional forms of representative and bureaucratic governance. At least since the 1950s, studies of urban politics have found that there are low levels of participation in city elections and meetings, and participation skews heavily toward the highly educated. A key challenge for all collaborative governance projects is to find new ways to design public engagement to broaden the set of people involved and ideas communicated. For example, deliberative polling used in the State of Texas to advise the selection of energy projects in the 1990s helped people overcome practical obstacles of participation, such as providing parents of young children with babysitters. Engaging with the same set of participants that show up in city council elections or to protest a local government action will only replicate the inequities evident in more traditional forms of representative or bureaucratic governance.

Gipuzkoa and other communities in Europe and around the world are in the early stages of the experimentation with collaborative governance. As we embark on this journey, it is useful to keep Elinor Ostrom's sage insight in mind: solving problems through collaborative, deliberative and polyarchic decision-making is *incremental and sequential*. A community first may try one idea, and, if that does not yield the desired results, it will experiment with another idea, adjusting to what it learned from its own experiences. With that in mind, the evaluation of the experiences in Gipuzkoa can inform both those in the region seeking to solve problems and those elsewhere in the world interested in the potential of collaborative governance.

Comment 12
Some reflections about the future of *Etorkizuna Eraikiz*

JAVIER LEZAUN, *Institute for Science, Innovation and Society, Oxford University, UK*

Etorkizuna Eraikiz revolves around the most precious – and fragile – object in democratic politics: the future, what is yet to come, as a matter of free, collective deliberation.

In times of uncertainty and seemingly constant crises, it is difficult to make the future the centrepiece of political debate. One tends to find comfort in the certainties of the past, a shared sense of history, the memories that ground our individual and collective sense of belonging. The future, in contrast, appears indeterminate, treacherous, likely calamitous. War, pandemics, economic downturns, the escalating climate crisis... it is hard to organise our politics around a hopeful engagement with the future, particularly when increasing precarity threatens the livelihood of the younger generations.

This predicament is compounded by the short-circuiting of our traditional mechanisms of collective debate and democratic participation. Growing inequality and political fragmentation foster disenchantment with representative institutions.

Gipuzkoa is exposed to these trends, as it grapples with the localised impact of systemic, planetary changes. *Etorkizuna Eraikiz* intervenes in this complex set of issues by experimenting with alternative arrangements for the design of public policies. The term 'collaborative governance' is a useful catch-phrase for this sort of initiative, but it does not fully capture the diversity of initiatives that have come together under the umbrella of *Etorkizuna Eraikiz* over the last decade.

Perhaps the most striking feature of this experience is its very origin: an institution like the Provincial Council of Gipuzkoa, with full authority to design and implement public policies, willingly sharing its executive power with civil society. In so doing, the institution makes itself accountable to the stakeholders – and citizens – who agree to take part in the myriad acts of debate and decision-making that follow, for all those actors are now in a position to judge whether the commitment to 'collaborative governance' leads to truly participatory processes and better public policies, or is simply a rhetorical strategy for partisan gain.

The scale of Gipuzkoa and its high level of social capital make this accountability much more genuine. This is a community of little more than 700,000 residents, evenly distributed in a small territory, and traversed by multiple forms of civic associationism and political activism. This means that the claims of any institution to inclusiveness can be easily put to the test. A process like *Etorkizuna Eraikiz* would quickly come to naught unless those claims were supported by effective participation – people would simply 'exit' these forums if their involvement did not render any concrete benefits to them. The fact that civic involvement in these initiatives has grown over time, and that none of the actors that engaged in these processes of collective reflection has walked away, should count as the primary success.

In addition to the experience of the different reference centres, labs and think tank, perhaps the most significant impact of *Etorkizuna Eraikiz* may be in its ability to change the administrative culture of the Council itself, in the extent to which collaborative governance is built into the habits of civil servants. This will determine whether the spirit (if not the actual programmes) of *Etorkizuna Eraikiz* will continue when the leadership of the Provincial Council changes.

The distinct social and political conditions of Gipuzkoa – a small and prosperous region with a high level of political autonomy, control over key tax revenues, entrepreneurial state institutions and relatively low levels of income inequality – make the experience of *Etorkizuna Eraikiz* not easily replicable in other contexts or jurisdictions. International observers can nevertheless draw practical lessons from the successes and failures in making specific issues – ageing and dependency, electric mobility, social use of the Basque language, employability and social exclusion, advanced manufacturing, etc. – tractable to public participation through reference centres and living labs. They will also be able to learn about how processes of 'invited participation' can generate genuine change in the thinking and workings of the institution that sets these processes in motion – or, alternatively, what are the factors that limit the potential of these processes and reduce them to mere acts of consultation or 'placation' (to use Arnstein's famous 'ladder of participation' scheme, Arnstein, 1969).

Going forward, there are several features of this experience that require further reflection. The first one is the role of formal institutions of public deliberation. Gipuzkoa has a Parliament that should in principle serve as the primary forum for discussing public policies. Yet *Etorkizuna Eraikiz* has operated largely outside this institutional channel of public debate, reaching out directly to civil society actors to formulate priorities and experiment with new ways of designing policy. The challenge here is common to most parliamentary institutions in liberal democracies, which are seen as represent-ing the rigid agendas of political parties rather than serving as a conduit for civil society concerns. *Etorkizuna Eraikiz* convened a forum with all political parties represented in the Provincial Parliament, but Parliament itself was not a decisive forum to articulate the aspirations expressed through *Etorkizuna Eraikiz*. How to reinvigorate formal institutions of public debate and make political parties more permeable to civil society agendas remains a key challenge in the effort to imbue institutions with the principles of participatory policy-making.

A second point of reflection is the definition of priorities for experimental, collaborative policy-making. *Etorkizuna Eraikiz* was conceived, organised and funded by the Provincial Council, and the choice of areas of work tracks closely the concerns of the Provincial Council itself. Public opinion surveys suggest that these concerns are broadly shared by the Gipuzkoan citizenry, but they are key socioeconomic issues – housing, precarity and working conditions, employer–employee relations – that do not lend themselves so easily to experimental formats of collaborative governance.

As *Etorkizuna Eraikiz* closes this cycle of activities, a clear trade-off becomes apparent. The institution at the heart of the initiative has shared some of its authority to define public policies. In return, it has gained greater access to the insights, aspirations and competencies of civil society actors. When the process is successful, this leads to a virtuous cycle in the relationship between institution and society: it reinforces civil society actors, generating greater pluralism in the identification of problems and solutions, and at the same time strengthens the role of the institution as an authoritative venue for collective, future-oriented deliberation.

Chapter 8
Conclusions: Pracademic lessons learned

GEERT BOUCKAERT, *KU Leuven, Belgium*
MARÍA JOSÉ CANEL, *University Complutense Madrid, Madrid, Spain*
XABIER BARANDIARÁN, *Diputación Foral de Gipuzkoa*

1. Introduction

It may be a wicked statement to say that wicked problems require wicked solutions. However, in an increasingly complex and polarised society, with major problems and challenges, it is obvious that solutions of the past will most probably not work for the future. It is also obvious that the academic field of public administration should reflect in a critical way to find (re-)newed solutions. It also means that policy-makers and politicians should start thinking and acting out of the box to ensure not only inclusive service delivery, but also governance of chronical crises, which will require social and digital innovations. The main ambition is to rethink our democratic politico-administrative system and how it is embedded in and interacts with our society at large.

This book is about a grand democratic reform programme in the Basque Gipuzkoa Province, and its transition towards collaborative governance. It is about explaining what collaborative governance is as a major transformation and transition of a system, how to understand what is going on and how it could happen; and hopefully, it is also about how to convince other governments to realise a major reform programme of collaborative governance, as a major part of a solution, to maintain and strengthen our democratic systems.

This reform programme is not just about improving services for citizens, which was a major focus of the so-called New Public Management reform movement. Nor is it just about enhancing networks as a tool to involve citizens in policy and delivery as co-production, which is still a major focus of the so-called New Public Governance. This reform programme addresses a "big governance question" (Roberts, 2020) of how to curb democratic fatigue and alienation. This grand question is raised by the leadership of the government and its provincial council. The grand reply to the question is "to reinforce and experiment with new models for promoting public policies […] empowering citizens and opening spaces for debate and decision-making [as] an essential step for ensuring the future of democracy" (Olano, 2022, p. 3).

This major reform programme already covers a period from 2016 to 2023, and will probably continue beyond. It 'survived' one election (this book goes to print six months before the 2023 provincial elections) and received broad support in the provincial council with a coalition government, also beyond the majority. This programme is remarkable for academia and practice, not just for its size, covering about 150 projects, but also for its broad policy field coverage, and its comprehensive and systematic governance approach, from a close interaction between executive politics and administration to actively including society, which sometimes had a majoritarian presence in the decision-making and the deliberative processes. It is also remarkable for its collaborative experimentation with societal participants across the entire territory of the province.

Most reform initiatives are about 'risk', with its assessment and control. However, EE is not just about 'risk' but about an increasing 'uncertainty' in our transforming society, and how to cope with this. EE with its collaborative governance paradigm opts explicitly for cooperation and deliberation and not for confrontation, polarisation and conflict. It opts explicitly for inclusion and not for exclusion. It opts explicitly for trust-driven institutions in both the direction from society to governance and *vice versa*, and also within the public sector, based on cooperation and deliberation.

The next pracademic debates will have to address the ultimate question of 'governance with or without democracy'. Globally, there seems to be a divergent system change and even a political competition, unfortunately also in the Western and even European world, between 'governance with democracy' versus 'governance without democracy'. This EE collaborative governance model opts for governance with and for democracy. It should result in a system where governance and democracy mutually reinforce one another within a legitimate and trustworthy state model which respects the rule of law.

The way EE has attempted to do so is what this book has analysed, and this concluding chapter tries to distil major lessons learned from the initiative. We label the chapter as 'pracademic' lessons since, as stated in the introductory chapter, the knowledge here produced emerges from a close interaction between those embedded in the day-to-day practice of CG and leading scholars in the world who study this approach.

The structure of this chapter is as follows. We first present a concluding summary of the three types of texts that compose this book: the chapters, the notes from the workshops and the scholars' comments. They are arranged around the three major topics: structure and institutionalisation of the CG model; relational aspects; and results. Since Workshop 3 looked at results through a trust lens, a specific relationship between CG and trust is presented. Finally, we provide several concluding hypothetical sentences which may serve as basis for further research on this project and on other developments in collaborative governance.

2.   *Etorkizuna Eraikiz*: from walking the talk to talking the walk

In this section, following the structure of the three parts, a concluding summary of what emerges from the interaction between practitioners and scholars is presented.

2.1.   Challenges of conceptualising and institutionalising collaborative governance

Part I addressed the model and its institutionalisation, trying to follow the journey from conceptualisation to practice, which includes registering, analysing and learning from the specific changes made to the initial approach.

Defining the 'what' is relevant for analysing the CG initiative, and this appears to be particularly the case for the EE reform, which in contrast to similar ones, is broad and comprehensive, including governance, markets and networks. It is a "constellation of projects", centres and strategies, creating an open and living system. It goes beyond a single network to comprise a dynamic "network of networks", including different sources of authority. In addition, discussions have categorised this initiative as a "relational model" based on clear structures and rules, but at the same time, relying on full commitment and strong relations among the different actors involved.

The process of CG development in EE is model-based, with three conceptualised spaces for reflection, experimentation and innovation. However, looking at the description of the different steps and evolutions throughout the implementation of the model shows that complexities are not absent in CG building. A systemic vision has been proven to be of help to articulate the development of the model, to develop meta-governance, and to deal with the tension between vertical and horizontal structures, as well as between efficiency, effectiveness and accountability. The observation of the journey from conceptualisation to practice has led workshop attendees to think that an emergent strategy better fits with CG building, or, following one scholar's metaphor, that jazz music is closer to what has happened in *Etorkizuna Eraikiz* than a symphony.

An overall conclusive remark from this first part on the model and its institutionalisation might come from a scholar's suggestion to take EE as a framework for learning and acting in order to address major challenges and paradoxes about building democracy. While CG is not a magic recipe for all the problems, it may help communities and governments around the world to keep on track when it comes to addressing current problems and challenges of modern governance.

2.2. Relational dimensions to learn and communicate about a culture of collaborative governance

Part II of this book has focused on relational dimensions to learn and communicate about a culture of collaborative governance. Three key thematic debates, issues and challenges emerge from the chapters, workshops and scholars' comments.

The first refers to the challenge of managing diversity, and more specifically, of developing dialogue and processing conflict in the attempt to involve many and diverse stakeholders for collaboration. It has been shown that when building collaborative governance, some kind of criteria for inclusion is established, and the endeavour of so doing encounters contradictions and self-exclusion (not only from citizens but also from politicians and civil servants); it even meets deliberate exclusion (particularly when there is a lack of reputation, a history of corruption and a lack of credibility). Methodologies of action research and action learning have been proven to be of help for the development of skills and competences that are needed for addressing these contradictions and building collaborative governance: to build spaces for critical listening and learning; to locate positive energy for change among members of an organisation and/or system, and to channel this energy into concrete steps and actions; and to facilitate policy-makers and stakeholders to work as a team in order to, ultimately, impact public policies. As scholars' comments show, facilitating these skills of alignment and conflict mediation are crucial to constructing a common ground for joint problem-solving, and this is one of the key challenges shown by different CG experiences across the world.

Collaborative governance challenges leadership, and this is the second crucial issue that emerges from the different texts. Scholars' comments have singled out the *Etorkizuna Eraikiz* initiative, in contrast to other initiatives, as being mainly inspired, launched and driven by politicians. This singularity leads to relevant questions in order to explore where leadership resides and comes from. Analysis shows that collaborative governance entails the development of different understandings and sources of leadership.

EE appears to be a laboratory for shifting from typical traditional leadership to some kind of leadership which comes not only from within the organisation but from outside it as well. EE departed from traditional hierarchy, but during the process of implementation leadership is being collectively built by different actors, which include professionals (experts and scholars have an influence), visionaries (there are single actors strongly portraying a view), and social actors (e.g. cooperatives). How communicating vessels between these different leaderships have operated is something that needs to be explored, and scholars' comments bring concepts which may better fit with a CG approach: interactive, collaborative, distributed and co-created leadership.

Finally, one key idea that emerges is that the challenge of communicating collaborative governance goes beyond crafting messages to 'sell' a government programme to different stakeholders. It has been shown that the understanding of communication in EE is based on the assumption that collaborative governance is not communicated but it is rather communication itself. Walking the talk and talking the walk coincide. The analysis has shown the difficulties and contradictions that arise in day-to-day practice when implementing this approach, and more specifically, when channelling messages to different stakeholders via institutional relations, the media and digital communication. The following elements appear to be crucial: solid narratives for aligning different stakeholders around common goals; segmenting the public and looking for their feedback; combining distributed and shared power with the necessary consistent coordination of communication among different and sometimes divergent actors; engaging the media's attention with policies which are mainly based on intangible aspects; and avoiding the risk of instrumentalising the initiative through self-promoting communication. Finally, a key challenge for building collaborative governance is that of combining substance with presentation, or in other words, of addressing gaps between real achievements and perceived achievements. To the extent that unseen collaborative governance may not exist, building collaborative governance entails placing emphasis on actions, facts and actual performance, but also and just as importantly on putting the initiative on the stage.

2.3. The endless challenge of looking for results, achievements and outcomes

Assessing a governmental reform, as can be derived from the multiple suggestions and ideas included in Workshop 3 as well as in the scholars' comments, is an endless endeavour which grasps the attention of both practitioners and scholars.

Evaluation is needed not only to account for outcomes, but also and first of all for self-understanding of what is being done. Therefore, evaluating entails including one's own organisation as one of the end-users of the evaluation.

Evaluating also entails taking into account not only direct but also indirect effects, being cautious about the awareness rates of the government initiative, collecting quantitative and qualitative data, and assessing relationships.

An overall conclusion about evaluating CG is that major attention has to be paid to assessing intangible outcomes: dialogue improvement, alignment, conflict management, legitimacy, leadership, citizen engagement, and trust, among others. One of the key challenges is therefore to make tangible the intangible, meaning to find metrics and objective indicators for intangible outcomes. This challenge implies registering gaps between real achievements and perceived achievements, as well as demonstrating the extent to which intangible resources actually transform tangible realities.

One key intangible outcome of CG is trust. Looking at trust requires putting the trust variable not only at the end, but also as a precondition for CG interventions, differentiating trust in politics from trust in public institutions, looking not only at self-reported trusting attitudes but also at trusting behaviours, and combining the emotional with the rational dimension. Here it is suggested to conduct survey experiments to get at causation; to do a difference-in-differences analysis of trust before and after EE, comparing outcomes in the region with those from other close regions; to use dynamic performance governance as a learning-oriented framework to performance governance; and to run analyses of alternatives.

Overall, and to the extent that CG transforms reality (or at least it attempts to do so), new ways of evaluating that capture transformed realities appear to be necessary.

3.   Looking at collaborative governance through a trust lens

The discussion on the causal interaction between governance and trust is complicated since trust as social capital is needed to develop effective governance, but also, as a consequence of effective governance, trust is a key objective. As such, trust is cause and effect of good-better-best but certainly, one hopes, of effective governance.

3.1. Trust and its different drivers and sources of trustworthiness

A consolidated map of the different drivers and sources of trustworthiness results in four key components, which can be given different labels according to the authors, but which can be clustered and summarised as ability, benevolence, integrity and participation (Colquitt *et al.*, 2007; Dietz, 2011; Lewicki *et al.*, 1998; OECD, 2022). These four dimensions correspond to the OECD trust model, which refers to reliability, responsiveness, openness, integrity and equal treatment, including political voice (OECD, 2022). Most of the research is based on trust of individuals in other individuals or in organisations and institutions and is therefore also relevant for our discussion on CG (Mayer *et al.*, 1995; Rousseau *et al.*, 1998). In line with EE, the OECD 2021 trust-survey confirms the importance of building trust in institutions to reinforce our democracies; it also shows the relevance of inclusion/exclusion for trust building (OECD, 2022).

Ability is about competences which are experienced and perceived. The bottom line of this debate is about the ability and capacity, about the reliability and responsiveness, to solve problems and deliver what is expected or promised. In a context of realising the 17 SDGs, the question arises whether the public sector is able to solve these problems by realising these objectives. There is a general understanding that this is not really the case and therefore collaboration is necessary between levels of government and with society. It is therefore also remarkable that SDG17 is about partnerships and cooperation. In this sense, CG becomes a SDG by itself, not just a tool or mechanism, but a system feature to ensure a global sustainable system (CEPA, 2018). The initiative looked at in this book shows that collaboration between different levels of government and with society might have an impact on the development of the 2030 Agenda for sustainability (see Appendix 9 for information about the contribution of EE to this agenda).

Benevolence is about a general experience and perception of goodwill, openness, fair and equal treatment by those in charge and in control, who do the right things in the right way, which means certainly and also respecting the rule of law and democratic decision-making. It is probably easier to assess 'benevolence' of all actors involved when CG is in place. By collaborating it is possible to observe and push for a benevolent culture which then becomes more trustworthy.

Integrity is also a crucial driver of trust. This is part of a logic of appropriateness, not just at the individual level of fraud and corruption, but also at the organisational level with a culture of service, openness and transparency, responsibility and accountability, fairness and honesty. Finally, it is also about integrity at the policy level by having inclusion, not exclusion from policies, as a tangible criterion. CG probably allows for more checks, formally but also informally, for integrity at the individual, organisational and policy level. This probably contributes to a general conviction that CG is a system that has (potentially) more integrity, and something of this kind should be taken into account when systematic assessment is done for EE.

A final element of trustworthiness is the feeling, experience and perception of inclusion through participation. A large part of certain target groups and populations feel the opposite and disconnect or get disconnected from our systems. One important aspect of participation as inclusion is access to services, which is not obvious for major policies such as health, education or justice (OECD, 2021b). Given CG's ambition to actively involve different groups of citizens, one could assume that CG, through participation, will (potentially and conditionally) boost levels of trust.

In larger and more fragmented systems, with actors that are unfamiliar with one another, institution-based trust is essential. This macro concept almost becomes a cultural feature of formal and informal norms and rules which affect attitudes and behaviours of citizens. This culture of trust in rules and their related institutions (or neo-institutions) differs significantly between countries, and sometimes also between regions in a country. CG will be impacted by different levels of institutional trust, since trusting rules and hierarchies also defines and frames these collaborations.

There is also a calculus-based trust, which is more utilitarian. A CG calculus-based trust implies and expects that collaborations will result in better services (Rousseau *et al.*, 1998). Finally, relationship-based trust refers to concrete interpersonal sources, and is also crucial in partnerships to develop policies and deliver services (Oomsels & Bouckaert, 2014). CG will benefit from these relation-based trust drivers and, as is shown in the next section, relationships are one of the predominant sources of trust in EE.

3.2.   Some data on EE and trust

While there is not yet data on trust and *Etorkizuna Eraikiz* which allow for a full account of the levels of trust associated with this initiative, the following comments can be made based on some quantitative and qualitative data that has been collected.

In surveys in Western liberal democracies, trust levels are in general higher for local governments than for central governments. Some of the reasons for this are the proximity of local government, but also the typology of tangible services delivered by local government (Bouckaert, 2023). Survey data collected by the *Sociómetro* (the PCG's unit surveying Gipuzkoan citizens) corroborate this: the level of trust in the municipality is the highest, and it declines as the level of government goes up (the *Diputación Foral de Gipuzkoa* is next, followed by the government of the autonomous community; finally, the central national government is at the lowest level of trust). There is also quantitative data that show that people aware of the *Etorkizuna Eraikiz* government initiative rate the institution higher in terms both of performance and of trust. These people also score higher in items looking at political interest and commitment, as well as at trust in other institutions. The question of causality remains about whether it is that being aware of EE leads citizens to rate institutions higher, or the opposite, that trusting citizens are more prone to be informed about these kinds of initiative.

There are also qualitative data collected with semi-structured interviews with different actors (politicians, civil servants and civil organisations) from EE, in which interviewees were asked about their relation to (dis)trust in the project: major drivers, obstacles, drawbacks and expectations (Barandiarán, Canel & Bouckaert, 2022). Analysis of the data reveals the development of strongly shared narratives and a normative framework about the concept, goals and benefits of collaborative governance, with special emphasis on the benefit of collaboration and participation. It shows also that relationships worked as a predominant source of trust over rules and structures; relationships as a trust source predominate even over calculus: to trust, participants seem to require a strong belief in the project by those in charge of it, rather than individual rewards.

4. Some conditions and mechanisms to replicate CG: pracademic lessons from EE

There is a significant literature on so-called best practices. The general fascination for these databases of best practices is obviously to be inspired, to learn and in some cases to replicate them. Unfortunately, best practices do not travel well, since there are contingencies which trigger the question of what are important and what are unimportant similarities and differences. In general, it is clear that blind copy-pasting is never a good idea. In most of these cases, these 'solutions' are not the right answers to the questions, or implementation is not possible because of differences in terms of starting points, resources and culture.

However, it makes sense to look at good-better-best practices in a comparative way to define conditions for 'replication' in some way. The 'replication' strategy could be based on principles or projects, it could be generic or specific, it could be based on content or on process. Our ambition is to present some mechanisms which we have been able to observe in the EE reform programme, and which we think are relevant for other liberal democracies within the OECD, and certainly in the EU, ranging from local to central government.

As was discussed in the workshops, the Basque Gipuzkoa region has its specificities in terms of its history, culture, size, wealth and population.

Nevertheless, some mechanisms emerge which help us understand the conditions under which collaborative governance could be part of the solution to change and upgrade the nature of our democratic systems to keep these functional, legitimate and trustworthy for the future. In this sense, collaborative governance will be part of the solution to our systemic challenges. Furthermore, it is pracademic conviction that collaborative governance will help realise the 17 Sustainable Development Goals within a democratic framework.

The following are hypothetical concluding sentences, and in this sense might work as propositions for further research. They synthesise what has emerged from the chapters, the interaction between scholars and practitioners at the workshops, and the scholars' comments. The sentences have been clustered around three governance levels: macro (the system), meso (policies), and micro (management). We present the sentences with a brief comment on the rationale.

4.1. Macro governance and the system

1) *The stronger the history of social capital and collaboration in civil society, the higher the chances of collaborative governance*

A path-dependency of cooperatives makes it possible to refer to historical good experiences and to extrapolate. However, CG is more than just some collaboration. It also requires the whole system to be aligned to a democratic culture of deliberation, decision-making and cooperation.

2) *Interiorising a new logic of collaborative governance requires developing a shared vision between the major political factions beyond elections*

Changing a culture takes time. To ensure an accumulating, sustainable and trustworthy practice of CG, it is essential that democratic majorities and oppositions take ownership of the new culture and practice, including beyond elections. Societal pressure for longer time cycles should push political pressure for election-based shorter time cycles.

3) *The more political and societal actors consider collaborative governance desirable and feasible, the higher the chances of collaborative governance*

One of the challenges is to increase the conviction that CG is desirable and also feasible. This means that thought experiments and historical examples should develop concrete cases in which 'solutions' are more sustainable and effective when made and implemented in a collaborative context than in a purely hierarchical way by the public sector.

4) *The more non-political actors are included in the political process, the higher the chances of collaborative governance*

Involving non-political actors in the political process allows for building another logic, as well as mutual understanding and trust, and creating shared ownership.

5) *A strong vision of and commitment to collaborative governance is necessary but not sufficient; there is also an urgent need to systemically and systematically institutionalise the inclusion and alignment of different stakeholders*

To avoid an off-and-on experience, it is important to create shared and accepted standard operating procedures which make common practices irreversible.

6) *Redistribution of power by empowered stakeholders for collaborative govern-ance should be considered*

Functional power sharing for effective governance depends on strong institu-tions, lower levels of mission, a voluntary base, experience of participants, existing diffused sources of power, and perceived cost–benefit calculations (Run *et al.*, 2018). However, there are still fundamental pending questions on the ultimate checks and balances between the executive and the legislative for ultimate responsibility and accountability. In addition, the changing role of political parties in CG models remains unsolved and needs to be addressed.

7) *Collaborative governance will be more sustainable and effective when there is not just and only a focus on a logic of consequences/results but more importantly and first of all a logic of appropriateness*

Demonstrating 'better' results in service delivery and policies is an obvious crucial component of the performance of governance systems. However, the legitimacy and trustworthiness of governance systems increasingly and crucially depend on the appropriateness of systems. Logics of appropriateness are about cultures of public values and general interest, transparency, fairness, inclusion, responsibility-related accountability, respect for diversity, etc.

When collaboration is brought to the core of governance, appropriateness becomes a prime focus.

8) *Collaborative governance needs a 'hierarchy' (like a 'rule of law'-driven democratic state) with 'markets' and 'networks'*

Effective CG cannot just rely on hierarchy, or just on the market (New Public Management), or just on networks (New Public Governance) as driving mechanisms. To combine and ensure inclusive service delivery, effective governance of chronic crises, and functional social and digital innovation, a neo-Weberian state model should be considered since it shapes a democratic and rule-of-law-based system which regulates and stimulates markets and networks. CG needs also meta-governance to use its authority in a democratic way within the rule of law to prevent the authoritarian version of hierarchy.

4.2. Meso governance and policies

9) *The more local knowledge is mobilised through dialogue, the greater the sustainable societal ownership of collaborative governance*

CG requires a lot of implicit, or tacit, and explicit (academic) knowledge on how the system really works. This requires combining and sharing different types of knowledge on what could work and on what will not work and why, by organising active interactions of, for example, action research (by universities), action learning, open platforms of communication and dialogue like think tanks, and experimentation.

10) *The more proactively local universities foster knowledge governance, the higher the chances of collaborative governance*

Universities are key players in designing, implementing and evaluating knowledge about policies, as well as the ways to govern this knowledge (experiments, surveys, action research and so on). As independent institutions, universities have the legitimacy to foster collaborative governance, as well as the capacity to contribute to the pracademic approach to building collaborative governance.

11) Within the policy cycle (design, decision, implementation and evaluation), the sooner key societal actors are involved, the higher the chances of collaborative governance

Often the collaborative part of governance comes too late in the cycle. If this involvement of societal actors is to be convincing and not just cosmetic, it is crucial to involve citizens and society as soon as possible.

12) The stronger the collaborative interaction and alignment of different levels of government, especially local governments, the stronger the collaborative governance

Local governments have a high level of proximity to citizens and stakeholders and therefore are crucial in CG. A value chain of service policies and delivery crosses various levels of government that should be connected. Multi-level collaborative governance is as strong as the weakest part of the chain.

13) The more interactive, distributed and collaborative leadership is, the higher the chances of collaborative governance

In CG it is not just about individuals (politicians, administration, society), but it is more about institutional and organisational leadership in a specific policy field. CG implies that a societal organisation could also take the lead in an interactive, distributed and collaborative way, but always within a framework of responsibility and accountability.

14) The better horizontal accountability is organised, the higher the chances of collaborative governance

Shared, distributed and collaborative leadership emphasises the horizontal relationships of accountability and shared responsibility. Formal leaders create conditions for participants to make meaningful contributions through collaboration and cultivate emergent leadership at different levels. Involved actors thus become leaders themselves within their sphere of influence. Developing this type of leadership at all levels of the collaborative governance system also requires visible, strong formal leaders with political and moral authority.

4.3. Micro governance and organisation

15) The higher the levels of internal and of external active collaborative listening and learning, the higher the chances of collaborative governance

Listening and learning is about feedback mechanisms which should impact processes. Active listening and learning is not just about waiting and hopefully seeing, but about proactively looking for this feedback. There should be coherence between internal and external since a CG regime has some blurred borderlines between inside and outside. The inside dimension is within the administration and also between politics and administration. The outside dimension is the politico-administrative system and society. Learning is not just about single-loop learning on reaching an objective, it is more about second-loop learning (changing and adjusting the objectives), and even about meta-learning (learning how to learn from one another in a two-way direction). In this sense CG is governmental social innovation.

16) The more and the sooner civil servants have a culture of change allowing empowered stakeholders, the higher the chances of collaborative governance

It takes time for a cultural change in the civil service. A CG administration requires all levels of civil servants to be included at the early stages of policy-making, as well as at the early stages of a CG reform.

17) The more different forms of communication for different purposes and different target groups, the higher the chances of collaborative governance

CG entails establishing relationships with new, diverse and probably mutually contradicting audiences. For these relationships to be established and enhanced, it appears to be key to segment the public, as well as to craft and channel the message accordingly. It is also key to look for the audiences' feedback in order to be better prepared to attune to their needs and expectations, as well as to develop the mutual understanding which is at the foundation of collaboration.

18) Communicating collaborative governance is more about acting together than about sending messages

Developing collaborative governance leads public authorities to interact more frequently with stakeholders, and this may transform an initial 'selling' communication attitude into a 'listening' attitude. The role of communication is thus more related to inviting people to act together and to undertake joint action than to unidirectionally inform about a project. By acting together communication develops; in other words, collaborative governance is in itself communication.

19) *The more tangible the intangible outcomes of collaborative projects, the easier it is to involve all target groups in collaborating*

Most CG outcomes are intangibles (legitimacy, dialogue, trust, etc.), and the interaction that is at the foundation of collaboration develops more easily when tangible benefits are visible. Communication should aim at showing how intangible outcomes help to transform realities.

20) *The more the making and the telling come together in communication, the higher the chances of collaborative governance.*

Communicating for building CG requires combining substance with presentation. Collaborative governance may not exist if it is unseen. Building CG entails placing emphasis on actions, facts and actual performance, but also, and just as importantly, on putting the initiative on the stage. The making and the telling come together in a CG approach.

5. Final remark

Having stated all the above hypothetical sentences, we would like to end this concluding chapter by asserting that collaborative governance is not a panacea. The list of challenging conditions for today's democracies is long: increasing polarisation; the changing nature of political parties; tensions between the executive, legislative and judicial powers; easier conditions for the dissemination of fake news; increasing populism; and so on. What we have learned from this close interaction between scholars and practitioners is that even when CG has the ambition to address all these key challenges in society, it is not able to solve all the problems. It may solve some, but may even cause new ones. CG is very conditional, as the 20 sentences above show.

EE has shown creativity in tackling some of the issues. It has operated as a framework not only for learning, but more importantly for acting. What we have experienced during the process of developing and looking together at this *Etorkizuna Eraikiz* initiative is that the more exposed to it people are, the more they are persuaded of its potentialities. In this sense, it could be stated that CG helps with moving from a self-fulfilling prophecy to a self-fulfilling practice. In other words, we have seen that by getting involved in the project, people jump from 'I/you govern collaboratively' to 'we all govern collaboratively', hence making this a CG approach spread over the system. But we are very much aware that there is still work in progress. By placing Chillida's 'embracement' sculpture on the cover of this book, we want to express our wish for CG to remain on this pracademic agenda for the coming years.

Appendices

Appendix 1. *Etorkizuna Eraikiz* website
Link to the *Etorkizuna Eraikiz* website homepage:
https://www.gip.eus/etorkizunaeraikiz

Appendix 2. The region of Gipuzkoa
Link to full information on the characteristics of the Gipuzkoa region:
https://www.gip.eus/gipuzkoa

Appendix 3. *Etorkizuna Eraikiz* projects
Link to *Etorkizuna Eraikiz* information on the projects, clustered by
citizens and experimental projects:
https://www.gip.eus/projects

Appendix 4. *Etorkizuna Eraikiz* listening space
Link to the EE listening space, which contains information
on think tanks:
https://www.gip.eus/listeningspace

Appendix 5. *Etorkizuna Eraikiz* reference centres
Link to the 11 *Etorkizuna Eraikiz* reference centres:
https://www.gip.eus/centres

Appendix 6. Status of *Etorkizuna Eraikiz*
Link to information about the status of achievements
of *Etorkizuna Eraikiz*:
https://www.gip.eus/status

Appendix 7. Report from the New Political Culture Deliberation Group
Link to the document New Political Culture Deliberation Group (2022).
*Building a New Political Culture in Gipuzkoa. Concepts, methodology and
experiences.* Donostia: Diputación Foral de Gipuzkoa:
https://www.gip.eus/documents

Appendix 8. *Etorkizuna Eraikiz* journal

Link to the *Etorkizuna Eraikiz* journal, *Orain & Etorkizuna*:
https://www.gip.eus/journal

Appendix 9. *Etorkizuna Eraikiz* and the 2030 SDGs Agenda

Link to information about the contribution of *Etorkizuna Eraikiz*
to the 2030 SDGs Agenda:
https://www.gip.eus/2030agenda

References

Acaroglu, L. (2017). *Tools for Systems Thinkers: The 6 Fundamental Concepts of Systems Thinking.* Retrieved from https://medium.com/disruptive-design/tools-for-systems-thinkers-the-6-fundamental-concepts-of-systems-thinking-379cdac3dc6a, 12 July 2022.

Agger, A., Damgaard, B., Krogh, A. H. & Sørensen, E. (Eds.) (2015). *Collaborative governance and public innovation in Northern Europe.* UAE: Bentham Science Publishers.

Agranoff, R. (2006). Inside collaborative networks: Ten lessons for public managers. *Public Administration Review,* 66(s1), 56–65.

Alburquerque, F. (2012). Desarrollo territorial. In Orkestra (Ed.), *Gipuzkoa Sarean Working Document.* Donostia-San Sebastián: Orkestra.

Angrist, J. D. & Pischke, J. S. (2014). *Mastering Metrics: The path from cause to effect.* Princeton: Princeton University Press.

Ansell, C. (2000). The networked polity: Regional development in Western Europe. *Governance,* 13(2), 279–291.

Ansell, C. (2008). Network institutionalism. In S. Binder, R. Rhodes & B. Rockman (Eds.), *The Oxford Handbook of Political Institutions* (pp. 75–89). Oxford: Oxford University Press.

Ansell, C. (2021). Coping with conceptual pluralism: Reflections on concept formation. *Public Performance and Management Review,* 44(5), 1118–1139.

Ansell, C. & Gash, A. (2008). Collaborative governance in theory and practice. *Journal of Public Administration Research and Theory,* 18(4), 543–571.

Ansell, C. & Gash, A. (2018). Collaborative platforms as a governance strategy. *Journal of Public Administration Research and Theory,* 28(1), 16–32.

Ansell, C., Sørensen, E. & Torfing, J. (2022). *Co-Creation for Sustainability: The UN SDGs and the Power of Local Partnerships.* Bingley: Emerald Publishing.

Ansell, C. & Torfing, J. (2015). How Does Collaborative Governance Scale? *Policy & Politics,* 48(3), 315–329.

Ansell, C. & Torfing, J. (2021). *Public Governance as Co-creation. Strategy for Revitalizing the Public Sector and Rejuvenating Democracy.* Cambridge: Cambridge University Press.

Aranguren, M. J. & Larrea, M. (2015). Territorial strategy: Deepening in the 'how'? In J. M. Valdaliso & J. R. Wilson (Eds.), *Strategies for Shaping Territorial Competitiveness* (pp. 55–72). London: Routledge.

Arellano, D., Sánchez, J. & Retana, B. (2014). ¿Una o varios tipos de gobernanza? *Cuadernos de Gobierno y Administración Pública,* 1(2), 117–137.

Arnstein, S. R. (1969). A ladder of citizen participation. *Journal of the American Institute of Planners,* 35(4), 216–224.

Arrona, A. & Larrea, M. (2018). Soft resistance, balancing relationality and criticality to institutionalize action research for territorial development. In K. Bartels & J. Wittmayer (Eds.), *Action Research in Policy Analysis: Critical and Relational Approaches to Sustainability Transitions* (pp. 134–152). Abingdon: Routledge.

Bang, H. P. & Dryberg, T. B. (2000). *Governance, Self-Representation and Democratic Imagination*. London: Routledge.

Barandiarán, X. (Ed.) (2022). *O&E: Orain eta Etorkizuna (Etorkizuna Eraikiz* journal), 1.

Barandiarán, X. (2022). General framework for transformation of the political culture: *Etorkizuna Eraikiz*. In Diputación Foral de Gipuzkoa (Ed.), *Building a New Political Culture in Gipuzkoa: Concepts, Methodology and Experiences* (pp. 9–13). Donostia: Diputación Foral de Gipuzkoa.

Barandiarán, X., Canel, M. J. & Bouckaert, G. (2022). ¿Qué mueve a confiar en la gobernanza colaborativa? Análisis de un programa gubernamental en el País Vasco. *Revista Española de Ciencia Política*, 60, 251-275.

Barandiarán, X. & Korta, K. (2011). *Capital Social y Valores en Gipuzkoa: Balance y Líneas Estratégicas de Actuación*. Donostia: Diputación Foral de Gipuzkoa.

Barandiarán, X., Murphy, A. & Canel, M. J. (2022). ¿Qué aporta la escucha al Capital Social? Lecciones de un proceso de aprendizaje de líderes públicos. *Gestión y Política Pública*, 31(1), 1–30.

Bastien, T. D. & Hostager, T. J. (1988). Jazz as a process of organizational innovation. *Communication Research*, 15(5), 582–602.

Bates, R. (1988). Contra contractarianism: some reflections on the New Institutionalism. *Politics & Society*, 16(2–3), 387–401.

Batory, A. & Svensson, S. (2017). Transforming into Open, Innovative and Collaborative Governments. Literature and report review, Work Package 2, Deliverable 2.1.

Batory, A. & Svensson, S. (2019). The fuzzy concept of collaborative governance: A systematic review of the state of the art. *Central European Journal of Public Policy*, 13(2), 28–39.

Bauman, Z. (2001). *En Busca de la Política*. Ciudad de México: Fondo de Cultura Económica.

Bhattacherjee, A. (2012). *Social Science Research*. University of South Florida, Global Text Project.

Bianchi, C. (2016). *Dynamic Performance Management*. Berlin: Springer International Publishing.

Bianchi, C. (2021). Fostering sustainable community outcomes through policy networks: A dynamic performance governance approach. In J. W. Meek (Ed.), *Handbook of Collaborative Public Management* (pp. 333–356). Cheltenham: Edward Elgar Publishing.

Bianchi, C. (2022). Enhancing policy design and sustainable community outcomes through collaborative platforms based on a Dynamic Performance Management & Governance approach. In B. G. Peters & G. Fontaine (Eds.), *Handbook of Policy Design* (pp. 411–433). Cheltenham: Edward Elgar Publishing.

Bianchi, C., Bereciartua, P., Vignieri, V. & Cohen, A. (2019). Enhancing urban brownfield regeneration to pursue sustainable community outcomes through Dynamic Performance Governance. *International Journal of Public Administration*, 44(2), 100–114.

Bianchi, C., Nasi, G. & Rivenbark, W. C. (2021). Implementing collaborative governance: Models, experiences, and challenges. *Public Management Review*, 23(11), 1581–1589.

Bingham, L. B. (2011). Collaborative governance. In M. Bevir (Ed.), *The SAGE Handbook of Governance* (pp. 386–401). London: Sage Publications.

Bingham, L. B., Nabatchi, T. & O'Leary, R. (2005). The new governance: Practices and processes for stakeholder and citizen participation in the work of government. *Public Administration Review*, 65(5), 547–558.

Blake, R. & Haroldsen, E. (1975). *A Taxonomy of Concepts in Communication*. New York: Nusting House.

Bolden, R. (2011). Distributed leadership in organizations: A review of theory and research. *International Journal of Management Reviews*, 13(3), 251–269.

Bossel, H. (1994). *Modeling and Simulation*. Boca Raton, FL: CRC Press, Taylor & Francis Group.

Botan, C. H. & Taylor, M. (2004). Public Relations: State of the field. *Journal of Communication*, 54, 645–661.

Bouckaert, G. (2023). Effective local governance. In F. Teles (Ed.), *Handbook on Local and Regional Governance* (pp. 27–39). Cheltenham: Edward Elgar Publishing.

Bouckaert, G. & Halligan, J. (2007). *Managing Performance: International Comparisons*. New York: Routledge.

Bourgon, J. (2011). *A New Synthesis of Public Administration: Serving in the 21st Century*. Washington, DC: McGill Queen's Press.

Bowden, J. (2009). Customer engagement: A framework for assessing customer-brand relationships. The case of the restaurant industry. *Journal of Hospitality Marketing & Management*, 18(6), 574–596.

Bradbury, H. (2022). *How to do Action Research for Transformations, at a Time of Eco-Social Crisis*. London: Edward Elgar Publishing.

Brogan, W. L. (1985). *Model Control Theory*. Upper Saddle River, NJ: Prentice Hall.

Brook, C. (2022). What's the use of action learning? *Action Learning*, 19(1), 1–2.

Brown, J. & Isaacs, D. (2005). The World Cafe shaping our futures through conversations that matter (1st ed.). Oakland, CA: Berrett-Koehler Publishers.

Bryson, J., Crosby, B. & Stone, M. (2015). Designing and implementing cross-sector collaborations: Needed and challenging. *Public Administration Review*, 75(5), 647–663.

Bryson, J., Crosby, B. & Stone, M. (2006). The design and implementation of cross-sector collaborations: Propositions from the literature. *Public Administration Review*, 66(1), 44–55.

Bryson, J. M., Cunningham, G. L. & Lokkesmoe, K. J. (2002). What to do when stakeholders matter? The case of problem formulation for the African American men project of Hennepin County, Minnesota. *Public Administration Review*, 62(5), 568-584.

Burns, T. & Flam, H. (1989). *The Shaping of Social Organization*. London: Sage Publications.

Canel, M. J. (1999). *Comunicación Política. Técnicas y Estrategias para la Sociedad de la Información*. Madrid: Tecnos.

Canel, M. J. (2010). *Comunicación de las Instituciones Públicas*. Madrid: Tecnos.

Canel, M. J., Barandiarán, X. & Murphy, A. (2019). Learning from society to build intangible value for territories: A Basque Country case of citizen engagement. Paper presented at the

2019 Annual Conference of the European Group of Public Administration (EGPA), Belfast, September.

Canel, M. J., Barandiarán, X. & Murphy, A. (2022). What does learning by listening bring to citizen engagement? Lessons from a government program. *Public Relations Review*, 48(1), 1–8.

Canel, M. J. & Luoma-aho, V. (2019). *Public Sector Communication. Closing Gaps between Public Sector Organizations and Citizens*. Wiley-Blackwell.

Canel, M. J., Luoma-aho, V. & Barandiarán, X. (2020). Public Sector Communication and publicly valuable intangible assets. In V. Luoma-aho & M. J. Canel (Eds.), *Handbook of Public Sector Communication* (pp. 100–114). New York: Wiley-Blackwell.

Canel, M. J. & Sanders, K. (2013). En busca de un modelo para el estudio de instituciones. In E. Gutiérrez García (Ed.), *Tendencias Emergentes en la Comunicación de Instituciones* (pp. 29–51). Barcelona: UOC.

Carroll, B. & Smolović, O. (2018). Mapping the aesthetics of leadership development through participant perspectives. *Management Learning*, 49(2), 187–203.

Carstensen, H. & Bason, C. (2012). Powering collaborative policy innovation: Can innovation labs help? *The Innovation Journal*, 17(2), article 4.

Castoriadis, C. (1983). *La Institución Imaginaria de la Sociedad*. Barcelona: Maxi-Tusquets.

CEPA (2018). Principles of effective governance for sustainable development. Official Record, 2018, Suppl. No. 24, E/2018/44-E/C.16/2018/8, para. 31. Economic and Social Council, UN, New York.

Chen, Q., Min, C., Zhang, W., Wang, G., Ma, X. & Evans, R. (2020). Unpacking the black box: How to promote citizen engagement through government social media during the COVID-19 crisis. *Computers in Human Behavior,* 110, 106380.

Chivers, M. & Pedler, M. (2004). *D.I.Y. Handbook for Action Learners*. London: Mersey Care NHS Foundation Trust.

Clarke, K. & Primo, D. (2012). *A Model Discipline. Political Science and the Logic of Representation*. Oxford: Oxford University Press.

Colquitt, J. A., Scott, B. A. A. & Lepine, J. A. A. (2007). Trust, trustworthiness, and trust propensity: A meta-analytic test of their unique relationships with risk taking and job performance. *Journal of Applied Psychology: An International Review*, 92(4), 909–927.

Cooper, T., Bryer, T. & Meek, J. (2006). Citizen-centered collaborative public management. *Public Administration Review*, 66, 76–88.

Costamagna, P. & Larrea, M. (2018). *Facilitative Actors of Territorial Development. A Social Construction-Based Approach*. Bilbao: Deusto University Press.

Crosby, B. & Bryson, J. (2010). Integrative leadership and the creation and maintenance of cross-sector collaborations. *The Leadership Quarterly*, 2, 211–230.

Crosby, B., Hart, P. & Torfing, J. (2017). Public value creation through collaborative innovation. *Public Management Review*, 19(5), 655–669.

Crue Universidades Españolas (2021). *Universidad 2030. Propuesta para el Debate*. Retrieved from https://www.crue.org/wp-content/uploads/2021/11/CRUE_UNIVERSIDAD2030_VER-SION-DIGITAL.pdf, 26 May 2022.

Delli Carpini, M., Cook, F. & Jacobs, L. (2004). Public deliberation, discursive participation, and citizen engagement. *Annual Review of Political Science*, 7, 315–344.

Dewey, J. (1939 [1988]). Experience, knowledge and value: A rejoiner. In J. A. Boydston (Ed.), *The Later Works of John Dewey, 1925–1953* (pp. 3–90). Carbondale, IL/Edwardsville, IL: Southern Illinois University Press.

Dietz, G. (2011). Going back to the source: Why do people trust each other? *Journal of Trust Research*, 1(2), 215–222.

DiMaggio, P. & Powell, W. (1983). The iron cage revisited: Institutional ssomorphism and collective rationality in organizational fields. *American Sociological Review*, 48(2), 147–160.

Diputación Foral de Gipuzkoa (2015). *Gipuzkoa Sarean. Bidean*. Donostia: Diputación Foral de Gipuzkoa.

Diputación Foral de Gipuzkoa (2020a). Etorkizuna Eraikiz Think Tank, New Political Culture Deliberation Group, Work Group's monthly meeting report, 6 September.

Diputación Foral de Gipuzkoa (2020b). *Etorkizuna Eraikiz. Lurralde Garapenerako Laborategia. 10 Urte Lankidetzazko Gobernantza Eraikitzen* [Etorkizuna Eraikiz. Territorial development laboratory. Ten years building collaborative governance]. Donostia: Diputación Foral de Gipuzkoa.

Diputación Foral de Gipuzkoa (2021a). Anticipatory Innovation Governance in Gipuzkoa. Internal report (OECD/OPSI), Paris.

Diputación Foral de Gipuzkoa (2021b). The status of *Etorkizuna Eraikiz* (2016–2020). Internal report.

Diputación Foral de Gipuzkoa (2022). *Etorkizuna Eraikiz* website. Retrieved from https://www. gipuzkoa.eus/en/web/council/etorkizuna-eraikiz, 25 October. 2022.

Doberstein, C. (2016). Designing collaborative governance decision-making in search of a 'collaborative advantage'. *Public Management Review*, 18(6), 819–841.

Donahue, J. D., Zeckhauser, R. J. & Breyer, S. (2012). *Collaborative Governance: Private Roles for Public Goals in Turbulent Times*. Princeton: Princeton University Press.

Dorf, M. & Sabel, C. (1998). *A Constitution of Democratic Experimentalism*. Cornell Law Faculty Publications, Paper 120.

Douglas, S. & Ansell, C. (2021). Getting a grip on the performance of collaborations: Examining collaborative performance regimes and collaborative performance summits. *Public Administration Review*, 81(5), 951–961.

Drath, W. H., McCauley, C. D., Palus, C. J., Van Velsor, E., O'Connor, P. M. G. & McGuire, J. B. (2008). Direction, alignment, commitment: Toward a more integrative ontology of leadership. *The Leadership Quarterly*, 19(6), 635–653.

Dupuy, C. & Defacqz, S. (2022). Citizens and the legitimacy outcomes of collaborative governance. An administrative burden perspective. *Public Management Review*, 24(5), 743–763.

Easterby-Smith, M., Araujo, L. & Burgoyne, J. (1999). *Organizational Learning and the Learning Organization : Developments in Theory and Practice*. London: Sage Publications.

Elkjaer, B. (2022). Taking stock of 'Organizational Learning': Looking back and moving forward. *Management Learning*, 53(3), 582–604.

Elster, J. (1989). Social norms and economic theory. *Journal of Economic Perspectives*, 3(4), 99–117.

Emerson, K. & Nabatchi, T. (2015a). *Collaborative Governance Regimes*. Washington, DC: Georgetown University Press.

Emerson, K. & Nabatchi, T. (2015b). Evaluating the productivity of collaborative governance regimes: A performance matrix. *Public Performance & Management Review*, 38(4), 717–747.

Emerson, K., Nabatchi, T. & Balogh, S. (2012). An integrative framework for collaborative governance. *Journal of Public Administration Research and Theory*, 22(1), 1–29.

Etorkizuna Eraikiz (2022). *Building a New Political Culture in Gipuzkoa. Concepts, Methodology and Experiences*. Donostia: Gipuzkoako Foru Aldundia.

Fagen, R. (1966). *Politics and Communication*. Boston: Little Brown & Co.

Florini, A. & Pauli, M. (2018). Collaborative governance for the Sustainable Development Goals. *Asia and the Pacific Policy Studies*, 5(3), 583–598.

Forcese, D. & Richer, S. (1973). *Social Research Methods*. Englewood Cliffs, NJ: Prentice Hall.

Forrester, J. W. (1994). Policies, decisions and information sources for modeling. In J. D. Morecroft & J. D. Sterman (Eds.), *Modeling for Learning Organizations*. Portland: Productivity Press.

Freund, J. (2018). *La Esencia de lo Político*. Madrid: Centro de Estudios Políticos y Constitucionales.

Fricke, W., Greenwood, D. J., Larrea, M. & Streck, D. (2022). On social productivity and future perspectives on action research. *International Journal of Action Research*, 18(1), 8–27.

Fukuyama, F. (2015). Why is democracy performing so poorly? *Journal of Democracy*, 26(1), 11–20.

Gaber, I. (2009). Exploring the paradox of liberal democracy: more political communications equals less public trust. *The Political Quarterly*, 80(1), 84–91.

Ghaffarzadegan, N., Lyneis, J. & Richardson, G. P. (2011). How small system dynamics models can help the public policy process. *System Dynamics Review*, 27, (1), 22–44.

Gough, D., Oliver, S. & Thomas, J. (2013). *An Introduction to Systematic Reviews*. London: Sage Publications.

Granovetter, M. (1985). Economic action and social structure: The problem of embeddedness. *American Journal of Sociology*, 91(3), 481–510.

Gray, B. (1989). *Collaborating: Finding Common Ground for Multiparty Problems*. San Francisco, CA: Jossey-Bass.

Greenwood, D. & Levin, M. (2007). *Introduction to Action Research* (2nd ed.). Thousand Oaks, CA: Sage Publications.

Greiner, L. (1972). Evolution and revolution as organizations grow. *Harvard Business Review*, 10, 4, 397-409.

Gugu, S. & Dal Molin, M. (2016). Collaborative local cultural governance: What works? The case of cultural districts in Italy. *Administration & Society*, 48(2), 237–262.

Gutiérrez García, E. (2013). *Tendencias Emergentes en la Comunicación de Instituciones*. Barcelona: UOC.

Hale, R., Norgate, C. & Traeger, J. (2018). From nurturing the H in HR to developing the D in OD – systemic benefits where action learning and organisational development combine. *Action Learning*, 15(2), 154–167.

Harmsworth, G., Awatere, S., Robb, M. & Landcare Research (2015). Māori Values and Perspectives to Inform Collaborative Processes. Landcare Research Manaaki Whenua Policy Brief, December.

Hartog, M. (2015). The art of jazz improvisation as an adaptive mechanism for civil servants in complex governance networks. *Applied Research Today*, 8, 72–85.

Hendriks, C. M. (2016). Coupling citizens and elites in deliberative systems: The role of institutional design. *European Journal of Political Research*, 55(1), 43–60.

Hendriks, C. M. & Lees-Marshment, J. (2019). Political leaders and public engagement: The hidden world of informal elite–citizen interaction. *Political Studies*, 67(3), 597–617.

Hjern, B. & Hull, C. (1982). Implementation research as empirical constitutionalism. *European Journal of Political Research*, 10, 105–115.

Hofstad, H., Sørensen, E., Torfing, J. & Vedeld, T. (2021). Leading co-creation for the green shift. *Public Money & Management*, 42, 1–10. DOI: 10.1080/09540962.2021.1992120

Hofstad, H. & Torfing, J. (2015). Collaborative innovation as a tool for environmental, economic and social sustainability in regional governance. *Scandinavian Journal of Public Administration*, 19(4), 49–70.

Huxham, C. & Vangen, S. (2013). *Managing to Collaborate: The Theory and Practice of Collaborative Advantage*. Abingdon: Routledge.

Hynes, W., Lees, M. & Müller, J. (Eds.) (2020). *Systemic Thinking for Policy Making: The Potential of Systems Analysis for Addressing Global Policy Challenges in the 21st Century. New Approaches to Economic Challenges*. Paris: OECD Publishing.

Imperial, M. T. (2022). Life cycle dynamics and developmental processes in collaborative partnerships: Examples from four watersheds in the U.S. *Environmental Management*, 27 August.

Imperial, M. T., Ospina, S., Johnston, E., O'Leary, R., Thomsen, J., Williams, P. & Johnson, S. (2016). Understanding leadership in a world of shared problems: Advancing network governance in large landscape conservation. *Frontiers in Ecology and the Environment*, 14(3), 126–134.

James, O., Jilke, S. & Van Ryzin, G. G. (2017). *Experiments in Public Management Research: Challenges and Contributions*. Cambridge: Cambridge University Press.

Johnston, K. & Taylor, M. (2018). Engagement as communication – pathways, possibilities, and future directions. In K. Johnston & M. Taylor (Eds.), *The Handbook of Communication Engagement* (pp. 1–15). New York: Wiley-Blackwell.

Joignant, A. (2019). *Acting Politics. A Critical Sociology of the Political Field*. Abingdon: Routledge.

Kapucu, N., Yuldashev, F. & Bakiev, E. (2016). Collaborative public management and collaborative governance: Conceptual similarities and differences. *European Journal of Economic and Political Studies*, 2(1), 39–60.

Karlsen, J. & Larrea, M. (2014). *Territorial Development and Action Research: Innovation through Dialogue*. Farnham: Gower.

Kattel, R. & Mazzucato, M. (2018). Mission-oriented innovation policy and dynamic capabilities in the public sector. IIPP Working Paper WP 2018-05.

Kivleniece, I. (2013). Public-private governance, uncertainty and longevity implications: Exploring the developing world's water sector partnerships. Paper presented at the 35th DRUID Celebration Conference, Barcelona, Spain.

Kolb, D. A. (2015). *Experiential Learning. Experience as the Source of Learning and Development.* Englewood Cliffs, NJ: Prentice Hall.

Lane, D. (1994). Modelling as learning: A consultancy methodology for enhancing learning in management teams. In J. D. Morecroft & J. D. Sterman (Eds.), *Modeling for Learning Organizations.* Portland: Productivity Press.

Lapassade, G. (1985). *Grupos, organizaciones e instituciones.* Barcelona: Gedisa.

Larrea, M. (2019). Una metodología para la construcción de gobernanza cooperativa. Compendio de los aprendizajes de una década de experimentación con la investigación acción para el desarrollo territorial en Gipuzkoa. *Cuadernos Orkestra*, 49, n.p.

Larrea, M., Bradbury, H. & Barandiarán, X. (2021). Action research and politics: power, love and inquiry in political transformations. *International Journal of Action Research*, 17(1), 41–58.

Larrea, M., Estensoro, M. & Sisti, E. (2018). The contribution of action research to Industry 4.0. policies: Bringing empowerment and democracy to the economic efficiency arena. *International Journal of Action Research*, 14(2–3), 164–180.

Larrea, M. & Karlsen, J. (2021). Think tanks for a new generation of regional innovation policies. *European Planning Studies*, 30(11), 2334–2351.

Latour, B. (2000). When things strike back: a possible contribution of 'science studies' to the social sciences. *The British Journal of Sociology*, 51(1), 107–123.

Lau, R. & Sears, D. (1986). *Political Cognition.* Hillsdale, NJ: Lawrence Erlbaum Associates.

Lave, C. & March, J. (1993). *An Introduction to Models in the Social Sciences.* Washington, DC: University Press of America.

Lee, S. (2022). When tensions become opportunities: Managing accountability demands in collaborative governance, *Journal of Public Administration Research and Theory*, 32(4), 641–655.

Lee, S. & Ospina, S. M. (2022). A framework for assessing accountability in collaborative governance: A process-based approach. *Perspectives on Public Management and Governance*, 5(1), 63–75.

Lewicki R., McAllister, D. J. H. & Bies, R. J. (1998). Trust and distrust: New relationships and realities. *Academy of Management Review*, 23(3), 438–458.

Lieberman, R. (2002). Ideas, institutions, and political order: Explaining political change. *American Political Science Review*, 96(4), 697–712.

Loge, P. & Caballero, A. (forthcoming 2023). *Uniting Competing Rhetorics of Basque Identity.* Bilbao: Agirre Lehendakaria Center.

Lourau, R. (1979). *El análisis institucional.* Buenos Aires: Amorrortu.

Lovari, A. & Parisi, L. (2015). Listening to digital publics. Investigating citizens' voices and engagement within Italian municipalities' Facebook pages. *Public Relations Review*, 41(2), 205–213.

Luhmann, N. (1988). Familiarity, confidence, trust. In D. Gambetta (Ed.), *Trust. Making and Breaking Cooperative Relations* (pp. 94–107). Oxford: Basil Blackwell.

Luoma-aho, V., Canel, M. J., Bowden, J., Ek, E. & Vainiomäki, V. (2021). Citizen engagement and the Covid-19 mask communication. *Sociologia della Communicazione*, 61, 20–35.

Martín Algarra, M. (2010). *Komunikazioaren teoria: proposamena*. Bilbao: Deustuko Unibertsitateko Argitalpenak. (Original in Spanish, 2008.)

Mayer, R. C., Davies, J. H. & Schoorman, F. D. (1995). An integrative view of organizational trust. *Academy of Management Review*, 20(3), 709–734.

McGee, M. C. (1975). In search of 'the people': A rhetorical alternative. *The Quarterly Journal of Speech*, 61(3), 235–249.

McGuire, M. (2006). Collaborative public management: Assessing what we know and how we know it. *Public Administration Review*, 65(5), 547–558.

Meadow, R. (1980). *Politics as Communication*. Norwood, NJ: Ablex Publishing.

Michels, A. (2016). Innovations in democratic governance: How does citizen participation contribute to a better democracy? *International Review of Administrative Sciences*, 77(2), 275–293.

Milward, H. B. & Provan, K. G. (2006). *A Manager's Guide to Choosing and Using Collaborative Networks*. Washington, DC: IBM Endowment for the Business of Government.

Minder, R. (2016). Chefs' camaraderie lifts Basque cuisine. *The New York Times*, 19 March.

Mintzberg H. (2009). *Managing*. San Francisco, CA: Berrett-Koehler.

Morecraft, J. & Sterman, J. (1994). *Modelling for Learning Organizations*. Abingdon: Routledge.

Morrison, F. (1991). *The Art of Modelling Dynamic Systems*. Mineaola, NY: Dover Publications.

Morse, R. S. (2011). The practice of collaborative governance. *Public Administration Review*, 71(6), 953–957.

Moynihan, D. (2008). *The Dynamics of Performance Management*. Washington, DC: Georgetown University Press.

Mudde, C. (2016). Europe's populist surge: A long time in the making. *Foreign Affairs*, 95(6), 25–30.

Mulgan, G. (2009). *The Art of Public Strategy. Mobilizing Power and Knowledge for the Common Good*. Oxford: Oxford University Press.

Murphy, A. (2009). Collaborative leadership and the importance of place based development. In Z. van Zwanenberg (Ed.), *Leadership for Social Care* (pp. 129–146). London: Jessica Kingsley Publishers.

Murphy, A. & Canel, M. J. (2020). *Manual de Action Learning para Gestores Públicos* [Action Learning Manual for Public Managers]. Madrid: INAP, Instituto Nacional de Admistración Pública.

Murphy, A., Canel, M. J. & Barandiarán, X. (2020). How do public leaders learn from society? A reflexive analysis of action learners. *Action Learning: Research and Practice*, 17(2), 172–185.

Nabatchi, T. (2022). Of Clocks and Clouds: Addressing Public Problems in the 21st Century. Keynote Talk, 16th Transatlantic Dialogue Conference, Roskilde, Denmark, June.

Nabatchi, T. & Leighninger, M. (2015). *Public Participation for 21st Century Democracy*. Hoboken, NJ: Jossey-Bass.

Najam, A. (1995). *Learning from the Literature on Policy Implementation: A Policy Perspective.* Working Paper WP-95-061. Laxenburg, Austria: International Institute for Applied Systems Analysis (IIASA).

Najam, A., Papa, M. & Taiyab, N. (2006). *Global Environmental Governance: A Reform Agenda.* Winnipeg, Canada: International Institute for Sustainable Development (IISD).

Nesta (2022). *A playbook for innovation learning.* Retrieved from https://states-of-change.org/resources/playbook-for-innovation-learning, 12ᵗʰ December 2022.

O&E (2022). *O&E: Orain eta Etorkizuna* (*Etorkizuna Eraikiz* journal).

O'Leary, R. (2014). *Collaborative Governance in New Zealand: Important Choices Ahead.* Wellington, New Zealand: Fulbright New Zealand.

O'Leary, R. & Blomgren Bingham, L. (2007). *A Manager's Guide to Resolving Conflicts in Collaborative Networks.* Washington, DC: IBM Center for the Business of Government.

OECD (2017). *Systems Approaches to Public Sector Challenges: Working with Change.* https://doi.org/10.1787/9789264279865-en 12/07/2022

OECD (2021a). Implementing the OECD Recommendation on Policy Coherence for Sustainable Development. Guidance Note COM/DCD/DAC/GOV/PGC (2021).

OECD (2021b). *Government at a Glance 2021.* Paris: OECD Publishing.

OECD (2022). *Building Trust to Reinforce Democracy: Main Findings from the 2021 Survey on Drivers of Trust in Public Institutions.* Paris: OECD Publishing. https://doi.org/10.1787/b407f99c-en

OECD *et al.* (2020), Introducing Systems Thinking into Public Sector Institutions: Learning by Doing? In W. Hynes, M. Lees & J. Müller (Eds.), *Systemic Thinking for Policy Making: The Potential of Systems Analysis for Addressing Global Policy Challenges in the 21st Century*, Paris: OECD Publishing. https://doi.org/10.1787/3a9acaa6-en. 12/07/2022

Olano, M. (2022). Preamble. In Diputación Foral de Gipuzkoa (Ed.), *Building a New Political Culture in Gipuzkoa. Concepts, methodology and experiences* (pp. 3–4). San Sebastián: Diputación Foral de Gipuzkoa.

Oomsels, P. & Bouckaert, G. (2014). Interorganizational Trust in Public Administration. *Public Performance and Management Review*, 37(4), 577–604.

Osborne, S. P. (2021). *Public Service Logic. Creating Value for Public Service Users, Citizens, and Society through Public Service Delivery.* New York: Routledge.

Ospina, S. M. (2017). Collective leadership and context in public administration: Bridging public leadership research and leadership studies. *Public Administration Review*, 77(2), 275–287.

Ospina, S. M. & Foldy, E. G. (2015). Leadership in a shared-power world. In J. Perry & R. Christensen (Eds.), *Handbook of Public Administration* (3rd ed. pp. 489–507). San Francisco, CA: Jossey Bass.

Ostrom, E. (1990). *Governing the Commons.* New York: Cambridge University Press.

Padgett, J. F. & Ansell, C. K. (1993). Robust action and the rise of the Medici, 1400–1434. *American Journal of Sociology*, 98(6), 1259–1319.

Papacharissi, Z. (2014). On networked publics and private spheres in social media. In J. Hunsinger & T. Senft (Eds.), *The Social Media Handbook* (1st ed., pp. 144–158). New York: Routledge.

Parés, M., S. M. Ospina & J. Subirats. (2017). *Social Innovation and Democratic Leadership: Communities Making Social Change from Below*. London: Edward Elgar Publishing.

Pedler, M. (2002). Accessing local knowledge: Action learning and organizational learning in Walsall. *Human Resource Development International*, 5(4), 523–540.

Pedler, M. (2008). Action learning for managers (2nd ed.). London: Routledge/Ashgate Publishing.

Pedler, M. (2020). On social action. *Action Learning*, 17(1), 1–9.

Pedler, M. & Abbott, C. (2013). *Facilitating Action Learning: A Facilitator's Guide*. Berkshire: McGraw-Hill Open University Press.

Pedler, M. & Brook, C. (2017). The innovation paradox: A selective review of the literature on action learning and innovation. *Action Learning*, 14(3), 216–229.

Peters, B. G., Pierre, J., Sørensen, E. & Torfing, J. (2022). *A Research Agenda for Governance*. Cheltenham: Edward Elgar Publishing.

Polanyi, K. (1944). *The Great Transformation: The Political and Economic Origins of Our Time*. Boston, MA: Beacon Press.

Popper, K. (1966). *Of Clouds and Clocks: An Approach to the Problem of Rationality and the Freedom of Man*. St. Louis, MO: Washington University.

Putnam, R. (2000). *Solo en la bolera. Colapso y resurgimiento de la comunidad norteamericana*. Barcelona: Galaxia Gutenberg.

Puttick, R., Baeck, P. & Colligan, P. (2014). *i-teams. The Teams and Funds Making Innovation Happen in Governments Around the World*. London: Nesta.

Rajala, T., Laihonen, H. & Haapala, P. (2018). Why is dialogue on performance challenging in the public sector? *Measuring Business Excellence*, 22(2), 117–129.

Ran, B. & Qi, H. (2019). The entangled twins: Power and trust in collaborative governance. *Administration and Society*, 51(4), 607-636.

Rauch, F., Schuster, A., Stern, T., Pribila, M. & Townsend, A. (Eds.) (2014). *Promoting Change through Action Research*. Rotterdam: Sense Publishers.

Reason, P. & Bradbury, H. (2001). Introduction. In P. Reason & H. Bradbury (Eds.), *The SAGE Handbook of Action Research, Participative Inquiry and Practice* (pp. 1–14). Los Angeles: Sage Publications.

Remler, D. K. & Van Ryzin, G. G. (2022). *Research Methods in Practice: Strategies for Description and Causation*. London: Sage Publications.

Revans, R. W. (1971). *Developing Effective Managers*. New York: Praeger.

Revans, R. W. (1982). *The Origins & Growth of Action Learning*. Bromley: Charwell Bratt.

Revans, R. W. (1998). *The ABC of Action Learning* (3rd ed.). London: Lemos & Crane.

Reynolds, S. (2015). The landscape of public sector innovation labs. *Design for Europe*, 13 August. Retrieved from http://www.designforeurope.eu/news-opinion/landscape-public-sector-innovation-labs, 12th December 2022.

Rhodes, B. (2022). This is no time for passive patriotism. *The Atlantic*, 8 January.

Rich, E. & Moberg, J. (2015). *Beyond Governance: Making Collective Governments Work*. London: Routledge.

Roberts, A. (2020). *Strategies for Governing: Reinventing Public Administration for a Dangerous Century*. Ithaca/London: Cornell University Press.

Rochlin, S., Zadek, S. & Forstater, M. (2008). Governing collaboration: Making partnerships accountable for delivering development. Health policy (Vol. 90). Amsterdam: The Netherlands. Retrieved from http://www.ncbi.nlm.nih.gov/pubmed/19271395

Rooduijn, M. (2018). What unites the voter bases of populist parties? Comparing the electorates of 15 populist parties. *European Political Science Review*, 10(3), 351–368.

Rosanvallon, P. & Goldhammer, A. (2008). *Counter-Democracy: Politics in an Age of Distrust*. Cambridge: Cambridge University Press.

Rousseau, D., Sitkin, S. B., Burt, R. S. & Camerer, C. (1998). Not so different after all: A cross-discipline view of trust. *Academy of Management Review*, 23(3), 393–404.

Royo, S. (2009). The politics of adjustment and coordination at the regional level: The Basque Country. Center for European Studies Working Paper Series #171.

Run, B., Huiting, Q. & Oszlak, O. (2018). Gobernanza colaborativa: las contingencias del poder compartido en Estado Abierto. *Revista sobre el Estado, la Administración y las Políticas Públicas*, 2(3), 47–90.

Sánchez Cuenca, I. (2022). *El desorden político*. Madrid: La Catarata.

Schumpeter, J. A. (1942). *Capitalism, Socialism and Democracy*. London/New York: Routledge.

Schütz, A. (1993). *La construcción significativa del mundo social*. Barcelona: Paidós. (Original in German, 1937.)

Scott, W. (2014). *Institutions and Organizations* (4th ed.). London: Sage Publications.

Selsky, J. W. & Parker, B. (2010). Platforms for cross-sector social partnerships: Prospective sensemaking devices for social benefit. *Journal of Business Ethics*, 94, 21–37.

Selznick, P. (1957). *Leadership in Administration: A Sociological Interpretation*. New York: Harper & Row.

Sheptulín, A. (1983). *El método dialéctico del conocimiento*. Moscú: Editorial Literatura Política.

Shudson, M. (1997). Sending a political message: Lessons from the American 1790s. *Media Culture and Society*, 19, 311–330.

Simon, H. (1979). Rational decision making in business organizations. *American Economics Review*, 69(4), 493–513.

Sirianni, C. (2010). *Investing in Democracy: Engaging Citizens in Collaborative Governance*. Washington DC: Brookings Institution Press.

Sloterdijk, P. (2011). *Bubbles, Spheres*. Volume I. Cambridge, MA: MIT Press.

Sørensen, E. (2020). *Interactive Political Leadership: The Role of Politicians in the Age of Governance*. Oxford: Oxford University Press.

Sørensen, E. & Torfing, J. (2005). The democratic anchorage of governance networks. *Scandinavian Political Studies*, 28(3), 195–218.

Sørensen, E. & Torfing, J. (2009). Making governance networks effective and democratic through metagovernance. *Public Administration*, 87(2), 234-258.

Sørensen, E. & Torfing, J. (2015). Enhancing public innovation through collaboration, leadership and new public governance. In A. Nicholls, J. Simon & M. Gabriel (Eds.), *New Frontiers in Social Innovation Research* (pp. 15-169). London: Palgrave Macmillan.

Sørensen, E. & Torfing, J. (2016). Political leadership in the age of interactive governance: Reflections on the political aspects of metagovernance. In J. Edelenbos & I. van Meerkerk (Eds.), *Critical Reflections on Interactive Governance: Self-Organization and Participation in Public Governance* (pp. 444–466). Brookfield, VT: Edward Elgar Publishing.

Sørensen, E. & Torfing, J. (2017). Metagoverning collaborative innovation in governance networks. *The American Review of Public Administration*, 47(7), 826–839.

Sørensen, E. & Torfing, J. (2018). The democratizing impact of governance networks: From pluralization, via democratic anchorage, to interactive political leadership. *Public Administration*, 96(2), 302–317.

Sørensen, E. & Torfing, J. (2019a). Towards robust hybrid democracy in Scandinavian municipalities? *Scandinavian Political Studies*, 42(1), 25–49.

Sørensen, E. & Torfing, J. (2019b). Designing institutional platforms and arenas for interactive political leadership. *Public Management Review*, 21(10), 1443-1463.

Sørensen, E. & Torfing, J. (2021). Accountable government through collaborative governance? *Administrative Sciences*, 11(4), 127–147.

Sørensen, E. & Torfing, J. (2022). Collective political intelligence as driver of effective, innovative and legitimate policy-making. In S. Boucher (Ed.), *Handbook of Collective Intelligence* (n.p.). Abingdon: Routledge.

Sørensen, E., Hendriks, C. M., Hertting, N. & Edelenbos, J. (2020). Political boundary spanning: Politicians at the interface between collaborative governance and representative democracy. *Policy and Society*, 39(4), 530–569.

Sranko, G. (2011). Collaborative governance and a strategic approach to facilitating change: Lessons learned from forest agreements in South East Queensland and the Great Bear Rainforest. *Interface*, 3(1), 210–239.

Stave, K. & Hopper, M. (2007). What constitutes systems thinking? A proposed taxonomy. In *Proceedings of the 25th International Conference of the System Dynamics Society*. Boston, MA, 29 July–3 August. Available at: https://www.researchgate.net/publication/255592974_What_Constitutes_Systems_Thinking_A_Proposed_Taxonomy, 12th December 2022.

Steelman, T., Nowell, B., Velez, A.-L. & Scott, R. (2021). Pathways of representation in network governance. *Journal of Public Administration Research and Theory*, 31(4), 723–739.

Strong, W. T. (1893). The fueros of Northern Spain. *Political Science Quarterly*, 317–334.

Taborsky, P. (2014). Is complexity a scientific concept? *Studies in History and Philosophy of Science*, 47, 51–59.

Torfing, J. (2016). *Collaborative Innovation in the Public Sector*. Washington, DC: Georgetown University Press.

Torfing, J. & Ansell, C. (2017). Strengthening political leadership and policy innovation through the expansion of collaborative forms of governance. *Public Management Review*, 19(1), 37–54.

Touriñán, J. M. (2020). La 'Tercera Misión' de la Universidad, transferencia de conocimiento y sociedades del conocimiento. Una aproximación desde la pedagogía. *Contextos Educativos,* 26, 41–81.

Townsend, A. (2014). Weaving the threads of practice and research. Reflections on fundamental features of action research. In F. Rauch *et al.* (Eds.), *Promoting Change through Action Research* (pp. 7–22). Rotterdam: Sense Publishers.

Ulibarri, N., Emerson, K., Imperial, M., Jager, N., Newig, J. & Weber, E. (2020). How does collaborative governance evolve? Insights from a medium-n case comparison. *Policy and Society,* 39(4), 617–637.

Urkiza, A. & Okarantza, L. (2022). Future & Culture. *O&E Orain eta Etorkizuna,* 1, 72–77.

Urra, M. (2017). Estado, mercado, academia … y comunidad. Una cuádruple hélice para el desarrollo integral y la innovación. Tesis de doctorado, Universidad Pontificia de Comillas.

van Dijk, R. & Van Dick, R. (2009). Navigating organizational change: Change leaders, employee resistance, and work-based identities. *Journal of Change Management,* 9(2), 143–163.

Vince, R. (2019). Institutional illogics: The unconscious and institutional analysis. *Organization Studies,* 40(7), 953–973.

Voets, J., Brandsen, T., Koliba, C. & Verschuere, B. (2021). Collaborative governance. In *Oxford Research Encyclopaedia of Politics.* Available at: https://oxfordre.com/politics/.

Vogelphol, T., Hirschl, B. & Meßmer, D. (2012). The institutional sustainability of public-private governance arrangements. The case of EU biofuels sustainability regulation. Paper presented at the Lund Conference on Earth System Governance, Lund, Sweden.

Vommaro, G. & Gené, M. (2016). *La vida social del mundo político: Investigaciones recientes en sociología política.* Buenos Aires: Ediciones UNGS.

Waardenburg, M., Groenleer, M., de Jong, J. & Keijser, B. (2020). Paradoxes of collaborative governance: Investigating the real-life dynamics of multi-agency collaborations using a quasi-experimental action-research approach. *Public Management Review,* 22(3), 386–407.

Wang, H. & Ran, B. (2021). Network governance and collaborative governance: A thematic analysis on their similarities, differences, and entanglements. *Public Management Review,* 1–25.

Weaver, R. M. (1953). *The Ethics of Rhetoric.* Brattleboro, VT: Echo Point Books & Media.

Weiss, C. H. (1979). The many meanings of research utilization. *Public Administration Review,* 39(5), 426-431.

Whyte, W. F. & Whyte, K. K. (2014). *Making Mondragon: The Growth and Dynamics of the Worker Cooperative Complex.* Cornell: Cornell University Press.

Wolton, D. (1992). *Elogio del gran público.* Barcelona: Gedisa.

Young, I. M. (2000). *Inclusion and Democracy.* Oxford: Oxford University Press.

Zuluaga, M. & Romo, G. (2017). La agenda pública en sus teorías y aproximaciones metodológicas. Una clasificación alternativa. *Revista Enfoques: Ciencia Política y Administración Pública,* 15(26), 13–35.

About the authors and contributors

AGUILAR, LUIS F. is National Researcher Emeritus (Mexico) in the field of Public Policy and Public Governance.

ANSOLABEHERE, STEPHEN is the Frank G. Thompson Professor of Government at Harvard University. He is an expert on democratic politics and communication, with a focus on elections, public opinion, representation and public engagement in policy-making and implementation in the energy transition in the United States.

ARZELUS, ANDER holds a degree in Economics from the University of Deusto and is an expert in territorial planning. He was vice-president of the Red Cross of Gipuzkoa for nine years, and since 1992 has been the head of the technical service in the Office of the Deputy General at the Provincial Council of Gipuzkoa. In recent years he has participated in the *Etorkizuna Eraikiz* steering committee.

ANDUEZA, UNAI is the Strategic Projects Managing Director in the Economic Promotion Department of Gipuzkoa, which is linked to some of the economic development reference centres of *Etorkizuna Eraikiz*. He holds an Industrial Engineering degree and a Master's degree in Management and Business Administration (Universidad de Navarra). He has a background in territorial development as he has worked for more than ten years in industrial economic development in a local agency in Gipuzkoa.

ARRONA, AINHOA is a researcher at Orkestra – Basque Institute of Competitiveness, Deusto Foundation. As a researcher focusing on research–policy interaction, public policy, territorial strategies and collaborative governance for regional development, she has participated since 2009 in action research processes of *Etorkizuna Eraikiz*.

BARANDIARÁN, XABIER is advisor to the Head of the Provincial Council of Gipuzkoa and one of the main promoters of the development of *Etorkizuna Eraikiz*. He holds a PhD in Sociology and is Associate Professor at the Faculty of Social and Human Sciences at the University of Deusto.

BIANCHI, CARMINE is professor at the University of Palermo (Italy). He focuses on innovative performance governance methods for enhancing stakeholders' learning in collaborative network policy analysis, for generating community outcomes and strengthening shared strategic resources.

BOUCKAERT, GEERT is professor at the KU Leuven Public Governance Institute (Leuven, Belgium). He is honorary professor at the Institute for Innovation and Public Purpose, University College London, and visiting professor at the University of Potsdam. ·

CABALLERO, ANDER is a visiting scholar at Harvard University, and Senior Fellow at the Agirre Lehendakaria Center. He is a consultant for *Etorkizuna Eraikiz*. He served as the representative of the Basque government to the US.

CANEL, MARÍA JOSÉ is Professor in Political and Public Sector Communication at the University Complutense Madrid (Spain) with a focus on intangible resources (trust, engagement, legitimacy and sustainability). She served as facilitator for action learning initiatives in *Etorkizuna Eraikiz*, and advised on its internal and external listening processes.

EIZAGUIRRE, ANDONI is a lecturer at Mondragon University, and a member of the Deliberation Group on New Political Culture of the *Etorkizuna Eraikiz* Think Tank.

ERRAZKIN, OLATZ holds a BA in law (UPV/EHU) and a Master's degree in Management and Business Administration (Mondragon). She has worked as a consultant assisting organisations in the strategic planning and future-oriented thinking. Since 2021, as the head of service of *Etorkizuna Eraikiz*, she has contributed to the development and implementation of this government reform.

ESPIAU, GORKA is Director at the Agirre Lehendakaria Center for Social and Political Studies (University of the Basque Country) and a member of the *Etorkizuna Eraikiz* Think Tank. He was Senior Advisor to the Executive Office of the Basque President, Professor of Practice at CIRM-McGill University,

Senior Fellow at the United States Institute of Peace, and Senior Associate to CICR (Columbia University).

GOIA, NAIARA is Managing Director at *Arantzazulab* reference centre on collaborative governance within *Etorkizuna Eraikiz*. Since autumn 2020, she is responsible for designing, implementing and developing the social innovation laboratory. She is an expert in innovation, networking and transformation strategies, with 20 years of experience in the area.

LAKIDAIN, ASIER works at *Sinnergiak* Social Innovation (UPV/EHU) as a research and field assistant. BA in Applied Sociology (UPNA) and Master's Degree in Social Policy and Social Research (UCL). He has participated in the *Etorkizuna Eraikiz* Think Tank.

LARREA, MIREN is senior researcher in Orkestra-Basque Institute of Competitiveness and editor in chief of *International Journal of Action Research*. She is an experienced facilitator of action research processes for territorial development. She coordinates the action research team in *Etorkizuna Eraikiz* Think Tank.

LEZAUN, JAVIER is Associate Professor in the School of Anthropology and Museum Ethnography and Director of the Institute for Science, Innovation and Society, Oxford University. His work explores the interplay of scientific and political change.

LOGE, PETER is an associate professor in the School of Media and Public Affairs at the George Washington University. He has worked in American politics for more than 30 years, including serving as a vice-president at the US Institute of Peace. His father's family came to the US from Pau in the early 20th century and Peter was raised on stories of the Basques.

LUOMA-AHO, VILMA is Professor of Corporate Communication, and Vice Dean of Education at Jyväskylä University School of Business and Economics (JSBE), Finland.

MUÑOA, ION is a PhD scholar at the University of Deusto, an advisor of the Provincial Council of Gipuzkoa, and a member of the *Etorkizuna Eraikiz* team. His areas of interest are public opinion, public communication and the quality of democracy.

MURPHY, ANNE is an expert in organisational learning with over 30 years' experience in applied and participative research in organisations. Since 2018, she has been involved in establishing, growing and consolidating *Ekinez Ikasi*, a programme of action learning in support of *Etorkizuna Eraikiz*.

NABATCHI, TINA is Joseph A. Strasser Endowed Professor in Public Administration and Director of the Program for the Advancement of Research on Conflict and Collaboration at the Syracuse University Maxwell School of Citizenship and Public Affairs. Her research centres on dispute resolution, public participation, collaborative governance and challenges in public administration.

NAJAM, ADIL is Dean Emeritus and Professor of international relations and of earth and environment at the Frederick S. Pardee School of Global Studies, Boston University. Earlier, he served as Vice Chancellor of the Lahore University of Management Sciences (LUMS) in Pakistan. He was also a Lead Author for the third and fourth Assessment Reports of the Intergovernmental Panel on Climate Change (IPCC)

OLANO, MARKEL has been president of Gipuzkoa for three legislative periods. Through *Etorkizuna Eraikiz*, he was able to activate a new form of governance with the citizens for a fairer, dynamic and more cohesive Gipuzkoa.

OSPINA, SONIA is a Professor of Public Management and Policy at the R.F. Wagner Graduate School of Public Service at New York University. Her present research interests include collective leadership and accountability in contexts of collaboration.

OYÓN, ELENA is a strategic thinker, doer and facilitator with a background in capacity building and organisational change. She has over ten years' experience of working in organisational learning, service development and innovation with a range of global organisations including UNICEF, Nesta, the British Council and multiple national-level governments.

POMARES, EGOITZ works as the Head of Research at *Sinnergiak* Social Innovation (UPV/EHU). PhD in Sociology from the University of the Basque Country (UPV/EHU). He has participated in the implementation and development of the *Etorkizuna Eraikiz* model.

SØRENSEN, EVA is professor at the Department of Social Sciences and Business, and at the Roskilde School of Governance at Roskilde University, Denmark. Her research focuses on citizen involvement, policy innovation, political leadership, co-creation, and meta- and network governance.

TAPIA, FERNANDO is a full-time lecturer at the Law Faculty of the University of the Basque Country and a member of the AKTIBA-IT research group. He is a member of the Deliberation Group on New Political Culture of the *Etorkizuna Eraikiz* Think Tank.

TORFING, JACOB is professor at the Department of Social Sciences and Business, and research director at the Roskilde School of Governance, at the Roskilde University, Denmark. He focuses on public-sector reforms, network governance, collaborative innovation and interactive political leadership. He is also professor at the Nord University, Norway.

UNCETA, ALFONSO is Professor of Sociology at the University of the Basque Country (UPV/EHU). He is the Director of *Sinnergiak* Social Innovation (UPV/EHU). Since 2016, he has contributed to the modelling and development of *Etorkizuna Eraikiz*.

VAN RYZIN, GREGG G. is a Professor in the School of Public Affairs and Administration (SPAA) at Rutgers University–Newark, USA, with expertise in behavioural science and research methods. He conducts empirical studies on performance measurement, citizen satisfaction with public services, co-production and trust in government.

ZURUTUZA, SEBASTIÁN holds a degree in Economics, specialising in Public Administration. He is Strategy Director of the Cabinet of the Deputy General of the Provincial Council of Gipuzkoa. Since July 2015, he has been part of the team that, under the leadership of the Deputy General, has promoted and coordinated *Etorkizuna Eraikiz*.